The Europeanization of Party Politics in Ireland, North and South

Edited by Katy Hayward and Mary C. Murphy

Taylor & Francis Group
LONDON AND NEW YORK

First published 2010 by Routledge
2 Park Square, Milton Park, Abingdon, Oxfordshire OX14 4RN

Simultaneously published in the USA and Canada
by Routledge
711 Third Avenue, New York, NY 10017

First issued in paperback 2014

Routledge is an imprint of the Taylor & Francis Group, an informa business

© 2010 Taylor & Francis

This book is a reproduction of *Irish Political Studies*, vol. 24, issue 4. The Publisher requests to those authors who may be citing this book to state, also, the bibliographical details of the special issue on which the book was based.

Typeset in Times by Value Chain, India

All rights reserved. No part of this book may be reprinted or reproduced or utilised in any form or by any electronic, mechanical, or other means, now known or hereafter invented, including photocopying and recording, or in any information storage or retrieval system, without permission in writing from the publishers.

British Library Cataloguing in Publication Data
A catalogue record for this book is available from the British Library

ISBN 13: 978-1-138-88235-5 (pbk)
ISBN 13: 978-0-415-57891-2 (hbk)

Contents

1. Party Politics and the EU in Ireland, North and South
   Mary C. Murphy and Katy Hayward   1

2. Ireland's EU Referendum Experience
   Jane O'Mahony   13

3. Irish Political Parties and Policy Stances on European Integration
   Kenneth Benoit   31

4. Irish Political Parties' Attitudes towards Neutrality and the Evolution of the EU's Foreign, Security and Defence Policies
   Karen Devine   51

5. Fianna Fáil: Tenacious Localism, Tenuous Europeanism
   Katy Hayward and Jonathan Fallon   75

6. Blissful Union? Fine Gael and the European Union
   Theresa Reidy   95

7. The Irish Labour Party: The Advantages, Disadvantages and Irrelevance of Europeanization?
   Michael Holmes   111

8. The Irish Green Party and Europe: An Unhappy Marriage?
   Nicole Bolleyer and Diana Panke   127

9. Sinn Féin's Approach to the EU: Still More 'Critical' than 'Engaged'?
   Agnès Maillot   143

10. 'Battling in Brussels': The DUP and the European Union
    Gladys Ganiel   159

11. Pragmatic Politics: The Ulster Unionist Party and the European Union
    Mary C. Murphy 173

12. The SDLP and the Europeanization of the Northern Ireland Problem
    P.J. McLoughlin 187

    Index 205

Party Politics and the EU in Ireland, North and South

MARY C. MURPHY* & KATY HAYWARD**
*University College Cork, Ireland; **Queen's University Belfast, Northern Ireland, UK

Introduction

Political party systems in both parts of Ireland – north and south – are typically regarded as unconventional. Neither has traditionally fitted neatly into the established party system models found in most other European states (for Republic of Ireland see Carty, 1976; Mair, 1979; Sinnott, 1984; for Northern Ireland see Mitchell, 1991, 1995). The uniqueness of the party systems in the Republic of Ireland and Northern Ireland has meant that, historically, studies of political parties and party systems, have tended to focus on the peculiarities and idiosyncrasies of each respective system.

The party system in the Republic of Ireland demonstrates a number of unusual characteristics. The strong presence of the centre is in contrast to many other European states. Indeed even the very character of centre parties in Ireland, i.e. Fianna Fáil and Fine Gael, means that they do not fit readily into the main European party families. The Irish party system is also unusual in having traditionally had only a small liberal party – now absent since the demise of the Progressive Democrats. The low levels of support for parties of the left, including the Labour Party and the Green Party, and the relatively high number of independents also mark Ireland's party system out as distinct. Although most authors accept that Ireland's party system is somewhat unusual relative to its European neighbours, there is some dispute as to the precise nature of this distinctiveness. Some have pointed to the impact of recent political developments on the party system, for example, and suggest a convergence between Ireland and other more standard European models (see summarized discussion by Weeks, 2009).

In Northern Ireland, the party system has been labelled a 'dual ethnic party system' (see Mitchell, 1991). The absence of a strong left–right divide is similarly evident here. The party system in Northern Ireland however, is constructed along different lines than that in the Republic. Party politics is polarized around a *profound* constitutional cleavage i.e. support for a united Ireland versus support for maintenance of the Union with the United Kingdom. With the exception of the Alliance Party of Northern Ireland (APNI) and the Green Party, the four largest parties draw electoral support from one of the two communities in Northern Ireland resulting in a party system which 'is plausibly represented as two systems, in which party competition occurs within nationalist and unionist blocs' (Evans & Duffy, 1997: 47). The impact of this party system structure is such that it serves to maintain, and may even exacerbate, the community divide in Northern Ireland. Attempts to win votes from the 'other' community are often viewed with suspicion by voters, and parties may be punished rather than rewarded for any such reconciliatory moves. In effect,

> The more serious consequence of intra-ethnic competition is that it makes conflict resolution much more difficult. The enlightened compromises required to resolve ethno-national conflicts are less likely to be forthcoming when there are rival parties in each bloc ready to profit by denouncing any deal as a 'sell-out'. (Mitchell, 1999: 114–115)

More recent studies have sought to downplay the perceived negative consequences of the Northern Ireland dual ethnic party system (see Mitchell *et al.*, 2009). Such views, however, do not detract from the enduringly distinctive nature of the party system.

Analysis of both the Irish and Northern Irish party systems have typically focused on historic and domestic influences in explaining the defining features of each. Consideration of external influences and in particular the impact of the European Union (EU) on either party system, or indeed on individual parties within each system, has been minimal. This volume addresses this omission and, in so doing, broadens the study and analysis of political parties and party systems on the island of Ireland. The papers which follow are rooted in the Europeanization literature (see below). They acknowledge and qualify the impact of the EU on the evolution of political parties and contribute to the development of a more complete and nuanced overview of political parties in both parts of Ireland.

Importantly, a distinction must be made between national and sub-national political parties. Ladrech and Mair's work focuses on the former. However all but one of the Northern Ireland political parties examined here are *sub-national* in nature. Authors such as Müller-Rommel (1998) and De Winter and Gomez-Reino (2000) have labelled these parties ethnoregional in character. In determining the extent to which such parties have (or have not) been Europeanized, it is necessary to acknowledge the particular political context within which they operate and the different opportunities Europe may present, when compared with national political parties. The accounts of Northern Ireland political parties which follow do not fit easily with more general commentaries on the Europeanization of ethnoregionalist parties (see De Winter and Gomez-Reino, 2000; Jolly, 2007). Northern Ireland's political parties have largely proved more resistant to Europeanizing influences than their counterparts elsewhere. In this respect, there is little evidence of radically changed attitudes towards Europe among Northern Ireland's political parties, nor is there any strong basis for suggesting that they have treated the EU as an essential arena for broadening political opportunities.

Europeanization

Attempts to identify and understand the impact which the EU may have on political systems is a relatively new area of political analysis. Although use of the term 'Europeanization' has increased since the late 1990s, there is no clear agreement on its precise meaning (see Featherstone, 2003; Mair, 2004). Cowles, Caporaso and Risse (2001) identify Europeanization as being focused on the development of distinct structures of governance at the European level. A more common interpretation of Europeanization, however, is advanced by authors including Ladrech (1994), Olsen (2002) and Radaelli (2000), who view the concept as referring to a process of national adaptation to the demands of EU membership. Analyses of the Europeanization of political parties tend to align more closely with the latter definition. A certain level of Europeanization is inevitable given the need to compete in European Parliament (EP) elections. Mair (2000) was among the first to examine the impact of European integration on political parties. In terms of the format and mechanics of party systems, he finds little evidence to suggest that Europe has had any tangible *direct* impact. He concludes that 'party systems appear to remain relatively impervious to the direct impact of Europeanization' (Mair, 2000: 47). He cautions, however, that the ability of political parties to resist Europeanization in this way risks undermining the relevance of conventional politics, and thus the democratic legitimacy of political parties themselves.

Mair's work was developed further by Ladrech (2002) who focuses more explicitly on the *indirect* impact of European integration on political parties. Ladrech (2002: 395) identifies European integration as an independent variable and 'increased government policy constraints and the public perception of growing irrelevance of conventional politics as dependent variables'. In this way, the Europeanization of political parties can be ascertained by systematically identifying and qualifying the responses of parties to this changed environment. Specifically, Ladrech (2002: 396–399) outlines five measurable areas where it may be possible to identify changes that reflect a process of Europeanization:

1. Programmatic change: modifications in party programmes (which can be measured qualitatively in terms of increased mention of the EU).
2. Organizational change: explicit statutory changes; changes in practices and power relations (possibly as a consequence of affiliation with European level institutions such as the EP).
3. Patterns of party competition: to the extent the EU becomes politicized in national politics, new voters may be targeted in an opportunistic strategy, either

in a pro- or anti-EU position (parties may choose to capitalize on the 'EU issue').
4. Party–government relations: participation of government leaders in EU forums may strain relations with the party on particular policies (EU participation may limit policy options causing a tension between party and leadership, and possibly leading to changes in manner of party management).
5. Relations beyond the national party system: promotion of new organizational and programmatic activities at a transnational level.

Ladrech's work reaches similar conclusions to Mair, i.e. the changed environment within which political parties operate results in processes of Europeanization which are largely subtle, rather than dramatic. The findings presented by the case studies from the island of Ireland in this volume do not depart in any substantial way from the more general observations made by Ladrech and Mair.

How Europeanized are Party Politics in Ireland?

Having outlined the meaning of 'Europeanization' and the nature of party systems both north and south in Ireland, we now present an overview of the papers contained in this volume. We do this by elaborating five common themes that have emerged in both the single-party studies and the comparative analyses presented here. These themes are: resistance, conditionality, pragmatism, (sub-)national priorities, and elite-led. We argue that the Europeanization of party politics in Ireland, north and south, has been characterized by these tendencies. These are not necessarily unique to this case study – indeed some of them are anticipated in the existing literature on Europeanization. Taken together, they reveal an approach to the European Union that reveals much about the process of European integration itself, as well as deepening our understanding of the nature of party politics within Ireland today.

Resistance

Ireland's recent experience of referendums on EU treaties confirms that political parties can no longer assume the existence of a positive public consensus on European integration (O'Mahony, 2009). This is perhaps unsurprising given that, as papers in this volume show, there has been a considerable and consistent degree of resistance to Europeanization in Ireland, north and south, since accession. The legacy of this is evident in the fact that some parties, particularly in Northern Ireland, have competed to be, in effect, the most critical (if not explicitly sceptical) of European integration. Moreover, there is no such active competition between parties for the label of being most pro-European. Parties appear to assume that few voters would be won over by the cause of Euro-enthusiasm. This is borne out by the example of the Irish Labour Party which, according to Holmes (2009), is substantially Europeanized but is yet to realize many electoral benefits for being so.

On the other hand, it is no coincidence that those parties most resistant to the EU are the ones which have a relatively unchanging and narrow support base and which are still quite unsure of their position in the wider sphere of party competition and constitutional battles. The resistance to Europeanization within some parties is based on the conviction that it strengthens their appeal and identity within this typical support base (particularly for the Democratic Unionist Party (DUP) and Sinn Féin). It is slightly ironic, if not altogether remarkable, that the DUP and Sinn Féin share the dubious label of being the parties that managed to turn Euroscepticism into a vote-winner. Their success in this regard, albeit in Northern Ireland, no doubt served to encourage the over-ambition of Declan Ganley's Libertas party, which came to so little in 2009. Indeed, the failure of Libertas in the 2009 European elections suggests that resistance to the European Union in Irish parties and among the Irish electorate is not first and foremost a 'European-oriented' matter. Instead, it is useful to conceive of the most overtly Euro-resistant parties, namely Sinn Féin, the DUP and the Green Party, primarily as anti-system parties which, as Mair (2000) argues, have come to object to European integration largely by force of habit.

This point of view is reinforced by the fact that when these parties gained governmental power and found themselves to be part of the 'system' they had made political fortunes out of opposing, they *all* modified their critical stances to become more engaged with the European Union (see Bolleyer & Panke, 2009; Ganiel, 2009; Maillot, 2009). Yet, from studies of the larger parties (which have greater experience of governance at national and EU levels), we can anticipate that the EU-engagement of these Euro-critical parties will remain carefully delimited according to party interests and that it will not necessarily have a trickle-down effect on their supporters. Grassroots (and consequently party) resistance to Europeanization is one explanation for the fact that national and local terms of debate and modes of operation continue to predominate for *all* parties, even when the purported subject and context is European integration itself.

Conditionality

The conditionality of the Europeanization of political parties in Ireland has two main dimensions. First, the degree and substance of Europeanization in parties' programmes and organization can vary according to the priorities of the time. Devine (2009) traces this process in action in relation to parties' interpretation of 'neutrality' and their approaches to European Security and Defence Policy. Moreover, Benoit's (2009) comparative overview of party positioning on European matters shows that the rise and fall of parties' interest in European matters (as indicated by mentions in party manifestoes) can happen in a fairly synchronized way. For example, among most parties in the Republic of Ireland, there was a peak in interest in European policy in the 1997 general election and a decline by 2002 (Benoit, 2009). This suggests that the referendum on the Treaty of Amsterdam and the first one on the Treaty of Nice generated very different effects on Irish party attitudes in comparison with each other, i.e. Amsterdam induced engagement and

Nice induced caution. These trends were fairly similar among the parties (particularly the three main southern parties). So, one version of conditionality means that 'Europeanization' is shaped according to the needs of the time.

Conditionality can also mean that Europeanization is secondary to party principles, i.e. Europeanization is conditional on meeting the specific interests of the political party in question. As Maillot (2009) argues in relation to the experience of Sinn Féin, any limited engagement by the party with the EU is conditional on such a move being seen to meet the (nationalist) interests of the party. Similarly, the DUP has found it necessary to justify engagement with the EU only insofar as it appears to serve the interests of unionist voters (Ganiel, 2009). Even the less Eurosceptic Ulster Unionist Party (UUP) has framed European integration as being acceptable only because it is to the *mutual advantage* of all participants in the venture, i.e. to each member-state (Murphy, 2009). Of course, such conditions are neither set independently nor assessed verifiably, but they are instead subject to the interpretation of the party elites at any one time. The experience of party politics in Ireland, north and south, shows that this privilege – of both setting and assessing the conditions for Europeanization – can be valued and exploited by party elites. In this way, Europeanization actually does become conditional on the interests of the parties.

What remains enigmatic is the degree to which these conditions themselves (and their interpretation) are indirectly shaped by the context of EU membership and participation. As noted above, all political parties in Ireland, north and south, have become engaged with the European Union, even if they object to some dimensions of its policy and decision-making. The effects of this engagement are not confined to a 'European' level. As seen in party positioning on the EU's Security and Defence Policy, resistance may be great among parties and conditions on engagement may be strict, but the ultimate outcome has been a move towards, not alienation from, the EU consensus (Devine, 2009).

Pragmatism

Devine's (2009) comparative study of the parties in the Republic on a single EU-related issue showed that programmatic change in light of Europeanization is not always connected to policy and is liable to fluctuate over time. Her study confirms Benoit's (2009) finding that the EU becomes particularly politicized as an issue of debate by parties around the times of referendums. Devine also argues that competition between parties themselves can induce shifts in party stances on EU-related issues. But this trend does not always indicate a movement towards deeper or positive 'Europeanization'. Instead, it may confirm that straightforward pragmatism characterizes Irish political parties' approach to the EU. This is more the case in some parties than others, but it is still true to say that an appraisal of the practical benefits of such a policy stance is the driving motivation. The adaptation of previously outspokenly critical unionist parties to participation in the European Parliament is difficult to interpret as anything other than pragmatic adjustment (see Murphy, 2009). Engagement with the EU by unionist parties remains selective and calculated (Ganiel, 2009). Even when we consider the most Euro-enthusiastic party on the island as a whole, the Social Democratic and Labour Party (SDLP), we note that the former leader John Hume was certainly ideologically-driven in his pro-Europeanism, but this was founded on the view of the EU as a crucial *resource* (McLoughlin, 2009). Hume saw the potential in the EU to make a practical difference to the situation in Northern Ireland. His idealizing of European integration was intended to have very 'real' rewards, be they publicity, funding, party contacts or, ultimately, Irish reunification.

In the south, Fine Gael has proudly contrasted its relatively consistent pro-Europeanism with what it suggests is the shameless expediency of Fianna Fáil – the implication being that Fine Gael is therefore more trustworthy and dependable in the longer term (Reidy, 2009). However, Reidy's analysis shows that the party's approach to European integration has not been significantly less 'rational' (as opposed to purely idealistic) than its competitors. Even the party with the proudest 'idealistic' credentials, the Green Party, has moved towards EU-engagement by prioritizing policy gains in significant areas (i.e. those important for their electoral mandate) over 'real democracy' grounded in the local sphere (which had previously been the primary focus of their objections to European integration) (Bolleyer & Panke, 2009). Ultimately it is clear that domestic calculations are the predominant deciding factors for all parties when it comes to policy moves on the EU, and these calculations are by and large made on the basis of pragmatism rather than principles (Murphy, 2009).

(Sub-)National Priorities

Identity and attachment to the nation are very strong in Ireland and certainly exceed identity with and attachment to the European Union, which are comparatively shallow and limited (Laffan & O'Mahony, 2008). The contrast with attitudes towards the EU is even greater when considering the 'local' dimension of Irish voters' political attachment and identity. This can be used to good effect when canvassing for local votes in a European election, for example (O'Mahony, 2009). The importance of the local profile and constituencies of support for Members of the European Parliament (MEPs) (at least in the south, the situation in Northern Ireland is somewhat different) is another indicator of the way in which the local dimension can feed into the European representation of Irish politics. But the strength of the sub-national level of politics for parties in Ireland can also have negative implications. To take the example of MEPs again, the lack of opportunity for them to influence decisions in the national sphere (see Hayward & Fallon, 2009) also constrains the influence of 'EU-level' democracy within their parties, either in terms of organization or policy. In participatory political events ostensibly about European integration, i.e. referendums on EU treaties or elections to the European Parliament, local or national concerns can easily overshadow all 'EU-relevant' topics. This does not necessarily make European elections 'second order' elections, but neither does it enable them to be purely issue-based (cf. Garry *et al.*, 2005).

Studies in this volume of even the most 'Europeanized' parties in Ireland show that the 'European' nature of referendums and elections generally has less of an impact than the current national topics, how mainstream parties are faring, and how local party campaigns are run (see Holmes, 2009; Reidy, 2009). Even John Hume's pro-integrationism was a *response* to the fact that his first priority was to Northern Ireland (McLoughlin, 2009). Sub-national priorities among party supporters and the prioritizing of national concerns by party elites places a limit on the Europeanization of party politics in general. Moreover, the insistence of most party leaders' right to 'mediate' the influence of the EU on the party/locality and to, in turn, represent them at the European level is further indication of why Europeanization is so limited in Irish party politics.

Elite-Led

The fact that what O'Mahony (2009) identifies as 'populist capture' – or the attraction of voters to Eurosceptic parties – takes place at the times of referendums on EU treaties in Ireland suggests that Europeanization has not become embedded among the Irish public. Moreover, the effects of 'elite withdrawal' in the first referendums on the Nice and Lisbon Treaties in Ireland indicate just how much Europeanization is an elite-led, elite-sustained project in Ireland (O'Mahony, 2009). Party leaders 'manage' incursion by the EU into the national arena and they do not want to allow it to compromise the party agenda (Murphy, 2009). Among the party elite, enthusiasm for the EU is generally overt compared to that of the 'grassroots' and yet this goes hand in hand with a strict control over policy change in response to Europeanization (Hayward & Fallon, 2009; Devine, 2009; Bolleyer & Panke, 2009). Thus, if we want to understand the scope and limitations of Europeanization on party politics in Ireland, we need to consider the prime position of the party elites in this process.

Europeanization has been hampered by the existence of a substantial (and some suggest growing) 'gap' between the political elite and the voting public. Party leaders in Ireland, north and south, have failed to enthuse voters about the importance and relevance of the EU, despite the regular tests posed by referendums on European treaties. Results aside, the low turnout rates in referendums on EU treaties do not reflect well on the ability of the leaders of the main parties to encourage their supporters to even make an appearance at the polling station (see Hayward & Fallon, 2009). This 'distance' between the elite and grassroots on the matter of Europe is arguably greater in the more pro-EU parties than in the Euro-critical ones. Hence, in the Labour Party, dissension over 'European' issues has been an indication of alienation between the party elite and its grassroots (Holmes, 2009); in Fine Gael, elite commitment contrasts with popular wariness (as revealed in party 'road shows' discussing the EU around the country) (Reidy, 2009); and in the SDLP, the loss of Hume as leader and MEP has drastically impaired the party's pro-European message, suggesting that attachment to Europe was not as deep-rooted in the party as some previously thought (McLoughlin, 2009). Even within the elite of a party, there can be significant differences over Europe. This may reflect the 'internalizing' within the party of general tensions in the Irish political sphere, for example disagreements between rural and urban or local and central political actors, as has been particularly damaging for Fianna Fáil in recent times (Hayward & Fallon, 2009). What these trends suggest is that Europeanization is secondary to the more immediate (in both time and geography) forces at work in the realm of party politics in Ireland. Debates about 'Europe' centre on a notion of European Union hewn from decades of experience but not (as O'Mahony (2009) confirms) from mountains of knowledge. It is a notion thrown into the public arena by necessity (as around referendums) or by expediency (as in opposition criticisms of government compromises in Brussels). Furthermore, it is a notion relatively untroubled by nuance and one defined primarily by party elites and their assessment of the interests of their support base.

Conclusions

This article has given a brief overview of the five main arguments highlighted by Ladrech (2002) and the different five themes elaborated here in this volume. We will now set the stage for the detailed studies collated here by drawing the two together. From the analysis of party politics on the island of Ireland, by both single-party and comparative studies, it is possible to deduce that the elements of Europeanization present in this case are of a different degree and nature to those in other member-states. This is to be expected. The outstanding difficulty is identifying whether the context (of Ireland or Northern Ireland) is more or less important than the subject (i.e. the particular party) in determining the effects of Europeanization. This is made all the more complex by the fact, noted above, that EU membership has irrevocably altered the political context and agenda in Ireland, north and south.

In relation to Ladrech's (2002) core points, we see that there is substantial variation between parties in terms of their programmatic, organizational, competitive, internal and transnational frameworks vis-à-vis the European Union. Overall, however, it is possible to suggest that programmatic change is limited in Ireland because parties tend to approach European integration from the basis of pragmatism rather than principle. Organizational change is constrained by the highly centralized party systems in Ireland and in Northern Ireland. In virtually all cases, the best that can be said of the EU is that it is an 'add-on' to the local/national framework for party organization. Similarly, as regards party competition, the EU has become an additional means of competition for most parties, not only as a forum (e.g. through elections to the European Parliament) but also as an 'issue' (as in referendums). Party/government relations can be tense, and this can certainly be exacerbated for many parties on the subject of the leadership's compromises and negotiations in Brussels. Finally, relations beyond the party system vary according to the pre-existing connections between parties and their European counterparts, which is easier for some parties (Greens, the 'Christian Democratic' Fine Gael) than for others (the DUP, Fianna Fáil) according to their ideological tradition rather than their conception of the EU.

We wish to conclude by making four points that may have relevance beyond the Irish case study and contribute to wider comprehension of Europeanization across the EU. First, the stimulus for the acceptance of Europeanization is to be found within the requirements and needs of the party at a particular point rather than from anything that occurs at the EU level. Secondly, we note that patterns of Europeanization fit closely with pre-existing patterns of party evolution. Yet there are some notable similarities in trends of discourse and policy change across all parties following their engagement with the EU, which does indicate that 'Europeanization' is rather greater than party interest writ large. Thirdly, the lack of a link between voting in referendums and voting in elections suggests that Europeanization is not actually first and foremost a *party* issue (Holmes, 2009). Engagement with the EU is overwhelmingly elite-led, knowledge of the EU is often mediated by political parties, and support for the EU is based on trust in political leaders. And yet voters are not following the example set by party elites vis-à-vis European integration as closely as they used to. The distance between central and local political interests, leadership and grassroots, is coming to bear on the power of political parties in determining the wider 'Europeanization' of the political sphere in Ireland. Finally, although local/national/party interests prevail over 'European' ones at every turn, some reconceptualization of these interests has undoubtedly occurred as a consequence of the small but significant Europeanization of the Irish political sphere that has already taken place.

References

Benoit, K. (2009) Irish political parties and policy stances on European integration, *Irish Political Studies*, 24(4), pp. 447–466.

Bolleyer, N. & Panke, D. (2009) The Irish Green Party and Europe: an unhappy marriage? *Irish Political Studies*, 24(4), pp. 543–557.

Carty, R.K. (1976) Social cleavages and party systems: a reconsideration of the Irish case, *European Journal of Political Research*, 4(2), pp. 195–203.

Cowles, M., Caporaso, J. & Risse, T. (Eds) (2001) *Transforming Europe: Europeanization and Domestic Change* (Ithaca, NY: Cornell University Press).

De Winter, L. & Gómez-Reino Cachefeiro, M. (2002) European integration and ethnoregionalist parties, *Party Politics*, 8(4), pp. 483–503.

Devine, K. (2009) Irish political parties' attitudes towards neutrality and the evolution of the EU's foreign, security and defence policies, *Irish Political Studies*, 24(4), pp. 467–489.

Evans, G. & Duffy, M. (1997) Beyond the sectarian divide: the social bases and political consequences of nationalist and unionist party competition in Northern Ireland, *British Journal of Political Science*, 27(1), pp. 47–81.

Featherstone, K. (2003) Introduction: in the name of 'Europe', in: K. Featherstone & C. Radaelli (Eds) *The Politics of Europeanization*, pp. 3–26 (Oxford: Oxford University Press).

Ganiel, G. (2009) 'Battling in Brussels': the DUP and the European Union, *Irish Political Studies*, 24(4), pp. 575–588.

Garry, J., Marsh, M. & Sinnott, R. (2005) 'Second-order' versus 'issue-voting' effects in EU referendums: evidence from the Irish Nice Treaty referendums, *European Union Politics*, 6(2), pp. 201–221.

Hayward, K. & Fallon, J. (2009) Fianna Fáil: tenacious localism, tenuous Europeanism, *Irish Political Studies*, 24(4), pp. 491–509.

Holmes, M. (2009) The Irish Labour Party: the advantages, disadvantages and irrelevance of Europeanization? *Irish Political Studies*, 24(4), pp. 527–541.
Jolly, S.K. (2007) The Europhile fringe? Regionalist party support for European integration, *European Union Politics*, 8(1), pp. 109–130.
Ladrech, R. (1994) The Europeanization of domestic politics and institutions: the case of France, *Journal of Common Market Studies*, 32(1), pp. 69–88.
Ladrech, R. (2002) Europeanization and political parties: towards a framework for analysis, *Party Politics*, 8(4), pp. 389–403.
Laffan, B. & O'Mahony, J. (2008) *Ireland and the European Union* (Basingstoke: Palgrave Macmillan).
Maillot, A. (2009) Sinn Féin's Approach to the EU: still more 'critical' than 'engaged'? *Irish Political Studies*, 24(4), pp. 559–574.
Mair, P. (1979) The autonomy of the political: the development of the Irish party system, *Comparative Politics*, 11(4), pp. 445–465.
Mair, P. (2000) The limited impact of Europe on national party systems, *West European Politics*, 23(4), pp. 27–51.
Mair, P. (2004) The Europeanization dimension, *Journal of European Public Policy*, 11(2), pp. 337–348.
McLoughlin, P.J. (2009) The SDLP and the Europeanization of the Northern Ireland problem, *Irish Political Studies*, 24(4), pp. 603–619.
Mitchell, P. (1991) Conflict regulation and party competition in Northern Ireland, *European Journal of Political Research*, 20(1), pp. 67–92.
Mitchell, P. (1995) Party competition in an ethnic dual party system, *Ethnic and Racial Studies*, 18(4), pp. 773–796.
Mitchell, P. (1999) The party system and party competition, in: P. Mitchell & R. Wilford (Eds) *Politics in Northern Ireland*, pp. 91–116 (Oxford: Westview Press).
Mitchell, P., Evans, G. & O'Leary, B. (2009) Extremist outbidding is not inevitable: tribune parties in Northern Ireland, *Political Studies*, 57(2), pp. 397–421.
Müller-Rommel, F. (1998) Ethnoregionalist parties in Western Europe: theoretical considerations and framework of analysis, in: L. De Winter & H. Türsan (Eds) *Regionalist Parties in Western Europe*, pp. 17–26 (London: Routledge).
Murphy, M.C. (2009) Pragmatic politics: the Ulster Unionist Party and the European Union, *Irish Political Studies*, 24(4), pp. 589–602.
O'Mahony, J. (2009) Ireland's EU referendum experience, *Irish Political Studies*, 24(4), pp. 429–446.
Olsen, J.P. (2002) The many faces of Europeanization, *Journal of Common Market Studies*, 40(5), pp. 921–952.
Radaelli, C. (2000) Whither Europeanization? Concept stretching and substantive change, *European Integration Online Papers (EioP)*, 4(8), available at: http://www.eiop.or.at/eiop/texte/2000-008a.htm (accessed July 2009).
Reidy, T. (2009) Blissful union? Fine Gael and the European Union, *Irish Political Studies*, 24(4), pp. 511–525.
Sinnott, R. (1984) Interpretations of the Irish party system, *European Journal of Political Research*, 12(3), pp. 289–307.
Weeks, L. (2009) The parties and party system, in: J. Coakley & M. Gallagher (Eds) *Politics in the Republic of Ireland*, 5th ed. (London: Routledge).

Ireland's EU Referendum Experience

JANE O'MAHONY
University of Kent, UK

ABSTRACT   *The purpose of this article is twofold. First, it surveys Ireland's European Union referendum experience, tracing the key actors, issues and political dynamics of seven European referendums from 1973 to 2008. It unpicks the institutional rules of the referendum game in Ireland stemming from the McKenna and Coughlan judgements, the operation of the Referendum Commission and the effect of this institutional environment on referendum campaigns and outcomes. Second, building on a framework originally developed by Darcy and Laver (1990), this article investigates the emergence of a dynamic in Irish referendums on EU treaties with two key elements: elite withdrawal and populist capture.*

Introduction

Until June 2001, Ireland's experience of European Union (EU) referendums was a positive one: referendums were comfortably carried, helping to copper-fasten Ireland's reputation as a constructive and *communautaire* EU member state. The supportive attitude of the electorate in referendums on accession, the Single European Act (SEA), Maastricht and Amsterdam treaties was mirrored by public opinion polls on the EU: a healthy majority of those surveyed declared themselves in favour of membership and appreciated the perceived benefits that membership brought Ireland. The rejection of the Nice Treaty by the electorate in 2001 was therefore a major shock to the political elites, and for the first time indicated that perhaps the Irish consensus on European matters could not be taken for granted. The success of the second Nice referendum in 2002 appeared to suggest that lessons were taken from the experience in 2001 and greater efforts were made to explain the relevant issues to the electorate. However, the decisive defeat of the Lisbon Treaty in June 2008 suggested that learning from Nice I was short-lived among Irish political elites (see Table 1).[1] With the second rejection of a European treaty by the Irish electorate in seven years, Ireland's EU referendum experience has been transformed.

The rejection of the Treaty of Lisbon in June 2008 marked a critical juncture in Ireland's relationship with the EU and at the same time brought two key issues sharply into focus: the Irish electorate's self-confessed lack of knowledge of the EU and evolving Irish attitudes towards European integration. An environment has emerged in which Irish referendums on EU treaties have become highly contested affairs.

14   J. O'Mahony

Looking at the Nice I and Lisbon I referendums in particular, a dynamic has become apparent with a number of common characteristics (Darcy & Laver, 1990; LeDuc, 2003; Moravcsik, 2008). As the experience of the French and Dutch referendums on the European Constitutional Treaty in 2005 show, these referendum characteristics are not unique to Ireland. In the Nice I and Lisbon I referendums, in the face of *de facto* elite withdrawal from the referendum playing field, a number of effectively-organized groups and political parties on the margins of the political system, often espousing populist and anti-establishment ideas, succeeded in capturing the referendum agenda. These actors capitalized on the fears and distrust of an electorate deficient in general knowledge about the EU and were facilitated by the complexity of the issues at stake and the institutional rules of the Irish referendum game.[2]

The purpose of this article is twofold. First, it offers a survey of Ireland's EU referendum experience, outlines why Irish governments hold referendums on EU treaties, provides an account of how the rules of the Irish referendum game evolved, and highlights the issues in each of the referendum campaigns. Second, it focuses on a referendum dynamic that has emerged in the Nice I and Lisbon I referendums, which involves the twin elements of elite withdrawal and populist capture. Implicit in this analysis is an investigation into whether the Irish electorate is becoming more Eurosceptic. In the Nice I referendum, it was evident that the success of the No vote as a percentage of the electorate was heavily influenced by the abstention of Yes voters, rather than an increase in the No vote as a percentage of the electorate *per se* (see Figure 1). However, a key difference between the Nice I and Lisbon

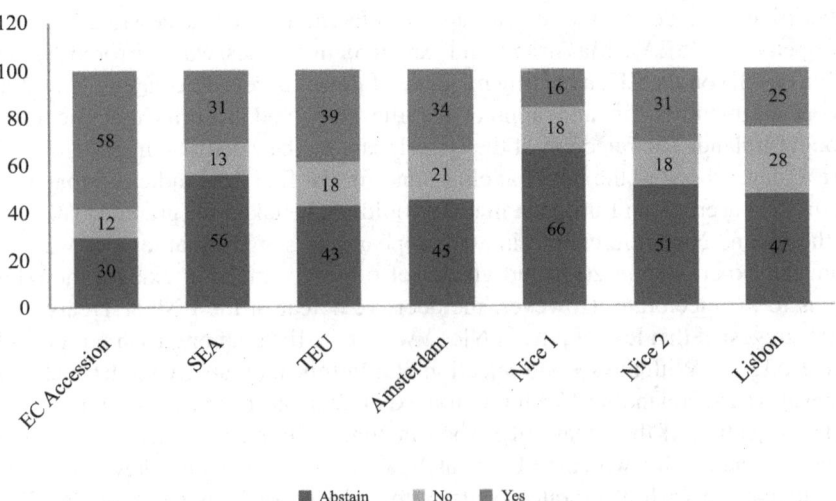

Figure 1. Yes, No and abstentions as proportions of the electorate in EU referendums in Ireland.
Source: Available at: www.ireland.com/focus/thelisbontreaty/analysis/graphics/#result (accessed June 2008).

Table 1. European referendum results, 1972–2008

Date	Issue	% Yes	% No	% Turnout	% Spoilt or blank papers
10.5.72	Accession to EEC	83.1	16.9	70.9	0.8
26.5.87	Ratify Single European Act	69.9	30.1	44.1	0.5
18.6.92	Ratify Maastricht Treaty	69.1	30.9	57.3	0.5
22.5.98	Ratify Amsterdam Treaty	61.7	38.3	56.2	2.2
7.6.01	Ratify Nice Treaty (first time)	46.1	53.9	34.8	1.5
20.10.02	Ratify Nice Treaty (second time)	62.9	37.1	48.5	0.4
12.06.08	Ratify Lisbon Treaty	46.6	53.4	53.1	0.4

I referendums is the increase in No voters as a proportion of the total electorate (from 18 percent at Nice I to 28 percent in June 2008). Although it was questionable whether Nice I proved the Irish electorate was becoming more Eurosceptic (Gilland, 2008: 120), recent *Eurobarometer* public opinion polls have certainly indicated that the Irish electorate is becoming increasingly cautious about European integration: public opinion is nuanced. This has significant implications not only for EU referendum campaigns in Ireland but, indeed, for the future course of Ireland's relationship with the EU.

Dynamics of Referendums in Europe

There has been a substantial increase in the number of referendums held throughout the world in recent years (LeDuc, 2003: 13; Qvortrup, 2005). Ireland is no exception to this phenomenon, as Figure 2 shows. The majority of referendums in Ireland, particularly since the 1960s, fall into one of two broad categories: those dealing with social-moral issues and those dealing with governance issues, including referendums on joining the European Economic Community (EEC) and subsequent EU treaties (Sinnott, 2002: 812). Supporters of the referendum device have argued that citizens' direct involvement in politics, through referendums, can supplement traditional forms of representative democracy (Qvortrup, 2005; Setälä, 2006). In an era where the traditional forms of political participation, such as voting in elections and membership of political parties, are seen to be in decline and trust in politicians is on the wane, direct participation of citizens in the political process through referendums can be seen to maximize legitimacy of decisions. They also have the potential to increase actual participation and involvement of citizens in the political process itself, engaging them as much as possible in the decision-making process (LeDuc 2003: 38). In this sense, voting in referendums becomes an active form of civic education (Barber, 1984; Qvortrup, 2005: 35).

Critics of the referendum device, however, focus on two general concerns. First, referendums are seen as privileging the rights of the majority over those of minorities. Second, instead of contributing to their civic education, voters in referendums 'routinely complain about insufficient information, confusing question wording, or contradictory lines of argument regarding the possible consequences of a referendum vote' (LeDuc, 2003: 43). In addition, voter turnout in referendums is typically lower than that in general elections (Butler & Ranney, 1994: 17). Indeed, Qvortrup (1998: 256) has found that a frequent use of referendums generally results in a drop in the turnout rate. The claims that referendums facilitate citizen participation in the political process and increase civic education must be seriously evaluated in this context.

Research on referendums, while limited in comparison to studies of voting behaviour in elections, has increased in recent years and focuses on why voters behave the way they do in referendums (LeDuc, 2003: 14). As regards EU referendums, political scientists are divided on the reasons why voters vote the way they do (Franklin, van der Eijk & Marsh, 1995; Svensson, 2002; Binzer Hobolt, 2003). Some focus on individuals' values and beliefs, arguing that voting behaviour in EU referendums reflects people's underlying broad attitudes towards Europe: it is voters' general views on Europe that influence how they vote (Svensson, 2002). Others argue that EU referendums work very much like second order European Parliament (EP) elections; an important factor in determining their outcomes can be support for, or opposition to, the party or parties in government at the time of the referendum (Franklin, van der Eijk & Marsh, 1995).

Campaign dynamics have also been investigated (Darcy & Laver, 1990; LeDuc, 2002, 2003). Referendums are often seen to provide a very volatile electoral environment, particularly in situations when political parties line up in a non-traditional manner (i.e. not on ideological or partisan lines). In such situations voters find it difficult to take cues or shortcuts from party positions, take more time to come to a decision, and that decision becomes highly unpredictable (LeDuc, 2003: 173; LeDuc, 2002: 727). In this context, the nature of the campaign becomes extremely important and the impact of opposition campaign strategies and tactics can play a crucial role in determining the outcome. While LeDuc acknowledges that the political context of each referendum can differ widely, a referendum dynamic, or at least a set of common patterns, can emerge (LeDuc, 2003: 15). In the face of broad consensus across the political spectrum, establishment elites often withdraw from the campaign arena, leaving the referendum field open to capture by what Darcy and Laver (1990) term 'fringe activists', frequently espousing populist or anti-establishment values. In the context of elite withdrawal from EU referendums in particular, the often emotive tactics of such groups – capitalizing on voter ignorance, the complexity of the issues and an underlying sense of political discontent amongst the electorate – can wrestle control of the referendum campaign from those who originally instigated it in the first place (Moravcsik, 2008). According to Darcy and Laver (1990: 16), 'as the going gets rough on one side, the elites withdraw, the spiral begins, the going gets rougher, and so on. Once the elites begin to back off, the voters too, become dubious and vote no'. As we will see in this survey of Ireland's EU referendum experience, such a referendum dynamic exists in Ireland, particularly since the Nice I referendum.

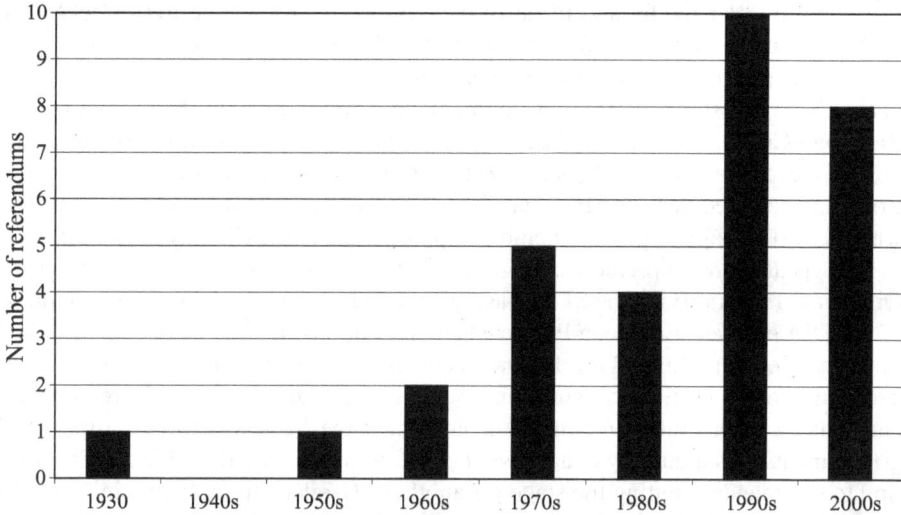

Figure 2. Number of referendums in Ireland per decade.

EU Referendums in Ireland

The reason behind the 1972 referendum on accession to the EEC was fairly straightforward: it was necessary in order to correct the conflict that the obligations of membership would cause for the Constitution, *Bunreacht na hÉireann*. Under the obligations of EEC membership and alongside the doctrine of supremacy of European law, legislative authority would no longer be solely invested in the Oireachtas and the European Court of Justice would be superior to the state's Supreme Court. Rather than amending each of the affected articles accordingly, the decision was taken to introduce a catch-all amendment (Article 29.4.3) allowing the state to join the EEC. The 1972 referendum has been the only time Irish political parties have divided on a European issue according to the (rather weak) left–right economic cleavage evident in Irish electoral politics (Sinnott, 2002; Gallagher, 2003): the parties of the centre-right/right (Fianna Fáil and Fine Gael), alongside business leaders and farmers' groups, strongly advocated membership of the Common Market, while parties of the left (primarily the Irish Labour Party and the Workers Party), alongside the civil society group the Common Market Study Group and the Irish Congress of Trade Unions, campaigned for a No vote. The mounting of a vigorous campaign by political parties and civil society groups which were clearly divided on the issue, together with wide public discussion of the issues, helped push turnout up (at 70.88 percent it is the highest level of turnout heretofore recorded in any referendum in Ireland) and the referendum was comfortably carried with 83.1 percent in favour.

By the time of the signature of the Single European Act (SEA) in 1986, the consensus amongst political and legal circles was that parliamentary approval was sufficient in order for Ireland to ratify the new treaty. After a period of delay, the SEA was put before the Dáil on 9 December 1986. However, concern in certain legal and academic circles as to the means used to ratify the SEA was growing and just before Christmas 1986, development economist and anti-EEC campaigner Raymond Crotty, backed by a larger group, challenged the constitutionality of the bill in the courts (McCutcheon, 1991). Crotty and fellow campaigner Anthony Coughlan believed that the SEA went far beyond what the Irish people consented to when they originally approved membership of the EEC in 1972 (Crotty, 1988: 104).

On appeal to the Supreme Court in early 1987, Crotty succeeded in stopping the Oireachtas from ratifying the SEA. Basing its judgments on the provisions in Title III of the SEA entitled 'European Political Cooperation', by a three-to-two majority the Supreme Court held that Title III was inconsistent with the Constitution as it was additional to the original constitutional sanction provided by the 1972 referendum and thus the Constitution required amendment if the SEA was to be ratified. The government moved quickly to approve legislation which would enable the Constitution to be amended, setting the stage for another EU-related referendum in 1987. As in 1972, the decision was taken to confine the 1987 referendum to the specific issue at hand, namely the amendment of the constitution in order to ratify the SEA, rather than introducing an all-encompassing amendment that would make all future referendums unnecessary. This political decision has meant that since 1987, ratification of European integration treaties in Ireland has been carried out by referendum.

The Rules of the Irish Referendum Game

The rules of the Irish referendum game were decided in the 1990s and stem directly from two court judgments referred to as the McKenna and Coughlan judgments respectively. During the 1992 Maastricht campaign the government came under fire from treaty opponents for the use of public funding in order to campaign for a Yes vote. Feeling hampered by their limited financial resources, especially in comparison with the resources held by the Yes side, anti-Maastricht groups criticized the decision by the state broadcaster Raidió Teilifís Éireann (RTÉ) to show a special government television appeal for a Yes vote without allowing equal airtime to the opposition campaign. In the run up to the 1995 divorce referendum, then Green Party Member of European Parliament (MEP) Patricia McKenna questioned the constitutionality of the use of public money by the government to campaign for a Yes vote. Such funding was declared unconstitutional as the Supreme Court ruled that the government was not entitled to use public money to put forward only one side of the case, since not all citizens would support one side. Thus, for each referendum since 1995, the government of the day has established a Referendum Commission whose function is to inform the public about the issues and arguments in a non-biased manner. The Commission is composed of non-political figures, and usually headed by either a former or current member of the judiciary nominated by the Chief Justice, alongside the Ombudsman, the Comptroller and Auditor General and other senior civil servants. One month before the Amsterdam referendum in

1998, in response to a request for judicial review by Anthony Coughlan, the High Court found that RTÉ's giving of airtime on the basis of electoral support for political parties resulted in inequality amounting to unconstitutional unfairness 'which would not have arisen had their starting point been to afford equality to each side of the argument to which there could only be a YES and NO answer' (Carney, 1998). The implication of this judgment (confirmed by the Supreme Court in January 2000) has been that in subsequent referendums, RTÉ has allotted equal broadcast airtime (i.e. on television or radio) to parties and groups advocating a Yes and No respectively, in any given campaign. Taken together, both judgments considerably altered the way EU referendums have since been conducted.

Elite Withdrawal

The SEA, the Treaty on European Union and Amsterdam Referendums

Between 1972 and 2008, Irish governments fought seven referendum campaigns asking the Irish electorate to ratify five EU treaties and a number of common characteristics in each of these referendum campaigns emerged. Turnout in EU referendums have typically been lower than at general elections, reaching a lowest point in June 2001 when 34.9 percent of the electorate turned out to vote on the Nice Treaty. Apart from the 1972 accession referendum, EU treaties have garnered broad support across the political establishment, including the mainstream political parties, trade unions and business organizations. Smaller political parties, ostensibly at the margins of the political spectrum, such as Sinn Féin, the Green Party and the Socialist Workers' Party and non-party political and civil society groups all have opposed EU referendums (this changed in 2008 when the Greens, now a partner in the Fianna Fáil-led government, did not campaign against the Lisbon Treaty).

Until Nice I, Irish governments and other pro-European campaigners were convincingly able to point to the benefits EU membership had brought Ireland, both in terms of direct financial transfers and in increased opportunities for Irish industry and workers. In alluding directly to this 'donor/recipient' narrative, they relied on the permissive consensus inherent in Irish public opinion on the EU, namely that citizens appreciated the considerable benefits Ireland had received from EU membership. Little effort was made to explain the issues at stake to the electorate. Political parties tended not to campaign actively in referendums.

The Single European Act referendum campaign is a case in point and set the tone for referendum campaigns to follow. While the Workers' Party and Sinn Féin campaigned for a No vote (the Labour Party did not adopt an official position due to internal differences), the main opposition came from groupings outside the party political system, including veteran anti-EU campaigner Anthony Coughlan. Those campaigning for a Yes vote argued that Ireland's membership of the European Community would be at stake and that damage would be done to the economy and employment if the referendum was defeated. Little effort was made to inform voters fully about the issues. In the end, the campaign was relatively short and the referendum was comfortably carried with an almost 70 percent Yes vote. The fall in turnout to 44 percent was more alarming however, and constituted at the time the second lowest ever turnout in a referendum (Gallagher, 1988: 80). The effect of the low turnout was that the Yes vote amounted to only 30.7 percent of the electorate, compared with 58.4 percent in 1972.

In some ways, the Maastricht referendum of 1992 could be said to have been merely a re-run of the SEA referendum. The referendum was comfortably carried (with 69.1 percent voting Yes) and the pro-European consensus amongst mainstream political parties and interest groups such as the trade unions was solidified as both the Labour Party and the Irish Congress of Trade Unions (ICTU) came out in favour, thus marking the first time that Labour had given official support to an initiative towards integration. What is notable about the Maastricht referendum campaign is not just the solidifying of a pro-European consensus amongst political parties (with the exception of the Green Party and Sinn Féin), but also the rise in importance of civil society groupings in the referendum campaign. In the Maastricht campaign, these groups included Anthony Coughlan's National Platform for Employment, Democracy and Neutrality (comprising other groups such as the People First/Meitheal organization and Irish Campaign for Nuclear Disarmament, CND). Neutrality, sovereignty and independence, and the threat integration posed to traditional, Catholic values were recurring motifs of the debate. The threat of possible conscription to a common European army was also mooted. The focus of the campaign was also deflected away from the content of the treaty itself towards issues such as the record financial sum negotiated by the then Taoiseach Albert Reynolds as part of the Delors II structural fund package and the controversial rulings on abortion by the High Court and Supreme Court in the 'X' case, which led to discussions on the treaty becoming embroiled in the issue of the introduction of abortion in Ireland.

The party-political pro-European consensus continued in the 1998 Amsterdam referendum as the leaders of the government coalition parties, Fianna Fáil and the Progressive Democrats, joined forces with Fine Gael, Labour and Democratic Left to host a press conference in which they jointly urged a Yes vote based on the economic and political benefits active EU membership would bring. A core tenet of their argument was that rejecting the treaty would hurt Ireland's position in the EU. Much of the debate during the campaign focused on the issue of neutrality with protagonists in favour of the treaty asserting that the treaty had no negative implications for neutrality. The Peace and Neutrality Alliance (PANA) chaired by Roger Cole opposed the treaty on the grounds of the threat it posed to Irish neutrality and much of the discussion during the campaign focused on Ireland's participation in the North Atlantic Treaty Organization's (NATO) Partnership for Peace framework.

While the referendum was comfortably carried with a 61.7 percent Yes vote, the No vote of just over 38 percent was the largest vote against EU integration hitherto recorded. With a turnout of 56.2 percent, the proportion of the electorate rejecting further integration reached a high of 21 percent, with 45 percent of the electorate choosing to abstain (see Figure 1). The Amsterdam referendum was the first EU referendum to take place under the auspices of the Referendum Commission. The

Referendum Commission's approach of making a public call for arguments from individuals, interest groups or parties, and then putting these together in leaflets, newspaper advertisements, and television and radio broadcasts was widely criticized, leading as it did to erroneous arguments being presented as facts. The material disseminated by the Commission was also criticized by some as turgid and confusing, turning off voters rather than enlightening them (Mansergh, 1999; Gallagher, 2003). The ineffectiveness of the Commission in informing voters of the issues at stake was highlighted even more when the results of an exit poll were published in May 1998. Asked 'why did you vote No against the Amsterdam Treaty', those polled cited a perceived lack of information as the main reason (Gilland, 1999: 435).

The Nice and Lisbon Referendums

The Nice I and Lisbon I referendums provide the most illuminating examples of Ireland's EU referendum dynamic, clearly illustrating the two characteristics of elite withdrawal and populist capture. At Nice I, the broad consensus across the political establishment in favour of ratification was again in evidence. The smaller parties of Sinn Féin, the Green Party and the Socialist Workers' party all campaigned against the treaty. The Nice Treaty was sold by Yes campaigners as being in Ireland's best interests, as it would facilitate the enlargement of the EU from 15 to 25 and thereby give Irish industry access to an enlarged single market. The referendum also took place on the same day as two other referendums on the International Criminal Court and the death penalty. With their eye on a general election in 2002, political parties advocating a Yes vote were reluctant to spend money campaigning and the message put forward to the voters was unclear. In contrast, No campaigners, including Anthony Coughlan's National Platform, the 'No to Nice' group (led by anti-abortion campaigner Justin Barrett), PANA and others ran a highly committed and visible campaign. Their main slogan 'if you don't know, vote No', echoed that of the Amsterdam referendum.

In the second Nice referendum in 2002, those advocating a Yes vote did not this time withdraw from the campaign arena. While the same No campaigners emerged to advocate another No vote, a re-engaged political elite was joined by a number of strongly committed civil society groups organized under the umbrella 'Irish Alliance for Europe'. Before the campaign proper began, the government moved to allay electorate fears, securing two declarations on Irish neutrality at the June 2002 Seville European Council summit. A National Forum on Europe was set up to communicate the issues to a wider public in advance of the second referendum, and national parliamentary scrutiny on EU matters was enhanced. With Minister for European Affairs Dick Roche taking the lead, government ministers and opposition politicians spoke to the issues within the treaty and firmly rebutted No campaigners' claims. Increased face-to-face political campaigning also took place which reduced room for No campaigns to instil fear in the electorate. On 18 October 2002, 49.5 percent of voters turned out to vote with 63 percent voting to ratify the treaty.

The referendum dynamic of elite withdrawal was even more in evidence in the first Lisbon referendum of June 2008. For those advocating a Yes vote, selling Lisbon was always going to be difficult. Unlike the single European market underlying the SEA or the common currency underlying the Maastricht Treaty, the Treaty of Lisbon contains no one 'grand' idea (Moravcsik, 2008). As an amending treaty, it sets out various incremental reforms to EU decision-making and policy-making procedures. It is arguable that, as the only member state to ratify the treaty by referendum, the Irish government was faced with an unenviable task. Early signs that ratification would be a challenge were also evident in public opinion polls. In a poll conducted in November 2007, only 25 percent of those surveyed said they would vote Yes to the new Treaty, while 13 percent intended to vote No and 62 percent said they did not know or had no opinion.[3]

The retreat of the political elite from the Lisbon campaign could be said to be a mixture of both accident and design. It became clear from early 2008 that the then Taoiseach Bertie Ahern was distracted from the business of government due to ongoing revelations at a judicial enquiry into planning matters. Amidst growing public disquiet, Ahern's position came under scrutiny. Confusion also existed as to when the referendum itself would be held as Ahern procrastinated in naming a date, eventually deciding on a date in June (Laffan & O'Mahony, 2008: 116). Between the announcement on 2 April 2008 of Ahern's intention to resign and the appointment of Brian Cowen as Taoiseach on 8 May 2008, a political vacuum emerged which was filled by effectively organized No campaigners. Passing Lisbon was the new Taoiseach's first priority but the campaign itself was set to be a short one of barely four weeks and, as new Minister for Foreign Affairs Micheál Martin was to subsequently acknowledge, the Government failed to run an effective campaign.[4] The Lisbon Treaty had the support of all main political parties, including the parliamentary Green Party. Sinn Féin was the only party in the Dáil to campaign against Lisbon.

The Yes campaign only ignited one week before the referendum date itself, when a TNS/MRBI poll clearly indicated that the referendum could be lost. In terms of campaign strategies and tactics, the Yes campaigners failed to construct a narrative on the treaty, simply urging voters to trust them and vote Yes. Yes posters expounded generic slogans such as 'Good for Ireland, Good for Europe', 'Europe, Let's be at the Heart of It' and controversially displayed photos of politicians, which were more akin to election campaign posters. Admissions by a number of politicians such as new Taoiseach Brian Cowen and European Commissioner Charlie McCreevy that they had not read the treaty in its entirety did not help the Yes campaign. Given the early foothold gained by the No campaign, the Yes side spent their time attempting to counter No arguments and misinformation. Infighting amongst the mainstream political parties (most notably Fianna Fáil and Fine Gael) also undermined the Yes campaign, as did the threat by sectional interests such as the farmers' organizations, most notably the Irish Farmers' Association (IFA), to withhold their support for the treaty unless a commitment was given by the government to veto ongoing World Trade Organization (WTO) talks should the ultimate deal undermine Irish farmers' interests.

Marsh et al. (2008: 5–11) have found that an important feature of Irish politics is the personal and local style of campaigning in general elections which consists of extensive door-to-door campaigning by party workers and the candidates themselves, the distribution of leaflets, putting up posters and canvassing at shopping centres, church gates, etc. Such campaigning has not been as common in referendums: 'traditionally political parties don't campaign door to door in referendums'.[5] Anecdotally, reports circulated that there was very limited door-to-door campaigning undertaken by the Yes side in the Lisbon referendum. In a parliamentary committee debate in the immediate aftermath of the referendum result, one politician referred directly to this: 'Nobody knocked on doors. People felt a massive deficit in engagement ... People are reassured by personal canvassing and explanations'.[6] In contrast, the National Forum on Europe road shows that took place around the country in the lead-up to and during the campaign appeared not to have had an impact on public knowledge and engagement as public attendance was low. According to Marian Harkin MEP: 'we go to meetings of the Forum on Europe and we are talking to ourselves'.[7]

Populist Capture

Low Levels of EU Knowledge

Research has shown that since the 1990s at least, knowledge of the EU amongst the Irish public is low (Laffan & O'Mahony, 2008: 128). In his 1995 study, Sinnott discovered that the positive perceptions of EU membership in Ireland were accompanied by relatively low levels of knowledge regarding the EU (Sinnott, 1995). Ireland ranked sixth overall out of all then 15 EU member states in actual levels of knowledge of how the EU functioned. In addition, Sinnott found a positive correlation between higher levels of knowledge of European affairs and a favourable attitude to European integration. Low levels of knowledge are also closely associated with social class and level of education. At the time of Lisbon I in 2008, it became clear that both the Irish electorate's objective (i.e. actual) and subjective (i.e. perceived) knowledge of the EU continued to be poor (Laffan & O'Mahony, 2008: 129). In *Eurobarometer* 69 (Spring 2008), three questions were fielded to those surveyed to test their knowledge on the EU.[8] In the survey Ireland was compared with Denmark: 29 percent of Irish respondents answered three questions correctly (compared with 40 percent of Danes); 28 percent of Irish respondents answered two questions correctly; 22 percent answered one question correctly and 22 percent gave no correct answer to the questions (in comparison with 10 percent of Danes).

In terms of knowledge of the Lisbon Treaty itself, a Referendum Commission opinion poll in late April 2008 found that just five percent of those polled believed they understood the treaty well or quite well (see Quinlan, 2009). A total of 15 percent understood it to some extent while 80 percent said they did not understand it particularly well or did not understand it at all (Referendum Commission, 2008). In the post-Lisbon survey undertaken by Millward Brown/IMS on behalf of the

Department of Foreign Affairs, the main reason behind abstention was lack of knowledge/understanding of the treaty (at 46 percent this was well in excess of any other reason). In terms of an understanding of the treaty at the time of the referendum, the researchers found:

1. 9 percent had a good understanding of what the treaty was about;
2. 31 percent understood some of the issues but not all;
3. 30 percent was only vaguely aware of the issues involved;
4. 30 percent did not know what the treaty was about at all.

Of those surveyed who said they voted Yes, 70 percent said that they either had a good understanding of the treaty or some understanding of the issues. In contrast, of those who said they voted No, 53 percent said they were either only vaguely aware of the issues or had no knowledge. As the Millward Brown/IMS report (2008) concluded: 'an EU knowledge deficit is clearly present which has undoubtedly contributed to the No vote [in Lisbon] ... Knowledge of EU institutions and how they work appears to be particularly low. The difficulty of advocating a referendum that is based on the premise of institutional reform in this environment is apparent'.

A common strategy of referendum opponents is to sow seeds of doubt about the motives of those proposing the referendum and possible unforeseen consequences of a positive referendum outcome. As analysts such as LeDuc (2003: 71) have observed, 'when voters become suspicious or uncertain, they tend to vote No'. In the context of the knowledge deficit amongst the Irish electorate as outlined above, the strategy of Lisbon No campaigners was to cherry-pick elements of the treaty and attack them, instilling fear into the minds of an electorate already displaying worries about Ireland's deteriorating economic climate and showing distrust in Irish parliamentary institutions (*Eurobarometer*, 2008). In this way, voters did not have the knowledge to hand to be able to properly scrutinize the various statements regarding the treaty put forward by the No campaigners (Moravcsik, 2008). Through the McKenna and Coughlan judgments, these fringe activists, often espousing populist sentiments, gained an important foothold in the media and succeeded in capturing the Lisbon campaign.

Populism and the No Campaigns

The populism of Irish No campaigners was most clearly evident in the Lisbon I referendum campaign. As a concept, populism is notoriously difficult to define. According to Canovan (1999: 3), populism in modern democratic societies is best seen as an appeal 'to the people' against both the established structure of power and the dominant ideas and values of the society. Indeed, what is often clearer is who and what populists are *against*, rather than what they are for (Mudde, 2004: 546). At its heart however, populism involves opposition between the 'people' and the 'elite'. In an era of declining participation in political parties, falling voter turnout and low levels of trust in politicians, populists attack the establishment for its corruption and lack of accountability to the people, far removed from the 'common' person (Abts & Rummens, 2007: 408). Populism can attach itself to many different ideologies and any economic programme, therefore populists can be found in any position on the left–right political spectrum. Populism is not confined to grass-roots movements led by charismatic leaders, members of the political establishment can also adopt 'populist' tactics with the use of simple, direct language that appeals directly to the people.

At first glance, the rise of populism in Western Europe has been a phenomenon that has taken place outside of Ireland, with the use of referendums on moral, social and European issues helping to insulate Irish electoral politics from it (Albertazzi & McDonnell, 2008: 2). However, that does not mean that populism does not exist in Ireland. Indeed, as an example, Fianna Fáil politicians in particular have adopted populist rhetoric in the past (the famous reference to Fianna Fáil as a movement rather than a political party for instance). Sinn Féin politicians also make use of populist rhetoric, particularly in relation to the EU (cf. McDonnell, 2008; O'Malley, 2008). In the Lisbon I campaign, populist sentiment became increasingly evident amongst opponents of the treaty, from both the left and the right. On the left was the Campaign Against the EU Constitution (CAEUC), a broad coalition of leftwing political parties, organizations, trade unionists and individuals who opposed the Lisbon Treaty. Couching their rhetoric in anti-establishment terms, these groups opposed the treaty on a number of fronts: it posed a threat to Irish sovereignty and independence (particularly in foreign policy terms as an attack on Irish neutrality), it undermined workers' rights, it would usher in the privatization of public services, and Ireland's right to levy taxes would be circumscribed. Finally, the treaty was presented as an 'anti-democratic constitutional treaty ... foisted upon the peoples of Europe by anti-democratic methods' (Campaign Against EU Constitution, 2008). Anthony Coughlan's National Platform also campaigned against Lisbon on the basis that it undermined Irish sovereignty and the principle of the equality of states in the EU.

As in the Netherlands, elements of the religious right have also opposed EU referendums in Ireland on the grounds that ratification of EU Treaties constitutes a threat to Irish Catholic values, by undermining the importance of family values, facilitating the introduction of abortion and challenging the right to life. During the Nice I and II referendum campaigns, the No to Nice group, led by longstanding conservative campaigner Justin Barrett, himself a former leader of Youth Defence, campaigned against the Nice Treaty on this and other issues. In 2008, Youth Defence re-emerged as *Cóir* (Justice) and opposed the Treaty of Lisbon on similar grounds. Going against the official position of the Irish Bishops, *Cóir* argued that the Charter of Fundamental Rights would force Ireland to legalize abortion, gay marriage, prostitution and euthanasia. *Cóir* also tapped into the 'anti-establishment, anti-authority and anti-politician' mood in the country (*Irish Times*, 7 June 2008) through their use of poster slogans such as 'Don't be Bullied, Vote No'.

In opposing the Lisbon Treaty, Declan Ganley and his small but tightly organized Libertas movement also made most use of populist rhetoric, combining anti-establishment sentiment with economic neo-liberalism and an emphasis on the benefits of 'entrepreneurship'. Ganley's stance stemmed from his opposition to the

Constitutional Treaty, which he called an 'attack on democracy in Europe and a subversion of Europe's citizenry' (Ganley, 2003: 3). For Ganley, the Constitutional Treaty represented the 'political bureaucracy's attempt to consolidate its hold over the decision-making process in the EU'. The crux of Libertas' campaign against the Lisbon Treaty in 2008 was that it was *de facto* a European constitution. Libertas undoubtedly ran a masterful and highly effective campaign, with sophisticated use of the internet amongst other media. Ganley welcomed the referendum result with rhetoric that exemplified his style throughout the campaign:

> This is democracy in action. It makes me proud to be Irish … The Irish sent a message to an unelected, unaccountable elite in Brussels that they need to listen to the will of the people … today is about the common sense and generosity of the Irish people in handing Europe back to the people it belongs to … A chasm is opening up between the political elites and the people of Europe. (Comments reported in *Irish Times*, 13 June 2008)

In late 2008, Ganley launched Libertas as a pan-European political party, contesting the 2009 European Parliament elections throughout Europe. Only French politician Philippe de Villiers was elected under the Libertas banner, Ganley himself failing to win a seat in Ireland's North West Constituency. Very late in the day Declan Ganley decided to re-enter the fray and oppose the Lisbon Treaty referendum again. The ignominious results for the party were closely followed by Ganley's announcement that he would not lead the party in campaigning for a No vote in the second referendum (*Irish Times*, 9 June 2009), a position he retracted just a few weeks prior to the Lisbon II vote.

Populist and anti-establishment argumentation in an EU referendum campaign is not unique to Ireland and the range of objections raised to EU treaties in Irish referendums have been echoed elsewhere. In the French referendum on the Constitutional Treaty in 2005, the No campaign brought together a 'fairly heterogeneous collection of minor fringe and/or radical anti-system parties placed disparately on the traditional left-right axis', from Philippe De Villiers (later of Libertas) and his far right, Eurosceptic *Mouvement pour la France,* to the Communist Revolutionary League and the anti-globalization organization *Attac* (Ivaldi, 2006: 55). These left-wing groups argued that the Constitutional Treaty promoted an Anglo-Saxon vision of a liberal free market Europe (Marthaler, 2005: 230). In the Dutch referendum of 2005, a similar range of groups from both left and right campaigned against the treaty. According to Harmsen (2005: 6), these groups consisted of three main strands: the populist left (such as the Socialist Party), the populist right (including the Pim Fortyn List and the Geert Wilders group) and small, traditional Protestant parties, who were critical of the absence of a reference to the EU's Christian heritage.

Euroscepticism in Ireland?

The shift in the No vote at Lisbon by 10 percent to 28 percent of the electorate prompted the question as to whether Euroscepticism is rising in Ireland. As a concept,

Euroscepticism can be viewed in a broad manner, either as an outright rejection of the EU and the process of European integration (so-called hard or principled Euroscepticism), or as opposition towards particular policy areas or developments (soft or contingent Euroscepticism) (Szczerbiak & Taggart, 2008; Sorensen, 2008: 6). In investigating Euroscepticism in Ireland it is also important to make the distinction between party Euroscepticism and scepticism amongst the electorate (Sczcerbiak & Taggart, 2000). Over time, the Green Party and Sinn Féin have provided the most audible voices critical to the EU amongst Irish political parties, falling into the 'soft' Eurosceptic camp in their opposition to aspects of EU integration (Gilland, 2008). Both parties have shifted over time, however, leading to the conclusion that their opposition to aspects of the EU is perhaps conditional. The transformation in the Green Party stance on the European Union since it entered government does suggest that small party opposition to the EU may be contingent (Laffan & O'Mahony, 2008). Following a poor general election campaign in 2007, Sinn Féin used the Lisbon I referendum to enhance the profile and positioning of the party in the Republic. The profile of the party may have benefited, but their electoral fortunes did not. The party returned only its MEP from Northern Ireland (Bairbre de Brún) to the European Parliament in 2009 after Mary Lou McDonald failed to regain her seat (in the Dublin constituency whose seat total had been reduced from four to three).

There remains widespread support for European integration amongst Irish people. Since the early 1980s, support for the EU rose from lower levels of support to very high levels, well above the EU average (Laffan & O'Mahony, 2008: 123). However, on some indicators, Irish support for integration is of a 'soft' and perhaps more conditional nature (*Eurobarometer*, 2008). Faced in 2004 with a hypothetical situation whereby the EU would be scrapped (the dissolution question), 54 percent of Irish respondents said they would be sorry, whereas 43 percent felt they would be either indifferent or did not know what to think – thus giving the impression that enthusiasm for the EU does not run all that deeply. Irish enthusiasm for certain aspects of integration, such as further political integration, is also more measured (Laffan & O'Mahony, 2008). For example, while attitudes to security and defence matters in general are more likely to be positive than negative, a large percentage of Irish people are unsure about these issues (as evidenced by the numbers of respondents who are reluctant to offer an opinion). According to the *Eurobarometer* poll published in the aftermath of the Lisbon I referendum, 'there is also evidence of a recent small but significant shift towards a preference for more national decision-making and away from EU decision-making on a range of issues, especially issues of taxation, agriculture and fisheries, immigration and energy' (*Eurobarometer*, 2008: 15). In addition, identification with Europe is low amongst Irish citizens. In the 2008 poll, 46 percent of those surveyed said they had little or no sense of attachment to the EU and 59 percent 'rejected the proffered degrees of European identity and opted for an exclusive Irish identity, second in frequency in this respect only to Britain (63 percent)' (*Eurobarometer*, 2008: 21). While on their own such findings do not point directly to rising Euroscepticism amongst the Irish electorate, they do illustrate that Irish support for European integration is nuanced.

Conclusion

In the second half of 2008, the use of the referendum device in ratifying EU treaties was seriously questioned as a solution to Ireland's 'Lisbon dilemma'. Indeed, the scope of the Crotty judgment and the possibility of parliamentary scrutiny of the Lisbon Treaty or aspects of the Lisbon Treaty were widely discussed (e.g. Barrett, 2008; Barrington, 2008; Cox, 2008; Fanning, 2008). The conduct of the referendum game in Ireland was also questioned, most particularly the role of the Referendum Commission. Based on overwhelming precedent, however, it has become embedded in Irish political culture that EU treaties are ratified by referendum and in December 2008 it became clear that the Lisbon Treaty would be put to the Irish electorate for a second time under the existing referendum rules (LeDuc, 2003: 186; Cox, 2008). As Minister for European Affairs, Dick Roche acknowledged, the challenge for the Fianna Fáil-Green coalition government in the Lisbon II referendum in this context involved constructing: 'a narrative for Europe that speaks to peoples' hearts, as well as to their pocketbooks' (Roche, 2008). The changed economic situation facing the country, the emergence of new, active campaign groups (both for and against) and the re-invigoration of existing pro-European civil society groups also meant that the 2009 referendum campaign on the Lisbon Treaty would be somewhat different to that of its forerunner.

Acknowledgements

The author would like to thank the editors, two anonymous referees, Michael Gallagher and Clive Church for their extremely helpful comments on previous versions of this article.

Notes

1. The second referendum on the Lisbon Treaty took place on 2 October 2009. The referendum was passed by 67.1% to 32.9% on a turnout of approximately 58% (source: RTÉ).
2. Darcy and Laver (1990: 16) based their analysis in part on the 1986 divorce referendum in Ireland and proposed that elite withdrawal in referendum campaigns consists of 'elite retreat brought about by community conflict' when the elite either loses or cedes control of the referendum campaign to ad hoc groups. While in the 1986 referendum campaign non-government political parties such as Fianna Fáil pledged neutrality on the issue and as such did not actively campaign in the Nice I and Lisbon I referendums, the political parties which did come out in favour of the treaty ran weak campaigns. I am very grateful to Michael Gallagher for clarification of this point.
3. TNS/MRBI *Irish Times* Poll, 5 November 2007.
4. As reported by Stephen Collins, *Irish Times*, 11 September 2008.
5. Micheál Martin, Minister for Foreign Affairs, RTÉ *Morning Ireland* programme, 30 July 2008.
6. John Perry TD, speaking at the Joint Committee on European Scrutiny - Joint Committee on European Affairs Lisbon discussion, 3 July 2008.
7. Marian Harkin, Independent MEP, speaking at the Joint Committee on European Scrutiny – Joint Committee on European Affairs Lisbon discussion, 3 July 2008.
8. Individuals surveyed were asked first about the number of states currently in the EU, second whether Switzerland was a member of the EU, and third about the rotating Presidency of the EU (a fourth was

also asked about the number of Eurozone countries. This question was excluded from the analysis as it was of a different order of difficulty) (*Eurobarometer*, 2008).

References

Abts, K. and Rummens, S. (2007) Populism versus democracy, *Political Studies*, 55, pp. 405–424.
Albertazzi, D. & McDonnell, D. (2008) Introduction: the sceptre and the spectre, in: D. Albertazzi & D. McDonnell (Eds) *Twenty-First Century Populism. The Spectre of Western European Democracy*, pp. 1–9 (Basingstoke: Palgrave).
Barber, B. (1984) *Strong Democracy: Participatory Politics for a New Age* (Berkeley, CA: University of California Press).
Barrett, G. (2008) Lisbon vote is not buck-passing by politicians, *Irish Times*, 24 April.
Barrington, R. (2008) Was holding referendum on Lisbon Treaty really necessary? *Irish Times*, 11 July.
Binzer Hobolt, S. (2003) Europe in question: referendum behaviour in Denmark and Ireland, paper presented at the 33rd Annual UACES conference, University of Newcastle upon Tyne, 2–4 September.
Butler, D. & Ranney, A. (Eds) (1994) *Referendums around the World: The Growing Use of Direct Democracy* (Basingstoke: Macmillan).
Campaign Against EU Constitution (2008) *Democracy Undermined*, available at: http://www.caeuc.org/index.php?q=node/9 (accessed August 2009).
Canovan, M. (1999) Trust the people! Populism and the two faces of democracy, *Political Studies*, 47, pp. 2–16.
Carney, J. (1998) High Court Judicial Review No. 1997 209 'Anthony Coughlan vs Broadcasting Complaints Commission, RTE and the Attorney General', 24 April.
Cox, P. (2008) Another Lisbon vote not a great option but it is a democratic one, *Irish Times*, 26 August.
Crotty, R. (1988) *A Radical's Response* (Dublin: Poolbeg).
Darcy, R. & Laver, M. (1990) Referendum dynamics and the Irish Divorce Amendment, *Public Opinion Quarterly*, 54(1), pp. 1–20.
Eurobarometer (2008) National Report: Ireland, *Eurobarometer*, 69(2).
Fanning, R. (2008) Lisbon vote is not democracy but an exercise in buck-passing, *Irish Times*, 22 April.
Franklin, M., van der Eijk, C. & Marsh, M. (1995) Referendum outcomes and trust in government: public support for Europe in the wake of Maastricht, *West European Politics*, 18(3), pp. 101–117.
Gallagher, M. (1988) The Single European Act Referendum, *Irish Political Studies*, 3, pp. 77–82.
Gallagher, M. (2003) Referendum Campaigns in Ireland, paper presented at the 8th International EISE Conference on 'Le campagne elettorali', Venice, 18–20 December.
Ganley, D. (2003) Europe's constitutional treaty: a threat to democracy and how to avoid it, *Newsletter for Foreign Policy Research Institute's Centre for the Study of America and the West*, 4(5).
Gilland, K. (1999) Referenda in the Republic of Ireland, *Electoral Studies*, 18(3), pp. 430–438.
Gilland, K. (2008) Shades of green: Euroscepticism in Irish political parties, in: A. Szczerbiak & P. Taggart (Eds) *Opposing Europe? The Comparative Party Politics of Euroscepticism. Volume 1 Case Studies and Country Surveys*, pp. 117–133 (Oxford: Oxford University Press).
Harmsen, R. (2005) The Dutch referendum on the ratification of the European Constitutional Treaty 1 June 2005, *EPERN Briefing Paper*, No. 13, Sussex European Institute.
Ivaldi, G. (2006) Beyond France's 2005 referendum on the European Constitutional Treaty: second order model, anti-establishment attitudes and the end of the alternative European utopia, *West European Politics*, 29(1), pp. 47–69.
Laffan, B. & O'Mahony, J. (2008) *Ireland and EU Membership* (Basingstoke: Palgrave).
LeDuc, L. (2002) Opinion change and voting behaviour in referendums, *European Journal of Political Research*, 41, pp. 711–732.
LeDuc, L. (2003) *The Politics of Direct Democracy: Referendums in Global Perspective* (Ontario: Broadview Press).
Mansergh, L. (1999) Two referendums and the referendum commission: the 1998 experience, *Irish Political Studies*, 14, pp. 123–131.

Marsh, M., Sinnott, R., Garry, J. & Kennedy, F. (2008) *The Irish Voter. The Nature of Electoral Competition in the Republic of Ireland* (Manchester: Manchester University Press).

Marthaler, S. (2005) The French referendum on ratification of the EU Constitutional Treaty, 29 May 2005, *Representation*, 41(3), pp. 230–239.

McCutcheon, P. (1991) The legal system, in: P. Keatinge (Ed.) *Ireland and EC Membership Evaluated*, pp. 209–229 (London: Pinter).

McDonnell, D. (2008) The Republic of Ireland: the dog that hasn't barked in the night?, in: D. Albertazzi & D. McDonnell (Eds) *Twenty-First Century Populism. The Spectre of Western European Democracy*, pp. 198–210 (Basingstoke: Palgrave).

Millward Brown/IMS (2008) *Post Lisbon Treaty Referendum Research Findings*. September, available at: www.dfa.ie/uploads/documents/Publications/Post%20Lisbon%20Treaty%20Referendum%20 Research%20Findings/final%20-%20post%20lisbon%20treaty%20referendum%20research%20 findings.pdf (accessed August 2009).

Moravcsik, A. (2008) Don't know? Vote no! *Prospect Magazine*, July.

Mudde, C. (2004) The populist zeitgeist, *Government and Opposition*, 39(4), pp. 542–563.

O'Malley, E. (2008) Why is there no radical right party in Ireland? *West European Politics*, 31(5), pp. 960–977.

Quinlan, S. (2009) The Lisbon Treaty Referendum 2008, *Irish Political Studies* 24(1), pp. 107–121.

Qvortrup, M. (1998) Voter-knowledge and participation: a comparative study of referendums in Denmark and Switzerland, *Representation*, 35(4), pp. 255–265.

Qvortrup, M. (2005) *A Comparative Study of Referendums: Government by the People*, 2nd ed. (Manchester: Manchester University Press).

Referendum Commission (2008) Press Release, 28 April, available at: http://www.lisbontreaty2008 (accessed 4 July 2008).

Roche, D. (2008) Speaking on RTÉ Prime Time, 28 August.

Setälä, M. (2006) National referendums in European democracies: recent developments, *Representation*, 42(1), pp. 13–23.

Sinnott, R. (1995) *Knowledge of the European Union in Irish Public Opinion: Sources and Implications* (Dublin: Institute for European Affairs).

Sinnott, R. (2002) Cleavages, parties and referendums: relationships between representative and direct democracy in the Republic of Ireland, *European Journal of Political Research*, 41, pp. 811–826.

Sorensen, C. (2008) Love me, love me not … a typology of public Euroscepticism, *EPERN Working Paper*, Sussex European Institute.

Svensson, P. (2002) Five Danish referendums on the European Community and Union: a critical assessment of the Franklin thesis, *European Journal of Political Research*, 41(6), pp. 733–750.

Szczerbiak, A. & Taggart, P. (2000) Opposing Europe: party systems and opposition in the Union, the Euro and Europeanisation, *Sussex European Institute Working Paper* 36, Sussex European Institute.

Irish Political Parties and Policy Stances on European Integration

KENNETH BENOIT
Trinity College, Dublin, Ireland

ABSTRACT *Support for the political and economic integration of Europe has formed an increasingly important policy issue for Irish political parties as the European Union has grown in importance at both the domestic and European level. This article examines the political positioning of Irish parties on the issue of European integration, comparing these positions across parties and across time. For data, it draws on expert surveys taken at each election since 1992, a time series of coded manifestos as well as a computerized content analysis of the 2007 party manifestos. The article also reports the results of a previously unpublished expert survey of Irish party positions on other political dimensions conducted by the author in 2007.*

Introduction

The ongoing project of European integration has had a tremendous impact on Irish social, political and economic life. Since joining the EU in 1973, Ireland has received over €20 billion in funding under the Structural and Cohesion Funds scheme, leading not only to a figurative transformation of the economic landscape, but also a literal transformation of the physical Irish landscape as transport, roads, tunnels and bridges were built or improved using EU funds.[1] Immigration as a result of the open EU labour market has also soared since the expansion of the EU eastward in 2004 and again in 2007, transforming the Irish social fabric and labour markets through an unprecedented infusion of immigration, legalized and facilitated by Ireland's membership of the European Union. Furthermore, this effect has continued to change and grow as the EU itself has changed and grown.

As a political issue, the expansion of European-level political institutions moved to the fore of the Irish issue space during the debate and first referendum on the Lisbon Treaty in June 2008. All major Irish political parties supported ratification of the treaty, yet this support belied subtle differences in party positioning on various aspects of support for the scope and pace of continuing European integration. Furthermore, the Irish voters' first rejection of the Lisbon Treaty demonstrated the potential political force of anti-European issue positions. This potential can only be expected to grow as debate continues over ratification of the Lisbon Treaty. Despite the pledge of the major parties to continue to support European integration, therefore, we should continue to expect differentiation in the political positions of Irish parties on the issue of Europe.

Party positions towards Europe have received extensive comparative study in the literature on European integration (Hooghe et al., 2002; Marks et al., 2002; Rohrschneider & Whitefield, 2007), yet with only a few exceptions (Holmes, 2005; Moxon-Browne, 2000), none has focused on the evolution of this issue among Irish parties. Party positions in Ireland have been presented before (Benoit & Laver, 2005, 2006; Laver, 1994, 1998), but have not focused specifically on policy towards Europe. This article explicitly targets the empirical record of Irish political party positioning on the issue of European integration by measuring and mapping these positions using empirical data on Irish party positions on European integration over time. Using estimates from the Comparative Manifesto Project (CMP) (Budge et al., 2001, Klingemann et al., 2006), I trace the salience of the EU issue in policy platforms dating back to the Treaty of Rome in 1957 when the issue first appeared in party manifestos. Using data from expert surveys conducted at the last four Irish elections, I also examine the position of Irish political parties on EU integration, as well as the relative importance of this dimension for each party. Finally, I also report the full results on all aspects of policy from a new expert survey of Irish party positions conducted in 2007.[2]

The Relative Salience of the European Issue

The motivations for and means by which parties position themselves on different political issues has been extensively examined in political science, including positioning on European integration (Marks et al., 2002; also see above). Apart from *positions* on an issue dimension, it is also possible to distinguish the relative *importance* of a given issue for a political party (Benoit & Laver, 2006). Issues that parties deem more important than others are likely to be those for which differences in positioning matter more, both to the party members and representatives as well as to their electorates. When viewed across parties, furthermore, some issues will emerge as more important than others in the overall political discourse. With the introduction of an unprecedented initiative for decentralizing government departments and agencies announced with the 2004 budget, for instance, decentralization policy grew in political importance relative to other issues in the Irish policy space. Similar events, typically coming from Europe in the form of treaties, agreements, and enlargement, have also resulted in changes over time in the relative salience of European integration as a political issue in Ireland. Using data on the salience of this issue over time, it is possible to measure and track these changes.

One way to look at this issue is through a comparative examination of Irish party manifestos over time. The Comparative Manifesto Project, a research effort that has been ongoing for several decades (Klingemann et al., 2006), provides such a measure in the form of their dataset of coded manifestos. The CMP divides each manifesto into discrete text units and then assigns each text unit a code from one of

56 policy categories. The CMP scheme includes two codes for the European issue, known as 'PER108: European integration: Positive' and 'PER110: European integration: Negative'.[3] If we consider the total occurrences of text units coded as belonging to one of these two categories, then we can measure their relative occurrence within each overall manifesto to form a picture of how important this issue has been in Irish party platforms over time.[4]

Figure 1 plots the total mention of either EU category over time, for the six major parties, from 1957. The labelled, dotted lines also indicate the dates of major referendums occurring in Ireland concerning European integration. Interestingly, there was almost no mention of the EU before Ireland joined in 1973, probably due to the fact that although all parties had campaigned intensively before the 1972 referendum on EU accession, the EU was not an issue in the election campaign that took place two months following EU accession. The EU issue remained more or less absent from party platforms until 1989, when it jumped significantly to more than 30

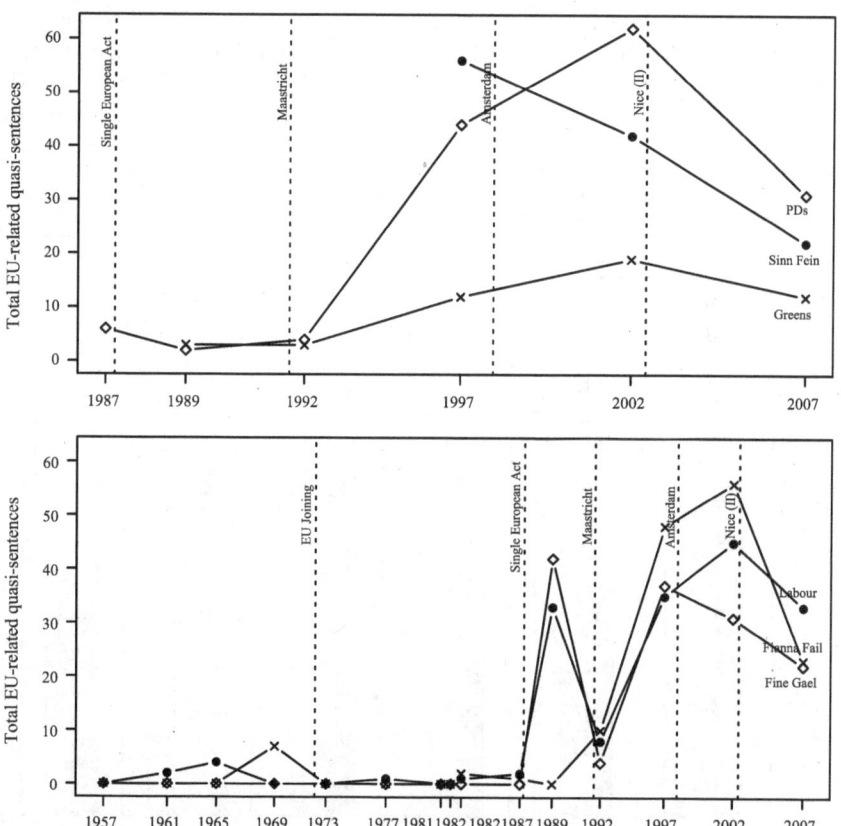

Figure 1. Total mentions of European integration (positive/108 or negative/110) in party manifestos, from CMP.
Note: Dotted lines indicate dates of referendums on European treaties.

mentions each in the Fianna Fáil and Fine Gael manifestos. This jump occurred in the wake of the referendum on the Single European Act (SEA) which took place soon after the 1987 elections. This referendum followed the decision of the Supreme Court in the Crotty case to require constitutional revision for approving European treaties such as the Single European Act and the Amsterdam, Maastricht, Nice, and Lisbon Treaties that followed.[5] The 1989 elections also occurred during negotiations on the shape of the Maastricht Treaty, the agreement that included the Economic and Monetary Union (EMU) and led to the creation of the Euro. By the time of the 1992 election, mentions of Europe had dropped again, possibly because this election came after the referendum on Maastricht had already passed to a Yes vote of 69.1 percent.

The last two elections in the top panel, as well as the bottom panel of Figure 1, show the expansion in debate over EU integration that took place in the 1997 and 2002 elections. To get a more nuanced picture of the relative importance of the EU as a political issue for these later elections, we can draw on four expert surveys of Irish party positions from studies conducted by Michael Laver (1994, 1998), Kenneth Benoit and Michael Laver (2006), and most recently, in 2007 by the author (see Appendix).[6] The relative importance of the EU policy dimension is plotted in Figure 2 as a barplot. Each bar shows, for the last four Irish elections, the level of importance attached to the European integration issue by the political parties. The importance scale runs from 1 (not at all important) to 20 (very important). The thin, capped lines on each bar show the

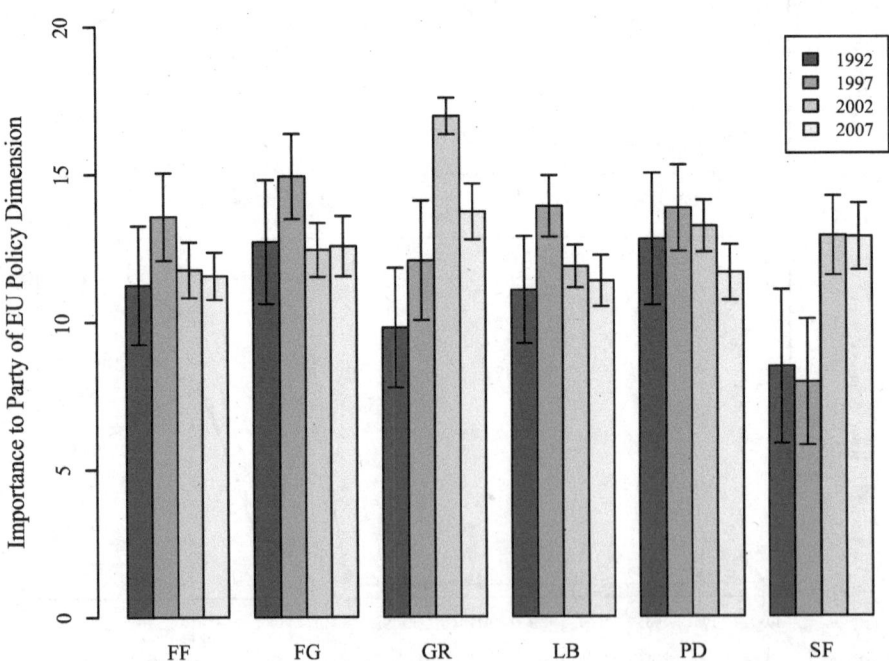

Figure 2. Importance of the EU policy dimension, 2002 and 2007, from Expert Surveys.
Note: Capped bars show 95 percent confidence intervals.

95 percent confidence interval for each measure, which comes from the mean of expert judgements, taking into account the number and variances of the expert placements.

The biggest changes in the importance of European integration as a political issue occurred in 1997, when most parties shifted by at least two points upward in the importance they attached to the European integration issue. Exceptions were the Progressive Democrats (PDs), for which the change was not statistically significant, and Sinn Féin, for which the importance of the EU issue fell marginally in 1997. The importance Sinn Féin placed on the European issue did change massively in 2002, however, when the EU suddenly became an issue of major importance for this party (see Maillot, 2009). The Green Party also shifted on the importance it attached to this issue in 2002, from around 13 points to around 17. Indeed, the Europe issue was important for all parties in 2002, given that every party mentioned the rejected first Nice Treaty referendum in their manifestos. In the 2007 election, there were few changes in the importance of the European issue among Irish parties. The Green Party seems to have regarded this issue as considerably less important than in 2002, while the PDs regarded it as nearly two points less important, although the PDs' change in importance could not be regarded as statistically significant. All things considered, 1997 seems to have seen the largest spike in the importance of the EU as a policy issue for Irish parties, with the notable exception of Sinn Féin.

Evidence of Changing Policy Positions

Apart from the importance that parties attach to the EU issue, they also adopt specific political *positions* on EU integration as a political dimension, typically favouring less or more integration, a reduction or expansion in the scope of EU authority, or keeping the EU's power base concentrated in national governments, versus granting more power to the EU through institutions such as direct election by EU electorates. Positioning on these issues can be compared over time for the last four elections using data from the expert surveys. Figure 3 tracks the changes in these positions from 1992 to 2007, showing the expert means in addition to the 95 percent confidence intervals represented by the shaded regions. Examining the main Irish parties, it is clear that two – the Greens and Sinn Féin – remained basically 'Eurosceptic' throughout the last four elections. Prior to their unprecedented participation in government following the 2007 elections and their qualified support for the Lisbon Treaty in 2008, the Greens had never before supported the ratification of an EU treaty (see Bolleyer & Panke, 2009). The Greens' 2007 position in fact shows a significant shift towards the middle position, a movement of nearly five points in the direction of favouring an expansion in the scope of EU authority. Sinn Féin has also consistently opposed greater European integration, traditionally favouring decentralization and the retention of national sovereignty. For the other main parties, some change is indicated, with many parties becoming considerably cooler on the EU issue, especially in the period from 1997 to 2002. The Progressive Democrats in particular experienced a large shift away from a previously strong pro-integrationist stance, but Fianna Fáil, Fine Gael and Labour also moved in this direction. Between

36 K. Benoit

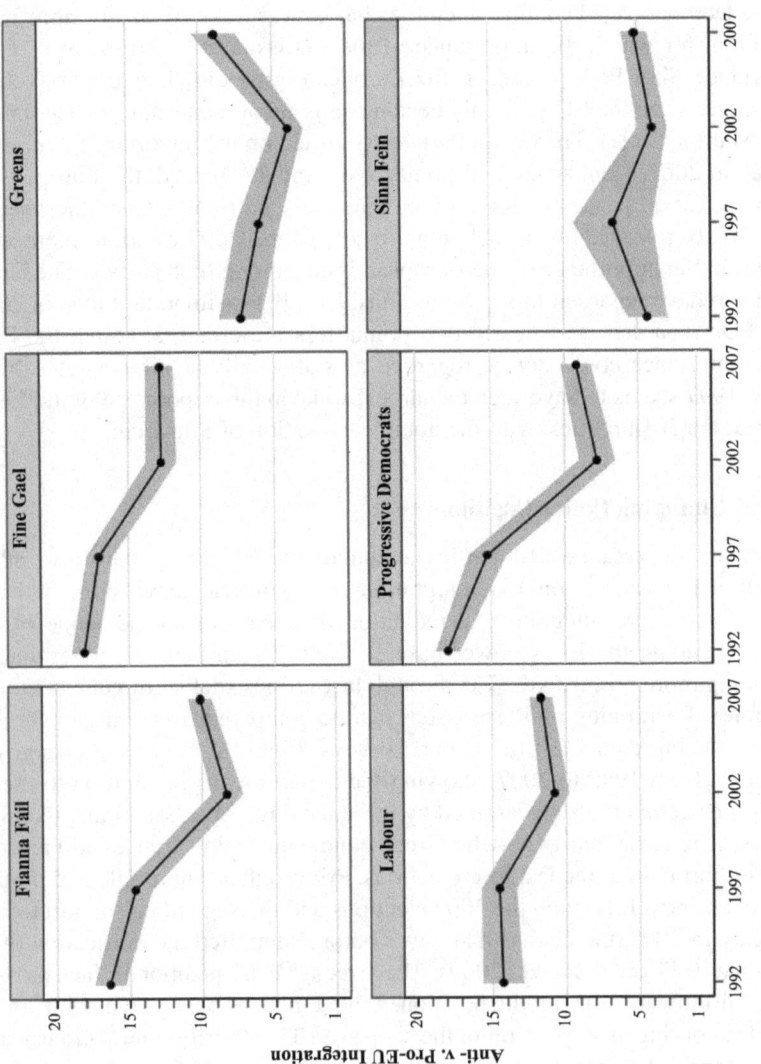

Figure 3. Irish party positioning on European integration, from Expert Surveys. *Note:* Shaded regions show 95 percent confidence intervals.

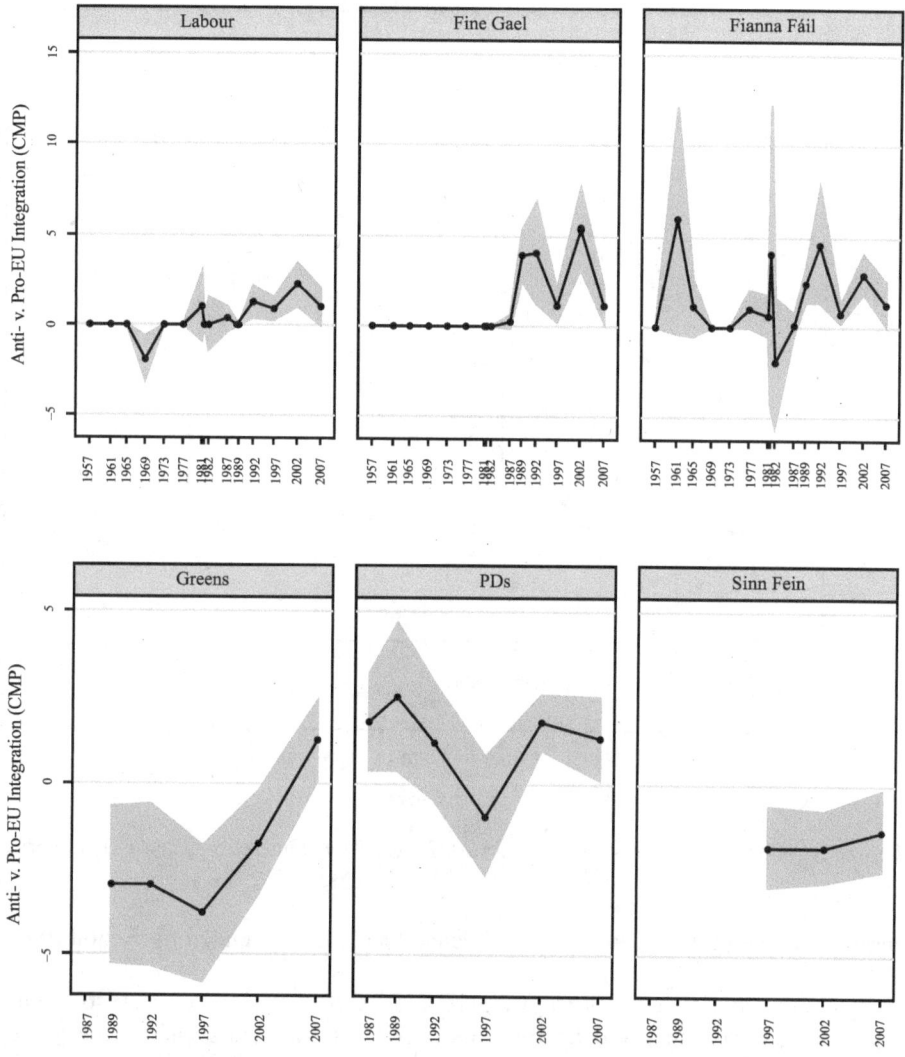

Figure 4. Positions on European integration, from CMP.
Note: Shaded CIs from Benoit *et al.* (2009).

2002 and 2007, only the Green Party exhibited a statistically significant change in its position on European integration, and then only from 2002 to 2007.

For a longer time series of positioning on European integration, we can turn to the CMP dataset. By subtracting the percentage of anti-EU mentions (PER110) from the percentage of pro-EU mentions (PER108), we can construct an anti- versus pro-EU policy measure spanning, at least theoretically, the [-100, 100] interval. Figure 4 plots the movement over time for the 'old' and 'newer' Irish parties, with the shaded

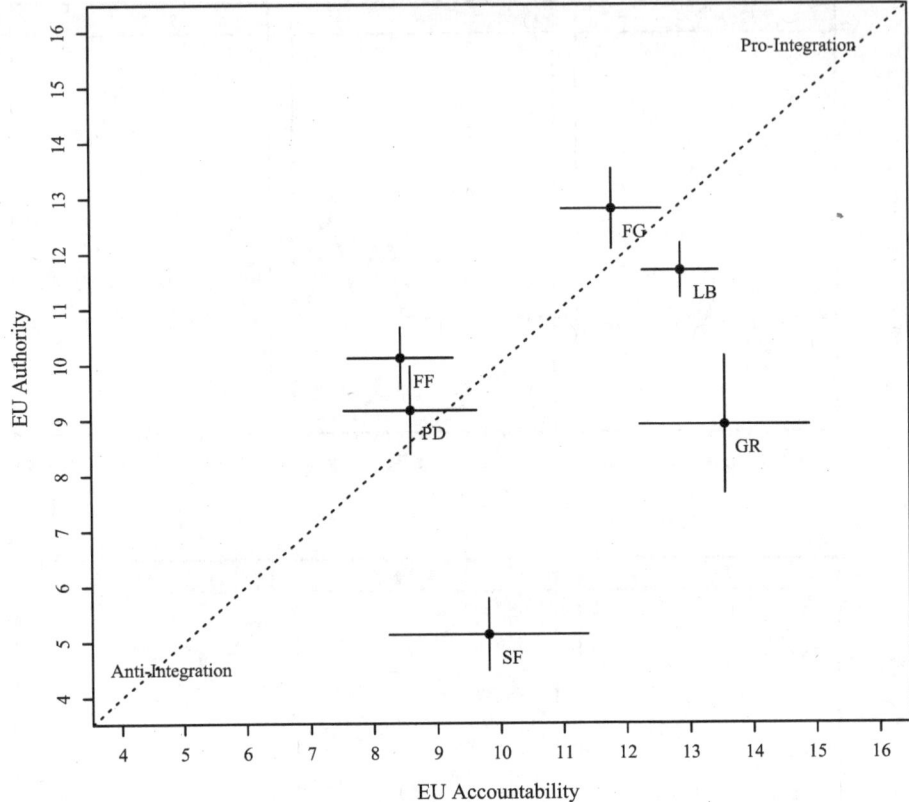

Figure 5. Comparing party positioning in 2007 on EU Accountability versus EU Authority. *Source:* 2007 Expert Survey.

regions indicating the 95 percent confidence bands (as computed by Benoit et al., 2009).

A few patterns are evident from Figure 4, as well as from its comparison to the comparable expert survey data from Figure 3. First, the data separates the parties into two groups, according to whether they favoured or opposed greater European integration. The two most 'Eurosceptic' parties are clearly the Greens and Sinn Féin, although the Greens made a weak shift towards a more pro-EU position in 2002. On the more pro-integration side were the other parties, with the PDs and Labour lower than Fianna Fáil, Fine Gael, at least in the 1990s. Second, given that the maximum value on the *y*-axis on European integration was about six (from 100), as a proportion of all manifesto statements European integration was relatively low on the agenda, and the only recent case being Fine Gael which reached six percent in 2002. Finally, in comparison with the expert survey results from Figure 5, the PDs appeared in 2002 to be more Eurosceptic according to the expert judgments than the manifesto scoring indicated. A similar difference is observable for Fianna

Fáil which was slightly Eurosceptic according to the experts in 2002 but was relatively pro-European in 2002 as judged by its manifesto score.

Dissecting the Dimensions of Support for Europe

The 2007 expert survey asked experts to judge parties on two separate dimensions of European policy, one relating to the scope over which the EU should have authority (restricted versus expanded), and the other relating to the degree of accountability (through national governments or direct) which should be granted to the institutions of the EU. The specific wording of these dimensions was:[7]

EU Authority:

'Favours increasing the range of areas in which the EU can set policy' (1), versus 'Favours reducing the range of areas in which the EU can set policy.' (20)

EU Accountability:

'Promotes the direct accountability of the EU to citizens via institutions such as the European Parliament.' (1), versus 'Promotes the indirect accountability of the EU to citizens via their own national governments.' (20)

By comparing the placements of parties on these two dimensions, we can attempt to determine whether these two dimensions in fact captured different positions among parties toward the EU, or whether by contrast they were measuring a single dimension of support or opposition to the European integration. Figure 5 plots the location of Irish parties according to their mean placements on the two EU dimensions from the 2007 expert survey, along with cross-hairs indicating the 95 percent confidence intervals of these positions. The two-dimensional placement reveals several interesting patterns.

First, it reveals that while Eurosceptic on the dimension of EU authority, both Sinn Féin and the Green Party are much more in favour of making the EU – whatever its scope of authority – much more directly accountable to EU citizens, even if this would ultimately increase at least the legitimacy (and hence authority) of the EU's institutions. Sinn Féin is almost twice as pro-European on the accountability issue (score of 9.8) than on the question of EU authority (score of 5.1); the Green Party is almost five points more pro-EU on accountability (13.6) than on authority (8.9). All other parties' positions were more or less the same on these two dimensions, as evidenced by their tight clustering around the dotted identity line.

Second, the two-dimensional configuration clearly reveals distinct clusters of parties, apart from the Greens and Sinn Féin. The incumbent coalition parties, Fianna Fáil and the PDs, were nearly in the middle of the range and indistinguishable on the (more politically salient) issue of EU authority. Fine Gael and Labour were also adjacent on both dimensions, and from their (just) overlapping confidence intervals we also see that their positions cannot be distinguished, at least statistically, on either dimension. Fine Gael and Labour were both considerably more pro-integration than Fianna Fáil and the PDs.

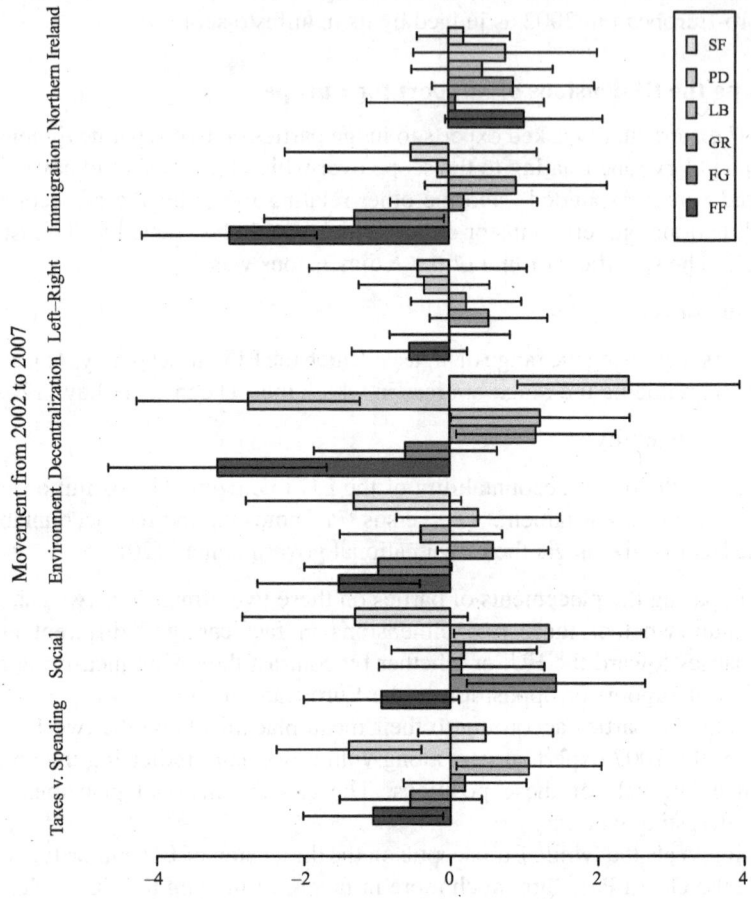

Figure 6. Changes in party positions, 2002 to 2007.

Other Policy Dimensions in the 2007 Elections

To provide some context for the changes we have observed in positioning on the issue of European integration, this section briefly discusses the positioning of Irish parties on non-European issues as well as the change in their positioning on these issues from 2002 to 2007.

The Appendix provides details of the 2007 survey, with numerical summaries presented in Tables 1 and 2. To compare these results to those from an expert survey taken at the 2002 election, Figure 6 plots the change in position from 2002 to 2007. The horizontal axis is the degree of (left–right) change as measured in 2007. On taxes versus spending, for instance, the Labour Party moved approximately one point to the right, while Fianna Fáil moved approximately one point to the left. The thin, capped lines drawn on each bar indicates the 95 percent confidence interval on a t-test of difference between the 2007 and 2002 expert mean placements. For both Labour and Fianna Fáil on taxes versus spending, for instance, it is possible to reject the null hypothesis of no change and to conclude that these parties' measured move leftward was in fact a real movement to the left, since the confidence interval does not overlap zero. Interpreting the bars this way, only the PDs also changed their position on this dimension, moving about 1.5 points to the left. For Sinn Féin, the Green Party, and Labour, none of the observed changes can be statistically distinguished from no change.

To summarize the change on the other dimensions, we observed no statistically significant change on the Northern Ireland issue, although all parties did move slightly toward a more pro-Unionist position. On the immigration issue, both Fianna Fáil and Fine Gael moved towards a more open position on immigration, with Fianna Fáil making a relatively large shift of three points in this direction. Fianna Fáil also moved significantly towards the more pro-environmental end of the environment dimension, by more than 1.5 points, with no statistically significant changes observed for any other parties on environmental policy. On social policy, both the PDs and Fine Gael moved slightly to the right, by nearly 1.5 points each; Sinn Féin and Fianna Fáil both moved slightly leftward on this dimension but these changes were not statistically significant.

The biggest change was observed on the decentralization policy dimension, a policy dimension which gained in salience following the announcement in 2004 of decentralization as an important component of government policy. Positioning on decentralization in 2007 basically divided the government and opposition parties. On the government side, both the PDs and Fianna Fáil moved significantly towards the pro-decentralization pole, by around three points each. On the opposition side, both Labour and the Green Party shifted about one point each towards the anti-decentralization pole, with both shifts statistically significant. An even bigger shift away from favouring decentralization was observed for Sinn Féin, which moved about 2.5 points away from its 2002 position.

On the overall left–right scale, which asked respondents to place the parties taking all aspects of party policy into account, no changes of either substantive or statistical significance were observed for any party.

Conclusions

From the examination of Irish party positions on European policy over time, several key conclusions can be highlighted. First, the examination of the Comparative Manifesto Project data clearly shows a rise in the prominence of Europe as a topic in party platforms from 1989 onward, while the issue received scant attention before this period. Mentions of the EU rose sharply in 1989 for the largest three parties. Mentions dropped in 1992, but then rose in importance from 1997 onward. As measured in the 1990s by expert surveys, the importance attached to policy toward

European integration rose sharply in the 1997 election, and returned to pre-1997 levels again in 2002. The exceptions to this pattern were the Greens and Sinn Féin, for whom the policy importance of European integration rose sharply between the 1997 and 2002 elections.

Second, all major parties experienced a move from relatively pro-European positions to more moderate positions on European integration between 1997 and 2002. Exceptions were Sinn Féin, whose policy position toward European integration was essentially unchanged, and the Green Party, which moved to a more moderate position on Europe from a Eurosceptic position held in 2002 and previous elections.

Third, a two-dimensional breakdown of attitudes toward the restriction or expansion of the scope of EU authority on one hand, versus the accountability of the EU to national governments versus directly to EU citizens on the other, shows three distinct clusters of parties. The first consists of Fine Gael and Labour, which are relatively pro-European on both scales. The second consists of FF and the PDs, which were centrist on both scales. The last group is made up of the Greens and Sinn Féin, both pro-accountability yet Eurosceptic on the scope of EU authority: mildly so for the Greens, extremely so for Sinn Féin.

Finally, examining the changes in policy positions on all other issues by comparing the 2007 and 2002 expert surveys, we see relatively few changes in policy by any parties. Exceptions were:

- Fianna Fáil moved to a more open position on immigration between 2002 and 2007, a shift of almost three points to the left on the 1–20 point expert survey scale, and to a slightly more pro-environment stance (a nearly two point leftward shift).
- Fine Gael moved slightly towards the more conservative end of the policy spectrum on the social liberalism dimension, a shift of around 1.5 points.
- The PDs and Fianna Fáil moved slightly to the left, and Labour slightly to the right, on the economic dimension of taxes v. spending.
- On decentralization policy, a dimension cast in a new light by the government announcement in 2003 of major new initiatives in this area, numerous parties changed their positions between 2002 and 2007. Sinn Féin became more opposed to decentralization policies, a statistically significant shift of almost three points, while the Greens and Fine Gael moved in this direction about one point each. Fianna Fáil and the PDs – the proponents of the new plans to shift significant parts of the Dublin-based state administrative apparatus to regional areas – show strong shifts of around three points each towards the pro-decentralization pole.

Acknowledgements

An earlier version of this paper was presented at the 25th Annual Conference of the Political Studies Association of Ireland, Dublin City University, 19–21 October, 2007. Support for this project was provided by the Institute for International Integration

Studies, Trinity College. Thanks to Tímea Kacskovics, Marina McGale and Nina Wiesenhomeier for assistance with data and various parts of the surveys, to Séin Ó Muineacháin for making available his coding of the 2007 Irish manifestos and for comments, and to Michael Gallagher for comments.

Notes

1. Data taken from the website of the National Development Plan, available at www.ndp.ie/view-doc.asp?fn=/documents/eu_structural_funds/overview/structural_funds.htm&mn=euso&nID=3> (accessed August 2009).
2. Unlike the discussion in other contributions to this edited issue, only political parties in the Republic of Ireland are considered here, regrettable but unavoidable limitation of the data used in this article.
3. The non-overlapping text units are known as 'quasi-sentences', the self-contained text units each expressing a distinct policy message that form the basic units of the CMP's coding scheme. The CMP coding scheme consists of 56 policy categories covering seven major policy areas. PER108 and PER110 fall under the broad category of 'internationalism'. For details see Klingemann et al. (2006) or Benoit et al. (2009).
4. The 2007 party positions come from a coding by Séin Ó Muineacháin.
5. More precisely, the Court determined that the provisions of Title III of the Single European Act required specific constitutional authorization, as it held that these provisions changed the substance of Irish membership in the European Community. Since this decision, Irish governments have chosen to pursue ratification through constitutional amendment, although parliamentary ratification technically remains an option. I thank an anonymous reviewer for clarifying this point.
6. The 1992 and 1997 expert surveys asked expert respondents to locate the main Irish parties on a single 1–20 point dimension of support for the European Union, worded as: 'Oppose more integration with the European Union (1) versus Promote more integration with the European Union (20).' The wording of the Benoit and Laver (2006) survey, conducted at the time of the 2002 election, was 'Favours a more powerful and centralised EU' (1) versus 'Opposes a more powerful and centralised EU' (20). The scale from the 2007 survey is detailed in the Appendix. For comparability the 2002 and 2007 dimensions were inverted to match the 1992 and 1997 scales, so that the 20 position represented the pro-integration pole.
7. As worded on the questionnaire, the EU Authority and EU Accountability dimensions were inverted, so that the (20) end of the scale represented the anti-EU integration position.

References

Benoit, K. & Laver, M. (2005) Mapping the Irish policy space: voter and party spaces in preferential elections, *Economic and Social Review*, 36(2), pp. 83–108.
Benoit, K. & Laver, M. (2006) *Party Policy in Modern Democracies* (London: Routledge).
Benoit, K., Mikhaylov, S. & Laver, M. (2009) Treating words as data with error: uncertainty in text statements of policy positions, *American Journal of Political Science*, 53(2), pp. 495–513.
Bolleyer, N. & Panke, D. (2009) The Irish Green Party: an unhappy marriage?, *Irish Political Studies*, 24(4), pp. 543–557.
Budge, I., Klingemann, H.-D., Volkens, A. Bara, J. & Tanenbaum, E. (2001) *Mapping Policy Preferences: Estimates for Parties, Electors, and Governments 1945–1998* (Oxford: Oxford University Press).
Holmes, M. (Ed.) (2005) *Ireland and the European Union: Nice, Enlargement and the Future of Europe* (Manchester: Manchester University Press).
Hooghe, L., Marks, G. & Wilson, C.J. (2002) Does left/right structure party positions on European integration?, *Comparative Political Studies*, 35(8), pp. 965–989.

Klingemann, H-D., Volkens, A., Bara, J., Budge, I. & McDonald, M. (2006) *Mapping Policy Preferences II: Estimates for Parties, Electors, and Governments in Eastern Europe, European Union and OECD 1990–2003* (Oxford: Oxford University Press).

Laver, M. (1994) Party positions and cabinet portfolios in Ireland, 1992, *Irish Political Studies,* 9, pp. 157–164.

Laver, M. (1998) Party policy in Ireland 1997: results from an expert survey, *Irish Political Studies,* 13, pp. 159–171.

Laver, M. & Hunt, B. (1992) *Party and Policy Competition* (New York: Routledge).

Maillot, A. (2009) Sinn Féin: still more 'critical' than 'engaged'? *Irish Political Studies,* 24(4), pp. 559–574.

Marks, G., Wilson, C.J. & Leonard, R. (2002) National political parties and European integration, *American Journal of Political Science,* 46(3), pp. 585–594.

Moxon-Browne, E. (2000) The Europeanisation of political parties: the case of the Irish Labour Party, in: J. Lorincz, (Ed.) *Studies on Common European Administration,* pp. 35–51 (Budapest: University of Economic Sciences).

Rohrschneider, R. & Whitefield, S. (2007) Representation in new democracies: party stances on European integration in post-Communist Eastern Europe, *Journal of Politics,* 69(4), pp. 1133–1146.

Appendix: Details of the 2007 Expert Survey

The expert survey of Irish party positions on policy was conducted during the period of two weeks before and roughly one month after the 2007 Irish general election which took place 24 May 2007. The survey closely followed the expert placement methodology used in previous surveys (Benoit & Laver, 2006; Laver, 1994, 1998; Laver & Hunt, 1992). Each policy dimension consisted of two endpoints anchored at 1 and 20, generally corresponding to the 'left' and 'right' positions respectively. Respondents were asked, for each policy dimension, to locate the main list of political parties on two scales, one indicating a party's *position*, and another indicating the *importance* that the party attached to this policy dimension.

A total of 237 experts were identified, based on the mailing list of the Political Studies Association of Ireland. These experts were invited to participate in the survey by email. The sample was randomly divided into two groups: 128 experts were contacted two weeks before the election, and 127 experts were contacted one week after the election. By clicking on a URL in the email containing a unique respondent identifier, each expert was directed to an online survey. A total of 54 valid surveys were received, for a response rate of 22.7 percent. The precise wording used in the scales is provided below.

Scale definitions:

Taxes versus spending:

Promotes raising taxes to increase public services. (1)
Promotes cutting public services to cut taxes. (20)

Social values:

Favours liberal policies on matters such as abortion, homosexuality, and euthanasia. (1)
Opposes liberal policies on matters such as abortion, homosexuality, and euthanasia. (20)

Deregulation:

Favours high levels of state regulation and control of the market. (1)
Favours deregulation of markets at every opportunity. (20)

Environment:

Supports protection of the environment, even at the cost of economic growth. (1)
Supports economic growth, even at the cost of damage to the environment. (20)

Decentralization:

Promotes decentralization of all administration and decision-making. (1)
Opposes any decentralization of administration and decision-making. (20)

Northern Ireland:

Opposes permanent British presence in Northern Ireland. (1)
Defends permanent British presence in Northern Ireland. (20)

Immigration:

Favours policies designed to help asylum seekers and immigrants integrate into Irish society. (1)
Favours policies designed to help asylum seekers and immigrants return to their country of origin. (20)

Left–Right:

Please locate each party on a general left-right dimension, taking all aspects of party policy into account.
Left. (1)
Right. (20)

Sympathy:

Taking all aspects of party policy into account, please score each party in terms of how close it is to your own personal views.
Same as respondent. (1)
Farthest from respondent. (20)

Policy Stances on European Integration 47

Table A1. Mean party positions, 95 percent parametric confidence intervals (based on t distributions) and sample sizes from 2007 expert survey

Policy Dimension	Party						
	Sinn Féin	Greens	Labour	Fine Gael	Fianna Fáil	PDs
Left–Right	**5.9**	**6.2**	**7.6**	**12.7**	**12.7**	**16.0**
	[4.9, 6.8]	[5.8, 6.7]	[7.1, 8.1]	[12.1, 13.4]	[12.2, 13.3]	[15.3, 16.8]
	52	54	54	54	54	54
Taxes v. Spending	**5.3**	**6.0**	**7.7**	**11.9**	**12.7**	**16.0**
	[4.6, 6.1]	[5.3, 6.6]	[6.9, 8.4]	[11.3, 12.5]	[12.1, 13.3]	[15.2, 16.9]
	53	52	53	54	53	53
Deregulation	**4.9**	**7.1**	**6.9**	**13.1**	**13.0**	**17.6**
	[4.2, 5.6]	[6.3, 7.9]	[6.2, 7.6]	[12.4, 13.8]	[12.3, 13.7]	[16.9, 18.2]
	54	51	53	54	53	54
Northern Ireland	**1.7**	**9.5**	**9.6**	**11.1**	**7.4**	**11.8**
	[1.2, 2.2]	[8.8, 10.3]	[8.9, 10.2]	[10.3, 11.8]	[6.6, 8.2]	[10.9, 12.7]
	54	43	52	54	54	52
EU: Authority	**5.1**	**8.9**	**11.7**	**12.8**	**10.1**	**9.2**
	[4.3, 5.9]	[7.5, 10.3]	[11.0, 12.4]	[11.9, 13.7]	[9.4, 10.8]	[8.2, 10.1]
	48	51	54	54	54	53
Immigration	**8.1**	**6.0**	**7.6**	**11.6**	**11.7**	**13.9**
	[6.9, 9.3]	[5.3, 6.8]	[6.6, 8.5]	[10.7, 12.5]	[10.8, 12.6]	[12.8, 15.1]
	48	51	52	54	54	53
Environment	**8.8**	**2.9**	**9.1**	**12.8**	**14.4**	**15.8**
	[8.0, 9.5]	[2.3, 3.5]	[8.4, 9.8]	[12.1, 13.5]	[13.6, 15.3]	[15.1, 16.6]
	48	54	53	52	54	53

(Continued)

Table A1. (Continued)

Policy Dimension	Party					
	Sinn Féin	Greens	Labour	Fine Gael	Fianna Fáil	PDs
Social	**8.3**	**5.8**	**6.2**	**12.9**	**13.9**	**8.3**
	[7.3, 9.2]	[5.1, 6.4]	[5.5, 6.9]	[12.2, 13.6]	[13.0, 14.7]	[7.4, 9.2]
	51	53	53	54	54	53
EU: Accountability	**9.8**	**13.6**	**12.9**	**11.8**	**8.4**	**8.6**
	[8.1, 11.5]	[12.1, 15.1]	[12.1, 13.6]	[10.8, 12.7]	[7.5, 9.4]	[7.4, 9.8]
	43	48	48	48	47	47
Decentralization	**9.0**	**5.7**	**9.8**	**11.2**	**9.9**	**9.2**
	[7.8, 10.3]	[4.8, 6.5]	[9.0, 10.7]	[10.4, 12.0]	[8.7, 11.0]	[8.1, 10.3]
	41	50	51	53	54	51
Sympathy	**14.2**	**7.9**	**7.4**	**10.9**	**12.3**	**13.7**
	[12.8, 15.6]	[6.9, 8.9]	[6.4, 8.5]	[9.8, 12.0]	[11.2, 13.5]	[12.1, 15.2]
	52	53	53	53	53	52
Vote Share 2007	6.9%	4.7%	10.1%	27.3%	41.6%	2.7%

Table A2. Mean party importance scores, 95 percent parametric confidence intervals (based on t distributions), and sample sizes from 2007 expert survey

Policy Dimension	Overall Importance [s.e.]	Party					
		Sinn Féin	Greens	Labour	Fine Gael	Fianna Fáil	PDs
Taxes v. Spending	13.7 [0.3]	13.4 [12.2, 14.6] 51	12.9 [11.7, 14.0] 50	13.4 [12.2, 14.7] 51	13.6 [12.8, 14.5] 52	13.8 [12.9, 14.7] 51	17.1 [16.3, 17.9] 52
Deregulation	13.5 [0.4]	12.9 [11.7, 14.2] 54	12.5 [11.3, 13.6] 51	15.0 [14.2, 15.7] 52	13.0 [12.2, 13.7] 53	13.4 [12.5, 14.2] 52	17.4 [16.6, 18.1] 54
Northern Ireland	12.4 [1.3]	19.3 [18.6, 20.0] 54	7.5 [6.1, 8.9] 43	9.4 [8.4, 10.4] 51	11.1 [10.0, 12.1] 53	13.5 [12.5, 14.5] 54	9.5 [8.4, 10.7] 50
EU: Authority	12.0 [0.3]	12.9 [11.7, 14.0] 47	13.7 [12.8, 14.7] 50	11.4 [10.5, 12.2] 53	12.6 [11.5, 13.6] 53	11.6 [10.8, 12.4] 53	11.7 [10.7, 12.6] 52
Immigration	11.8 [0.3]	11.4 [10.2, 12.5] 48	11.2 [10.1, 12.3] 50	13.1 [12.4, 13.8] 51	11.8 [10.9, 12.8] 53	11.5 [10.7, 12.4] 53	13.5 [12.3, 14.6] 52
Environment	11.5 [0.9]	9.9 [8.7, 11.1] 46	19.2 [18.8, 19.6] 53	11.4 [10.7, 12.1] 51	10.9 [10.0, 11.7] 51	11.4 [10.2, 12.6] 53	11.5 [10.1, 12.9] 52
Social	11.4 [0.4]	9.2 [8.2, 10.2] 49	11.7 [10.6, 12.8] 53	12.9 [11.9, 13.9] 51	11.4 [10.4, 12.4] 53	11.4 [10.4, 12.5] 54	11.2 [10.2, 12.3] 53

(Continued)

Table A2. (*Continued*)

Policy Dimension	Overall Importance [s.e.]	Party						
		Sinn Féin	Greens	Labour	Fine Gael	Fianna Fáil	PDs
EU: Accountability	**10.8** [0.3]	**11.0** [9.6, 12.5] 42	**13.2** [11.9, 14.6] 44	**10.6** [9.6, 11.6] 45	**11.0** [9.7, 12.3] 46	**10.4** [9.2, 11.6] 45	**10.3** [9.1, 11.4] 45
Decentralization	**10.4** [0.5]	**10.1** [8.4, 11.7] 40	**12.5** [11.3, 13.8] 51	**10.1** [9.0, 11.1] 48	**9.2** [8.2, 10.2] 50	**11.1** [10.0, 12.3] 52	**10.2** [8.9, 11.5] 51

Irish Political Parties' Attitudes towards Neutrality and the Evolution of the EU's Foreign, Security and Defence Policies

KAREN DEVINE
Dublin City University, Ireland

ABSTRACT *This article traces the evolution of attitudes and policies of Irish political parties towards Irish neutrality and the European Union Common Foreign and Security Policy (CFSP) and the European Security and Defence Policy (ESDP) across four decades. The article provides conceptual snapshots of the position of parties' policies along two policy dimensions. The first dimension captures policies of limited 'military' neutrality and 'positive'/ 'active' neutrality. The second dimension captures minimalist EU foreign and security policy, defined as 'civilian' or 'soft' security policy, to a maximalist EU CFSP/ESDP 'hard security' policy amounting to a 'militarized' EU. The positioning starts with the campaign for Irish membership of the European Economic Community (EEC), focusing on the accession negotiations and the 1972 referendum campaign and finishes with an analysis of parties' positions on the Security and Defence Policy aspects of the Lisbon Treaty in 2008. Evidence shows the positions of the larger parties of Fianna Fáil, Fine Gael and the Labour Party shifted away from fundamental neutrality to embrace treaty-based progress towards a maximalist EU ESDP. Over the same time period, the smaller parties of Sinn Féin and the Green Party were more consistent in their adherence to positive neutrality and in their opposition to the development of a maximalist EU ESDP. The forces of Europeanization have been evident in influencing evolving party discourses in Ireland. Much of this influence has been occasioned by the impact of participation in government on parties and the sporadic requirement to engage with referendum campaigns. The process of Europeanization has thus been subtle and muted and has interacted in intricate ways with domestic party agendas and objectives.*

Introduction

Foreign, security and defence policy are matters of 'high politics', traditionally perceived as separate from 'domestic' political concerns (such as healthcare, education, employment and taxation) that are broadly accessible to the public through direct experience and ready information. Yet, although neutrality is seldom an electoral issue in Ireland, the topic does influence voter behaviour in referendums on European integration treaties in particular. Smaller parties, especially, may perceive indirect electoral benefits through the adoption of specific foreign, security and defence policy positions during referendum campaigns. Indeed, theoretically speaking, there is a growing opportunity for wider party competition in Ireland in the realm of foreign, security and defence policy because the EU has not yet managed to secure ultimate competence in the area. This is an opportune time to examine party positions on neutrality and the EU's Common Foreign and Security Policy/ European Security and Defence Policy (CFSP/ESDP). The Lisbon Treaty sets out a legal base for comprehensive EU competence in foreign, security and defence policy, making neutrality and ESDP very significant, live issues in Ireland and across Europe.

In formulating their positions on neutrality and a common foreign, security and defence policy, Irish parties must confront multiple dynamics of the EU's CFSP/ ESDP. First, there are the diverse policy agendas in this field held by governments of fellow member-states, each with distinct historical traditions in matters of war and peace and cultural–domestic concepts of civil–military tenets, and each enjoying varying levels of 'permissive consensus' from public opinion. Each state also has its own important partnerships and relations with other non-EU states and international security and military organizations; in particular, states' positions in relation to the United States of America and the North Atlantic Treaty Organization (NATO) appear to be key dynamics of EU security and defence policy. Political parties confront a second, more serious institutional challenge through the intergovernmental organization of decision-making on CFSP/ESDP. The ESDP agenda is set by the European Council and decisions are taken by member-states through the Council of Ministers, rather than using the 'community method' that involves the European Parliament, the European Court of Justice and the European Commission. The two Council bodies 'meet behind closed doors and release the absolute minimum amount of information'(de Rossa, *Dáil Debates* 424: 1851, 3 November 1992). As a result, political parties suffer an acute information deficit in this area of policy and cannot influence policy unless they are in government. A third challenge comes from the changing nature of the EU itself, as it moves from its original 'soft' civilian ethos to the post-Nice extensions into 'hard' military power, along with parallel attempts to achieve a new political, constitutional union (Deighton, 2002: 726). The final dynamic for consideration is the security environment, i.e. the perceived threats to European security and defence and the designation of the appropriate role for the EU in response to such threats. Irish political parties must respond to all these factors in order to form coherent policy positions on neutrality and the EU's CFSP/ESDP.

Europeanization Factors Influencing Party Positions on Neutrality and ESDP

Identifying the evolving positions of all Irish parties on neutrality and the EU's CFSP/ESDP across four decades facilitates consideration of the extent to which a process of 'Europeanization' of Ireland's political parties may be evident. A range of influences, many of them domestic, are notable. They include the party leader's own personal values and preferences, party positioning and identity in terms of -

electoral competition, a party's position in government or on the opposition benches, party membership and the perceived policy preferences of Irish voters. These domestic influences inevitably interact with forces emanating from Europe to produce changes that are compatible with a process of Europeanization (Ladrech, 2002: 396). All of Ireland's political parties have, over time, modified their positions on neutrality and the ESDP. A conceptual matrix comprising two 'discursive' dimensions is used in this article to map the positions of Irish political parties regarding the EU's CFSP/ESDP and Irish neutrality. These dimensions are: (1) limited ('civilian/peacekeeping') to maximalist ('militarized/unlimited action') CFSP/ESDP, and (2) limited ('military') neutrality to maximalist ('positive/ 'active') neutrality. Positions are identified by focusing on the meaning of Irish neutrality, in terms of values and policy content, and the development of ESDP, incorporating the conceptual permutations and boundaries of this new policy area (instead of using a quantitative 'word score' approach that records the frequency of key words in party manifestoes). A conceptual approach helps to flesh out the subtleties involved in the use of the word 'neutrality' in party political discourse and to more accurately reflect parties' policy positions in their political context. The 'discourse' data used to configure party positions on the conceptual matrix are election manifestoes, policy papers, Ardfheiseanna (party conferences), press releases, referendum campaign material and, in particular, discourses and debates in the Houses of the Oireachtas. This overview thus provides a basis for determining the extent to which parties have experienced programmatic change, which is, according to Ladrech (2002) an important indicator of a process of Europeanization. Determining whether or not political parties have been 'Europeanized' with respect to their changed discourse on neutrality and ESDP is dependent on what influenced that change – EU or domestic factors. In this regard, the context within which change occurred is important.

The Context of Party Positions

Divergence of Neutrality Concepts

Although Irish attitudes to European integration are well understood (see Kennedy & Sinnott, 2007), academics, elites and government have argued that public thinking on neutrality is 'extraordinarily ill-defined', that a crystallized meaning of neutrality among the public does not exist (Gilland, 2001: 151) and that public attitudes to neutrality are 'confused' (FitzGerald, 1996) and non-rational (Everts, 2000: 178–179). However, more recent academic research has indicated that the public have consistently adhered to a clear-cut concept of 'active' or 'positive' neutrality. Furthermore, this adherence is 'rational' (Page & Shapiro, 1992: 36, 281) because the concept embodies the core values and beliefs (i.e. independence and identity) of Irish people in international affairs and foreign policy and in relation to the use of military force (Devine, 2008: 480; Keatinge, 1984: 99; Keatinge, 1996: 112–113; Government of Ireland, 1996: 119).

The 2001/2002 Irish Social and Political Attitudes Survey (ISPAS) survey showed that the strongest public support for neutrality is for a concept embodying the following foreign policy goals (Devine, 2008: 471):

- non-involvement in war
- independence
- impartiality
- peace-promotion
- self-defence only
- non-aggression
- not supporting big powers
- making our own decisions
- UN peace-keeping only

An analysis of survey responses gathered in April 1985, May and June 1992, together with the 2001/2002 responses, indicates that this meaning of Irish neutrality is reasonably stable over time (Devine, 2008: 472). This 'fundamental', 'active' or 'positive' concept supported by the public (herein known as 'Irish neutrality') is radically different from the so-called 'military' neutrality concept – amounting to non-membership of a military alliance – that appears in the discourse of the larger political parties such as Fianna Fáil and Fine Gael. These 'active' and 'military' neutrality concepts reflect differing foreign policy agendas (see also Keatinge, 1996: 111; 1984: 32, 118–119; McSweeney, 1988: 208; Fanning, 1996: 147), which may explain why parties in government are accused of 'fudging' the issue of neutrality; they are playing what Robert Putnam (1988) calls a 'two-level game', caught between the European Council and Council of Ministers' maximalist ESDP agenda driven by larger states such as France and Germany, and the domestic context of the public's 'active neutrality' agenda.

Compatibility of Neutrality Concepts with ESDP

Twenty-five years ago, Patrick Keatinge (1984: 44) noted, 'the futures posited by the European Community's style of integration and by permanent neutrality are mutually exclusive'. This incompatibility appears to be acknowledged in the Irish public's voting behaviour in referendums: neutrality has been among the top substantive policy reasons for voting against successive treaties furthering defence integration, e.g. the Single European Act (SEA) (Jones, 1987); Maastricht Treaty (Coghlan, 1992); Amsterdam Treaty (Sinnott, 1998a), Nice Treaty (Sinnott, 2001; Jupp, 2002) and the Lisbon Treaty (DFA, 2008: 14). Evidently, a proportion of Irish voters have consistently demonstrated a belief that further EU integration in the area of foreign, security and defence policy is incompatible with the concept of neutrality they support.

There is debate over the compatibility of several elements of the Common Security and Defence Policy (CSDP) proposed in the Lisbon Treaty with neutrality. For example, the Irish government has argued that 'military' neutrality is safeguarded, whilst legal analysts have pointed to some incompatibilities. For example, Hummer (2006: 67, 69) argues that the Article (42[7]) of the Consolidated Treaties amended by the Lisbon Treaty that contains a 'mutual defence clause' (Barroso, 2007) means that 'there remains no doubt that the neutral and non-aligned Member states are under the obligation to mutual (military) assistance in the case of armed attack' and that the solidarity obligations of CSDP are also clearly against neutrality law. Examining the positions of the political parties on neutrality and the ESDP from a legal perspective would indicate that parties may have difficulty in occupying more than one quadrant of the following conceptual matrices.

Party Positions in the 1970s

In the 1970s, the process of Ireland's accession to the then European Economic Community (EEC) raised the issue of Irish neutrality in the context of European common defence. From the outset of the negotiations to join the EEC, there was secrecy about what was agreed, specifically: about what Fianna Fáil had committed Ireland to in relation to neutrality and a future EU defence policy (e.g. Dillon, *Dáil Debates* 196: 3375–3382, 26 July 1962; Browne, *Dáil Debates* 196: 3501–3503, 26 July 1962; Dillon, *Dáil Debates* 198: 1341, 1346, 13 December 1962). For example, Senator Mary Robinson lamented the narrowness of the debate on Ireland's membership of the EEC, dealing with just economic aspects rather than wider political implications (*Seanad Debates* 69: 1292, 11 March 1971). She argued,

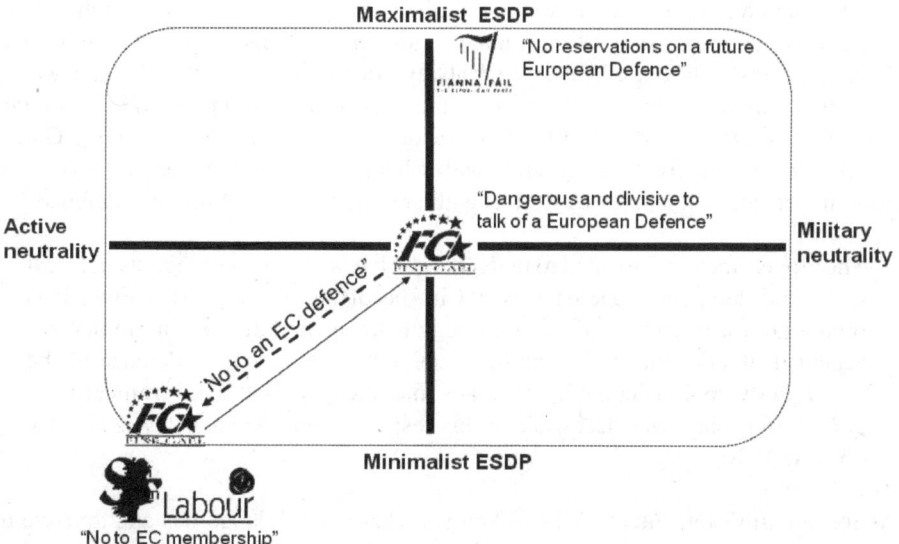

Figure 1. Irish parties' positions on neutrality and ESDP – 1970s.

it would be much stronger to have a genuine policy on neutrality, to state it now, and to state it as part of our commitment to the development of the European Community. This is a matter which should not be neglected. We should know what the intention of the Government is in this area.

A marked feature of this era was the disappearance of the word 'neutrality' from the governing parties' foreign policy discourse. For example, Minister for Foreign Affairs Patrick Hillery stressed Fianna Fáil's view that 'the foreign policy of a small democratic country like ours is not a single, grand design', and that the government 'should not and could not impose an arbitrary and abstract foreign policy' on Ireland's relations with Britain, the European Community, the United Nations and the developing world (*Dáil Debates* 260: 405, 18 April 1972). Hillery also argued that three issues – the assertion of its identity, the recognition of that identity by others, and the promotion and development of exchanges with other nations – are basic aspects of any country's relations with the world (*Dáil Debates* 260: 384). These, he concluded, 'indicate ... the general aim and direction of our foreign relations'. Hillery surmised that, 'our foreign relations and our foreign policy should, after all, in the long run, express the character, values and concerns of the Irish people in their dealings with the world' (*Dáil Debates* 260: 406). This new pre-accession discourse departed from past speeches by substituting the word 'identity' for 'neutrality' and they did not elaborate on Irish people's values, character and concerns, although the identity of the state and the people's values have consistently been viewed as being embodied in Irish neutrality (e.g. from Traynor, *Dáil Debates* 125: 1754, 1 May 1951; Cowan, *Dáil Debates* 138: 832–833, 29 April 1953; to Government of Ireland, 1996: 15; Ahern, 1999).

If Fianna Fáil in government were determined to avoid any talk of neutrality, Fine Gael, in government from 1973, wanted to smother any discussion of a future EU defence policy. Although Hillery had always denied offering that Ireland would enter into military commitments during the accession negotiations (*Dáil Debates* 259: 2444–2445, 23 March 1972), as shadow foreign minister in 1970, Garret FitzGerald was clearly uncomfortable with what he perceived Fianna Fáil had given away in pre-accession talks, as well as with any discussion of European defence:

> The Government have failed to understand what is involved as regards political unity and defence ... Defence is not in the offing at the present time. It is premature for us to talk about involving ourselves in defence commitments. I accept if this becomes a full political union that the common defence of the Community could become an issue at sometime. I think the government have gone further than was necessary in this respect. (*Dáil Debates* 247: 2009–10, 25 June 1970)

As foreign minister, FitzGerald's policy was that it was 'dangerous and divisive to talk about European defence' (*Irish Times*, 4 July 1975), partly due to fears of damage to EEC-US relations (*Irish Times*, 3 July 1975), thus making talk about

European defence during that era effectively 'taboo' (*Irish Times*, 4 July 1975). Sinnott (1998b: 6) observes that this trend is evident in all Ireland's referendums on European treaties precisely because of the sensitivity of the topic:

> it is usually assumed that neutrality is the great obstacle that, as far as Ireland is concerned, EU treaty changes must surmount or circumvent. This assumption results in much tiptoeing around, both by diplomats in the negotiation process and by politicians in the ratification debates.

Such deliberate silences maintained by the two largest political parties set the parameters of (the lack of) debate on Irish neutrality and EEC defence in the 1970s (and place them at the central point of the relative dimensions on Figure 1).

A second element of the strategy used both by Fianna Fáil and Fine Gael during the early 1970s was to differentiate NATO from a future EU military alliance – 'joining NATO and partaking in an eventual European defence arrangement are two entirely different things, and it is Government policy to keep them that way' (*Irish Times*, 4 July 1975). Use of the words 'pre-existing' military alliance distinguished the former (NATO) from the latter. In the 1980s, both parties claimed retrospectively that their *de facto* position at that time was that Ireland's neutrality would be waived in favour of joining a new *sui generis* EU military alliance – separate from NATO or the Western European Union (WEU) – in the future as part of a common security and defence policy; the only policy differences were the conditions under which this would happen. For example, Fianna Fáil in opposition claimed they had consistently followed a policy of being willing to contemplate security and defence integration once socio-economic equalization of regions throughout the EEC had been achieved (Lenihan, *Dáil Debates* 330: 130–31, 20 October 1981). Fine Gael would have Ireland participate in a European Community common defence policy once the EEC had evolved into 'a genuine federation of (sic) confederation, with a common foreign policy' (FitzGerald, *Dáil Debates* 334: 813, 11 May 1982). What was remarkable, given their respective policies of silence on neutrality and ESDP in the 1970s, was that both parties claimed public support for their positions. Two questions are raised with respect to the validity of their claims: did the parties in government put this commitment to an EU defence clearly to the people in 1970, and was it an essential part of the 1972 referendum campaign?

In fact, a third aspect of party policy that complemented the strategy of secrecy surrounding accession negotiations (O'Leary, *Dáil Debates* 230: 989, 26 July 1967; Tully, *Dáil Debates* 230: 1084–1085, 26 July 1967) and the disappearance of neutrality and EEC defence from party political discourse, was an apparent decision to minimize debates on Irish neutrality and the security and defence policy implications of EEC membership during the accession referendum (Curley, 1995; for reasons see Keogh, 1997: pts 23–24). According to media commentators, the issue was not mentioned in the White Paper on the terms of entry and did not play a central role in the referendum debate (Kennedy, *Irish Times*, 11 July

1975). This is confirmed by a number of academic analyses: Karsh (1988: 168–169) notes 'the dismissive attitude of the Irish proponents of EEC membership to the possibility of Ireland's entanglement within the political and military designs of the European Communities', and Hakovirta (1988: 131) surmises 'the question of neutrality was never very important in the arguments presented by the Irish government for EC membership, or even in the Irish EC debate in general'. The 1972 public debate on EEC membership concentrated on the economic implications of membership (Salmon, 1989: 214) whilst political consequences were not explored in any depth (Keatinge, 1973: 36). Hederman (1983: 109, 71, 146–147) indicates that, in public debate on Irish membership, any incompatibility between these goals (of EEC membership and neutrality) was not pressed home to the Irish people.

The 1972 referendum campaign attracted a 71 percent turnout at the polls, with accession to the EEC favoured by 83 percent of votes. With respect to neutrality and ESDP, Keatinge (1984: 28) surmises, 'the decisive vote of the electorate in favour of membership of the European Community is explained by the quantifiable expectations of economic gain rather than by views, one way or another, on neutrality'. The Labour Party was the only large political party to campaign against accession and instead advocated associate membership, mainly on economic grounds of unfavourable terms of accession and perceived neo-colonialism of the EC, but also due to fears regarding Irish neutrality. The party was particularly anxious over the governmental silence on neutrality and future European defence commitments and pressed the Government on the issue, eliciting the reply: 'When the Taoiseach opened the debate, and I think it is clearly stated in the White Paper, he said that there are no military or defence commitments whatsoever in Ireland's acceptance of the Treaties of Rome and Paris. *Our obligations as a member of the Communities will not entail such commitments*' (emphasis added) (Hillery, *Dáil Debates* 259: 2445, 23 March 1972). The government approach – to refer to the lack of military obligations in the text of the treaties and to deny that an agreement was made during the Irish negotiations for EEC membership to cede Irish neutrality for a future common European defence policy – did not dissuade the Labour Party from continuing to protest over what it perceived as the government's relinquishing of sovereignty and neutrality (Cruise O'Brien, *Dáil Debates* 259: 2208–2209, 23 March 1972). After the referendum, the party accepted the electorate's decision, adopted a role of critical participation in the European Community (Keatinge, 1973: 258) and soon after entered into coalition government with Fine Gael.

Irish political parties' foreign policies were formulated by either a small group under the foreign affairs spokesperson, or even the spokesperson alone; most parliamentary members of the larger parties have little or no role in the discussion of foreign policy (Keatinge, 1973: 263). It is clear that the participation of governing party leaders and foreign policy elites in EEC forums influenced Fianna Fáil party discourse. This is compatible with a process of Europeanization, although it did not appear to manifest itself in terms of strained relations within the party (see Ladrech,

2002: 398). It did, however, reflect a movement away from earlier party programmatic positions. Fianna Fáil was in government during Ireland's three attempts to join the EEC; after each round of accession negotiations, party leaders were probably more willing to secretly cede on policies important to the party in order to secure the ultimate goal of membership. This is reflected in the persistent criticism of Fianna Fáil by the opposition parties for allegedly ceding neutrality as a principle of Irish foreign policy.

Party Positions in the 1980s

The 1980s saw the European Economic Community attempt to develop a common position on foreign policy through the development of 'European Political Co-operation'; this dynamic formed the basis of the Supreme Court's decision in the Crotty case to mandate a referendum in Ireland on the SEA in 1986. This era provides opportunities to study the content of the parties' concepts of ESDP and Irish neutrality through the pressures of Ireland's EEC membership and attempts to respond to 'external' foreign policy events such as the Falklands War.

Oscillations in the neutrality concepts of the larger parties, generally coinciding with change in government, reflected some evidence of 'party competition' inducing shifts in parties' positions in the 1980s, indicated by the dotted lines in Figure 2. Once in opposition, each of the larger parties claimed to occupy a more 'fundamental' neutrality position than the party in government, knowingly appealing to the domestic constituency while freed from competing pressures from the European Council.

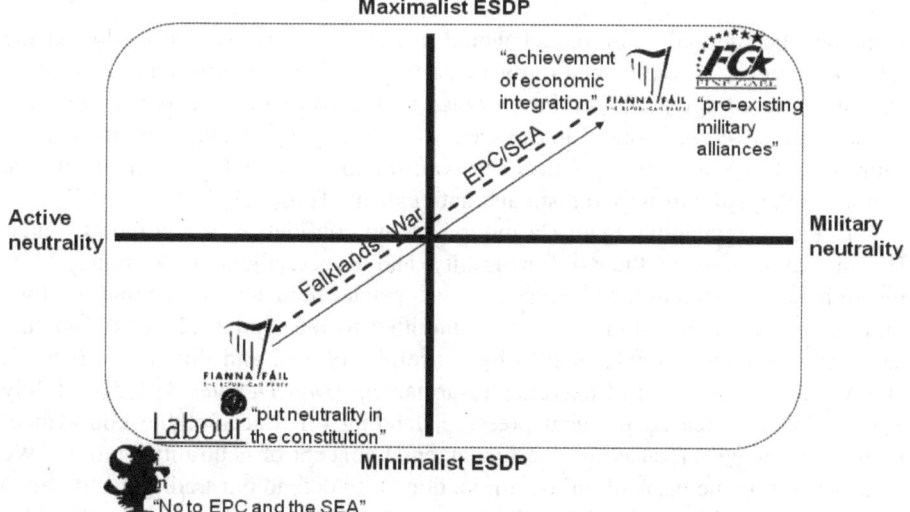

Figure 2. Irish parties' positions on neutrality and ESDP – 1980s.

Fianna Fáil and Oscillating Concepts of Neutrality

Fianna Fáil continued the tradition established in the 1970s of avoiding reference to the word 'neutrality' whilst in government, e.g. a key speech on defence contained one mention of the word (*Dáil Debates* 327, 11 March 1981). Taoiseach Charles Haughey outlined Fianna Fáil's policy as committing the state politically to the EEC but militarily to the United Nations (UN) (*Dáil Debates* 327: 1395, 11 March 1981). Although he noted that Ireland's UN peacekeeping would be jeopardized if Ireland joined a military alliance, Haughey declared that if the EEC evolved into a full political union, Ireland would accept obligations arising, even if these included defence (*Dáil Debates* 327: 1398, 1396).

Fianna Fáil's long-standing approach of ceding neutrality in favour of European defence appeared to be reversed during the Falklands War. In this case, the party appeared to favour neutrality and reject a common EEC policy. After the escalation of the Falklands dispute (war had not been officially declared), Fianna Fáil, having just regained the reins of power, sought to 'reassert our traditional policy of neutrality', arguing that 'the people of this country are deeply attached to our neutrality, and they are not prepared to see it eroded' (Haughey, *Dáil Debates* 334: 804, 11 May 1982). This recovered 'neutrality' justified Haughey's decision to withdraw EEC sanctions against Argentina, because:

> there were indications that diplomatic and economic pressure was simply viewed as complementary to military action ... As a neutral country, we are not prepared to back military action ... The Community has no role in the military sphere and it would be better for European unity and solidarity if it were not seen to take actions supportive of or complementary to military action. (*Dáil Debates* 334: 800, 802, 804, 11 May 1982)

Although the rational actor model would assume that Fianna Fáil evaluated the relative value of invoking neutrality in particular circumstances and chose their strategies accordingly, analysts have argued that the decision to exercise 'an independent and sovereign policy' in this case was driven only in small part to enhance support for Haughey's own political survival, and more likely by the effects of core political beliefs of anti-imperialism and nationalism (Tonra, 1996: 149–150).

Nonetheless, speaking against a motion of 'no confidence' a few months later, Haughey avoided using the word 'neutrality' and instead talked of 'our policy ... of remaining aloof from military alliances', 'independence in action', having 'our own view of international affairs', being 'committed to the United Nations' and 'the settlement of international disputes by peaceful, political and diplomatic means', and promoting the cause of universal disarmament (*Dáil Debates* 337: 562, 1 July 1982). Under increased political pressure, fending off a second 'no confidence' motion, Haughey refocused on the fundamental concept of neutrality, stating, 'We seek support on the basis of our determination ... to defend our tradition and policy of neutrality' (*Dáil Debates* 338: 649, 3 November 1982) and berated Fine Gael for misrepresenting his government's motives in the Falklands affair. In December

1982, Fianna Fáil lost the general election and a coalition of Labour and Fine Gael took office.

In opposition, Fianna Fáil put forward 'a policy of positive neutrality' (Haughey, *Dáil Debates* 359: 1976, 1977–1978, 26 June 1985) during a Dáil debate on the Dooge Report, advocating 'a firm position of principle that we are opposed to defence being discussed by the Community' on the basis that 'the last thing the world needs today is a reinforcement of military blocs or the creation of new ones'. The party rejected the CFSP obligation to be bound to 'common positions in keeping with majority opinion' because 'a common foreign policy is incompatible with our neutrality' (Haughey, *Dáil Debates* 359: 1978). Fianna Fáil also claimed that the SEA posed challenges 'to our neutrality' (Haughey, *Dáil Debates* 370: 1923–1924, 9 December 1986), noting 'a persistent and worrying tendency to try to blur the distinction between the Community and the Western Alliance' (WEU) and attempts to include military aspects of security in European Political Cooperation. On the basis that 'we have reached, perhaps gone beyond, what is strictly compatible with neutrality', Fianna Fáil demanded a declaration that the SEA 'does not and cannot affect our long-established policy of neutrality … and does not affect Ireland's capacity to act or refrain from acting in any way affecting our status of neutrality' (Haughey, *Dáil Debates* 370: 1925). But, back in government three months later, the party supported the SEA and the party leader's discourse reverted to the former policy of 'military neutrality' (Haughey, *Dáil Debates* 371: 2187, 22 April 1987).

Fine Gael and Oscillating Concepts of Neutrality

At the end of the 1970s into the early 1980s, Fine Gael's foreign affairs spokesperson Richie Ryan advocated a policy of fundamental neutrality at all times, regarding neutrality as the cornerstone of Irish foreign policy and arguing against Ireland's participation in a future common European defence (e.g. Ryan, *Dáil Debates* 314: 1943, 31 May 1979; *Irish Times*, 9 January 1981). Fine Gael pointed to the reversal of Fianna Fáil policy on neutrality, arguing that a 'fundamentalist position' on neutrality as espoused by de Valera was overturned by Seán Lemass and Patrick Hillery in their statements committing Ireland to a future common defence force of the EEC (FitzGerald, *Dáil Debates* 327: 1423–1424, 11 March 1981). Fine Gael party discourse during this time contained the supposition that 'fundamental' Irish neutrality is incompatible with a maximalist EU common defence policy.

However, Fine Gael's own fundamentalist position on neutrality was reversed under Garret FitzGerald's leadership of the party and copper-fastened with the appointment of James Dooge as Foreign Minister in 1982. 'Party-government relations' in the framework of a two-level game stands out as a significant factor in Fine Gael's handling of neutrality and the ESDP during this era. For example, the party leader Garret FitzGerald (1988: 29; 1995) expressed personal difficulties in having to remain silent at Council discussions of security and defence in the 1980s; he did so because he felt public opinion was against such discussions and favoured neutrality. The 'organizational change' dynamic may have influenced cabinet government formation in 1982. As Taoiseach, FitzGerald wanted to have an Irish foreign minister in favour of European defence integration at the Council of Ministers table. To achieve this, he appointed James Dooge as a senator, in order to later appoint him as foreign minister ahead of any elected TD colleagues – specifically, Richie Ryan, who was an obvious candidate for the position but was sidelined ostensibly because of his pro-neutrality stance (Haughey, *Dáil Debates* 330: 119, 20 October 1981).

Under FitzGerald, Fine Gael articulated a narrow concept of 'military neutrality', (conceived in realist 'balance of power' and Cold War contexts (*Dáil Debates* 327: 1424–1425, 11 March 1981)), meaning 'non-participation in a military alliance … not a member of NATO, WEU or any other alliance'. This was primarily due to pressure from public opinion and because staying outside of these military alliances allowed Ireland to play a more useful role in promoting world peace (*Dáil Debates* 327: 1423, 1420). As a foreign policy vehicle, military neutrality facilitated the following 'positive merits' of Irish foreign policy: UN peacekeeping, the 1961 nuclear non proliferation treaty, decolonization initiatives, opposing South African apartheid, accepting refugees, opposing US funding of South American paramilitaries, increasing aid to the Third World, and supporting Palestinian self-determination (*Dáil Debates* 327: 1425–1426).

Labour Party in the 1980s

For the Labour Party, its version of neutrality was neither a pragmatic policy nor a refusal to join a military bloc but a principled stance and active political philosophy that would always be relevant in a world of great power politics (Cluskey, *Dáil Debates* 327: 1402; Quinn, *Dáil Debates* 327: 1440, 1442). This 'active' neutrality, seen as a 'fundamentally held belief' of Irish people and an assertion of independence, implied a total commitment to peace (Quinn, *Dáil Debates* 327: 1441–1442). The Labour Party positioned itself as having the longest and deepest commitment to neutrality (Cluskey, *Dáil Debates* 327: 1402).

The party differed from Fianna Fáil and Fine Gael in seeing neutrality as nonnegotiable and wanting to ensure the EEC understood that Ireland would not give up neutrality for a common defence policy (placing it in the bottom left-hand quadrant of Figures 1 and 2). Neutrality was the primary objective of Irish foreign policy, over and above arriving at a common position or engaging in cooperation with other EEC members that might compromise, in particular, a neutral Irish position in relation to armaments, development and relations with the Third World. For Labour, 'Ireland neutral, positively pursuing its policy of neutrality at the United Nations and within the EEC – both at the Council of Ministers' level and at the technical level of European political co-operation – has a positive contribution to make, if we have the guts to make it' (Quinn, *Dáil Debates* 327: 1445–1446). The Labour Party further distinguished itself from the larger parties by arguing that neutrality should be affirmed permanently by amendment of the constitution (Quinn, *Dáil Debates* 327: 1440). The issue of neutrality exemplified tensions in 'party-government relations' arising from a process of Europeanization, e.g. when in government, the

Labour leadership supported ratification of the SEA whilst the party's rank and file opposed it on the grounds that its provisions posed a threat to Irish neutrality (Moxon-Browne, 1999: 5). The party withstood the tensions, but later modified and clarified its position on Europe and EU foreign policy in ways which would minimize the potential for future internal difficulties. It was argued that participation in government and the closer engagement with the EU which this implied effectively obliged the Labour Party to countenance and implement programmatic change.

Party Positions in the 1990s

Against the background of the end of the Cold War, the 1992 Maastricht Treaty introduced a Common Foreign and Security Policy (CFSP) that proposed the 'eventual framing' of a common defence policy; this was revised further in the 'progressive framing' of the policy under the 1997 Amsterdam Treaty. The latter introduced a CFSP 'policy unit' infrastructure, a new post of High Representative for CFSP, a deeper relationship with the WEU military alliance with provisions for future integration into the EU (the WEU–EU merger was subsequently initiated by a European Council decision at Helsinki in 1999), a new decision-making mechanism to avoid possible vetoes on proposed EU actions through abstention, and a remit of 'Petersberg tasks', including humanitarian and rescue tasks, peacekeeping tasks and tasks of combat forces in crisis management, including peacemaking. Taken together, these provisions signalled the material intent of the new political entity called the European Union to achieve a common foreign policy, coupled with a so-called 'crisis management' military bite. In Ireland, neutrality and EU defence policy issues started to show signs of politicization, mainly due to the activities of interest groups. Following from the 1995 McKenna judgement and 1998 Referendum Act, a

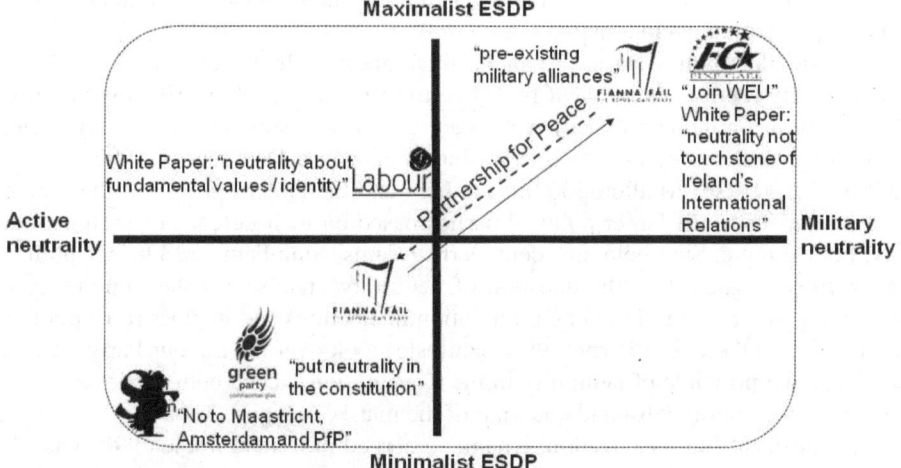

Figure 3. Irish parties' positions on neutrality and ESDP – 1990s.

newly-created Referendum Commission was charged with the task of providing information on both sides of the debate in the Treaty of Amsterdam referendum campaign.

Oscillations between concepts of 'military' and 'active' neutrality plus accusations of secrecy over European defence policy continued to characterize large parties' behaviour upon leaving office. For example, Fine Gael accused the Fianna Fáil government of being committed to hiding the reality of discussions at an EU level on new security arrangements (*Beyond Neutrality,* 2006: 6). In opposition, Fianna Fáil assumed the mantle of 'chief architect and defender of neutrality' (*Irish Times,* 16 April 1997) and promised to hold a referendum on membership of NATO's Partnership for Peace – 'seen by other countries as a gratuitous signal that Ireland is moving away from its neutrality and towards gradual incorporation into NATO and WEU in due course' (*Irish Times,* 29 March 1996). But within months of returning to power, Fianna Fáil led the government in joining Partnership for Peace in 1999, without a referendum.

In the meantime, Ireland's first White Paper on Foreign Policy (Government of Ireland, 1996) produced by the 'Rainbow Coalition' government had belied the tension between the Labour Party's 'fundamental' neutrality discourse ('the values that underlie Ireland's policy of neutrality have therefore informed almost every aspect of our foreign policy', Government of Ireland, 1996: 119) and Fine Gael's narrow concept of 'military' neutrality ('Many have come to regard neutrality as a touchstone of our entire approach to international relations, eventhough [sic], in reality, much of our policy is not dependent on our non-membership of a military alliance', Government of Ireland, 1996: 51). With respect to positions on ESDP, the Rainbow Coalition's White Paper (1996: 120, 139) rejected full membership of the Western European Union and the assumption of its mutual defence clause noting it 'would not be compatible with an intention to remain neutral' (1996: 120), but committed Ireland to participation in the Petersberg tasks in the area of humanitarian and peacekeeping operations.

The smaller parties started to make their mark in Irish politics in the 1990s: Green Party representation went from one to two TDs in 1997 whilst two Member of European Parliament (MEP) seats were gained and subsequently retained until 2004 (see Bolleyer & Panke, 2009). Sinn Féin won a Dáil seat in 1997 and two MEPs in 2004 (see Maillot, 2009). Sinn Féin and the Greens promoted themselves as alternatives to the larger political parties based on their defence of Irish neutrality. For example, Sinn Féin president Gerry Adams (Sinn Féin Ard Fheis, Dublin, 8 May 1999) argued that 'the question of neutrality underscores the importance of providing voters with Sinn Féin as an option in elections and in grass roots political activity', and the Green Party (1997 manifesto) took over the Labour Party's call to enshrine the principle of neutrality in the Constitution (hence both parties are positioned in the bottom left-hand quadrant of the matrix in Figure 3).

A significant Europeanization dynamic emerged in Ireland in the 1990s with the increased politicization of the neutrality/ESDP issue, namely in the form of changes in ideological distance separating political parties and the emergence of

European-centred dimensions of party competition (Mair, 2000: 30). This process of politicization of the EU by political parties was mostly confined to referendum periods, with little evidence of parties competing on EU issues during elections. Nevertheless, the u-turn by Fianna Fáil on Partnership for Peace membership and Fine Gael's shift to a less forthright position (one of silent hostility) on neutrality show the political calculations made by the two largest parties in attempts to differentiate themselves along this increasingly important European-centred policy dimension during referendum campaigns. Similarly, Sinn Féin highlighted its adherence to positive or 'active' neutrality given the vacuum left by the drift of rival left-wing parties, Labour and Democratic Left, towards maximalist ESDP.

EU Referendums

Referendums tend to force political parties to indicate policy positions through a decision to campaign for or against a treaty. On 8 June 1992, a week after the Danes rejected the Maastricht Treaty, Fianna Fáil, Fine Gael, Labour and the Progressive Democrats came together to call for a Yes vote in the Maastricht Treaty referendum. Particularly notable is the move of Labour from opposition in 1972, to a split in 1987, to advocating a Yes in 1992 but allowing conscientious objection (Franklin, Marsh & McLaren, 1994: 465). Moxon-Browne (1999: 7) argues that the elite leadership drove the policy change. The Green Party, Sinn Féin, the Workers' Party and the new Democratic Left campaigned against the treaty and its CFSP provisions. The referendum was carried with 68.7 percent in favour, based on a turnout of 57.3 percent.

Democratic Left shifted its position by the time of the May 1998 referendum on the Amsterdam Treaty, joining Labour, Fianna Fáil, Fine Gael and the Progressive Democrats in advocating a Yes vote. De Rossa's turnaround – from demanding a renegotiation of the Single European Act (*Dáil Debates* 371: 2127, 9 April 1987) and campaigning for a No vote on the Maastricht Treaty in 1992 to support for the Amsterdam Treaty – was premised on the argument that the prospect of EU militarization had been abandoned (*Irish Times*, 5 May 1998). After Democratic Left merged with Labour in January 1999, De Rossa had apparently become convinced by the need for an EU CFSP and called for a redefinition of neutrality to enable Ireland's full participation in it (*Irish Times*, 30 March 1999). This exemplifies the ways in which party elites involved in negotiations of the treaty at the European level appeared to adopt a cabinet-type responsibility to ensure ratification, regardless of clashes with party policy or the need to reverse previous policy positions.

The Amsterdam Treaty provisions on a potential WEU–EU merger prompted the Fianna Fáil-led government to promise a referendum in Ireland if 'the issue [of European defence] should arise in the future' (Ahern, 1998). The larger parties viewed Amsterdam's Petersberg tasks as 'consistent with the tradition of military neutrality' (Ahern, 2000). Based on support for 'active' neutrality, the Greens were against the tasks which they interpreted as allowing unlimited EU military action and marking a shift in Irish foreign policy away from UN peacekeeping (*Irish*

Times, 27 January 1998). The smaller parties of Sinn Féin, the Green Party and the Socialist Party campaigned against the treaty partly due to perceived negative implications for Irish neutrality. In doing so, they appeared to represent a significant constituency, because 'neutrality' was the top substantive policy reason for voting 'no' in the referendum (just behind 'lack of information'), according to a *Prime Time*/Raidió Teilifís Éireann (RTÉ) Exit Poll (22 May 1998).

Policy Changes

Fine Gael fought the 1994 European Parliament elections on a platform of 'full membership of the WEU', but subsequently retreated from what was seen as a 'foolhardy position' (*Irish Times*, 12 June 1995) – although the party continued to put forward motions for full membership of the WEU at Ardfheiseanna (*Irish Times*, 20 March 1996). The party's *Beyond Neutrality* (Fine Gael, 2000: 5) policy document declared, 'Ireland must now define the circumstances in which it would be willing to depart from neutrality and take part in an EU defence entity' and sought to have the WEU's article V mutual defence clause (enshrining a guarantee to automatically afford 'all the military and other aid and assistance' at member-states' disposal to a member-state suffering an attack) into a protocol instead of a full treaty provision in the next EU Treaty so that it would be invoked on a case-by-case basis rather than apply automatically to all states. This shift in programmatic content arguably provides evidence of Europeanization effects on party elite given that a majority of party members favoured the retention of neutrality (Marsh, 2002: 161).

Fianna Fáil in government refused to offer their position on a future European defence policy prior to the summit on the Maastricht Treaty in 1991 – it simply noted that the draft document did not involve Ireland in a mutual defence commitment or membership in a military alliance (Haughey, *Dáil Debates* 413: 1384–1186, 28 November 1991). In opposition, however, the party favoured an EU common defence policy in their 1995 foreign policy document but rejected within this any obligation to come to the aid of another member under attack (*Irish Times*, 7 November 1995), thereby preserving the option of a somewhat credible 'military' neutrality discourse.

Party Positions in the 2000s

In the 2000s, the EU enlarged to include 12 new members. The experience of war in the Balkans led to an agreement by the European Council on November 2000 to create a 60,000-strong European Rapid Reaction Force for crisis-management operations outside the EU; this was subsequently revised in November 2004 into 13 1,500-strong Battlegroups to carry out the Petersberg tasks, giving material effect to the EU's ESDP. The Irish government pledged 850 troops to the Battlegroups, and joined the Nordic Battlegroup in 2008 (with a political limit placed on missions through the 'triple lock' of requiring a UN mandate, government and Dáil approval). The Nice Treaty agreed in December 2000 contained a number of ESDP developments

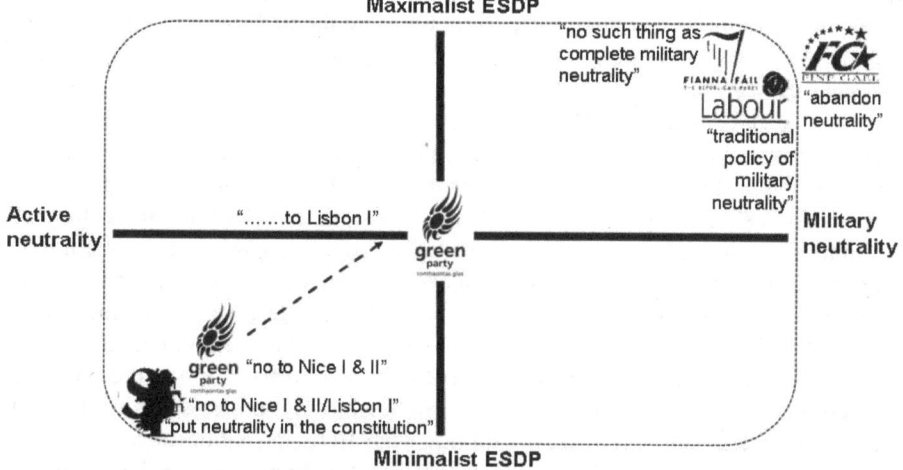

Figure 4. Irish parties' positions on neutrality and ESDP – 2000s.

including the incorporation of the WEU into the EU, a political and security committee, a military committee and military staff, and 'enhanced cooperation' in CFSP. The 9/11 terrorist attacks on the USA and subsequent invasions of Afghanistan and Iraq by US-led coalition forces were followed by the creation of new security strategies by the US in 2002 and the EU in 2003. In Ireland, the narrowing gap between Yes and No votes in referendums since Maastricht preceded the failure of the Nice Treaty referendum in June 2001 (with a vote of 53.9 percent against on a relatively low turnout of 35 percent) and was brought about in part by perceived threats to neutrality (Sinnott, 2001: v). The Nice Treaty was ratified by a second referendum in October 2002 (by 62.9 percent on a turnout of 49.5 percent) but the spectre of neutrality returned to haunt the 2008 referendum on the Lisbon Treaty (which was rejected by 53.4 percent on a turnout of 53.1 percent). This final section analyses the divisive role of the issue of neutrality in the referendums on the Nice and Lisbon Treaties.

Nice Referendums

Although Fine Gael had criticized the document as 'one of the weakest negotiating outcomes achieved by an Irish government in the European forum' (Bruton, *Dáil Debates*, 528: 453, 13 December 2000), it and all the larger parties, plus the religious, cultural, business, employer and trade union elite, were in favour of ratification of the Nice Treaty in the June 2001 referendum. With respect to ESDP, the government had claimed a crucial victory in ensuring that closer co-operation could not apply to measures having military or defence implications (Ahern, *Dáil Debates* 528: 450, 452, 13 December 2000). But the threat to Irish neutrality continued to be a primary justification for opposition to treaty ratification by both Sinn Féin and the Green Party, the latter reiterating a 'total rejection of the EU's Petersberg Tasks, the rapid reaction force established to carry them out and all the military hardware committee structures that have been put in place by the EU' and calling for a protocol in the treaty 'exempting Ireland from involvement in EU military efforts' (Sargent, *Dáil Debates* 528: 461, 13 December 2000).

After the defeat of the 2001 referendum, there were two statements relating to Irish neutrality in the proposal before the people again in October 2002. First, the so-called 'Seville Declarations': statements by the Irish government and EU member-states claiming there was nothing in the treaty that would affect Ireland's 'military' neutrality. Secondly, a new subsection to the proposed Amendment to the Constitution: 'The State shall not adopt a decision taken by the European Council to establish a common defence ... where that common defence would include the state' (Article 29.4.9). The Declarations and the new amendment did not address the publicly-supported concept of 'active' neutrality but rather applied the narrowest concept of 'military' neutrality, i.e. non-membership of a pre-existing military alliance such as the WEU or NATO (although the EU's definition of a common or collective defence is 'participation in the defence of Europe under the Treaties of Brussels and Washington which stipulate that in the event of aggression, the signatory states are required to provide assistance'; see http://europa.eu/scadplus/glossary/collective_defence_en.htm). The issue of divergent concepts of positive/active neutrality and military neutrality highlighted by the Green Party (Boyle, *Dáil Eireann* 554: 401, 11 September 2002) was crucial in understanding the positions of the Yes and No sides in the second referendum campaign. Notably, when pressed to define its own concept of neutrality, Fianna Fáil avoided a direct response, simply admitting that 'we do not have anything like an appropriate definition' (Roche, *Dáil Debates* 554: 413). The Nice Treaty was passed this time (62.9 percent in favour on a turnout of 49.5 percent), aided by the notable (albeit legally spurious) Yes argument that the treaty was necessary for enlargement (to the extent that the government (Ahern, *Dáil Debates* 553: 74, 6 June 2002) and Department of Foreign Affairs (2007: 7) called it 'the Nice Treaty on enlargement').

Party Policy Changes

The most significant policy change announced on behalf of a party was Fine Gael's reported call for the abandonment of Irish neutrality (*Irish Times*, 30 May 2003) prompted by the 2003 re-launch of *Beyond Neutrality*. Certainly, its 2007 election manifesto stated, 'we believe Ireland should be a full participant in an EU security and defence arrangement' (Fine Gael, 2007). Although Fianna Fáil did not outline an explicit position on the matter, party discourse signalled further narrowing of the limited concept of 'military' neutrality. Indeed, the Minister for Defence, Michael Smith, was reported as saying, 'There is no such thing as, if you like, complete military neutrality' (*Irish Times*, 18 January 2003). In the context of the WEU–EU merger and negotiations to place the WEU's Article V mutual defence clause into an 'opt-in' protocol in the new EU Constitution (Convention Report, 20 December 2002: 12), Fianna Fáil reduced the notion of neutrality to one of 'non-membership of military alliance, and specifically, non-membership of an alliance *with a mutual defence commitment*' (Cowen, *Dáil Debates* 563: 722, 20 March 2003, emphasis added).

From its position of opposition, and supported by the Green Party and the Socialist Party, Sinn Féin took a proposed Private Members' Bill to put neutrality into the Constitution to a second stage in the Dáil (Ó Caoláin, *Dáil Debates* 561: 992, 18 February 2003). Sinn Féin's 'Positive Neutrality in Action' policy document (2004: 15, 9–10) outlines the party's concept of neutrality and argues that: 'there is no legitimate role for the European Union in military and defence matters'. Instead, the party advocates 'UN primacy', specifying that 'International peacekeeping and conflict resolution should happen under the auspices of the United Nations' (2004: 9–10). The document (2004: 10–13) notes the differences between the larger parties' concept of 'military' neutrality and its conception of positive neutrality, encompassing the minimum definition defined in the Hague Conventions and rejecting others' attempts to define neutrality negatively as pacifism, ambivalence and isolationism (2004: 10–11). Positive neutrality includes a guiding 'human security' doctrine, nuclear disarmament, a refusal to get drawn into military conflicts as a result of standing military alliances or mutual defence pacts, active promotion of the primacy of the UN, and a pursuit of (non-military) alliances with other progressive neutral states. Such elements distinguish the party from others and position it in the bottom left-hand corner of the matrix in Figure 4.

Positions on the Constitution/Lisbon Treaty ESDP Provisions

The ESDP provisions in the failed European Constitution (rejected in French and Dutch referendums in 2005) were revived through the Lisbon Treaty agreed in December 2007. The provisions make a commitment to a more assertive EU role in security and defence matters, including solidarity and mutual defence clauses, a common arms policy, Permanent Structured Cooperation in defence, and extensions to the Petersberg tasks (to include conflict prevention, joint disarmament operations and post-conflict stabilization, in part to support third countries in their fight against terrorism). Although Fianna Fáil re-stated their opposition to the EU turning itself into a military alliance (*Irish Times*, 18 January 2003) and whilst in opposition (Ahern, *Dáil Debates* 473: 608, 19 December 1996) and in government (Andrews, *Dáil Debates* 506: 197–198, 15 June 1999) in the 1990s had specifically rejected plans for the WEU–EU merger and the inclusion of alliance obligations in a Treaty, the party merely noted 'aspects of the [draft ESDP provisions in the Defence Working Group 'Barnier'] Report which raise issues for Ireland. These include reference to a mutual assistance or mutual defence clause'. The party stated that this proposal, along with the armaments policy and the lifting of the ban on enhanced cooperation in defence 'will need to be carefully studied' (Roche, 2002). The party's message during the referendum campaign was that Ireland's neutrality is not threatened by the Lisbon Treaty (O'Dea, 2008). Fianna Fáil, Fine Gael and Labour campaigned in favour of the treaty (see Quinlan, 2009). Sinn Féin was the only parliamentary party to campaign against the Lisbon Treaty.

Similarly to Sinn Féin, the Green Party had advocated a 'positive' concept of neutrality in their 2007 election manifesto, distinguished from successive governments' definition of non-membership of military alliances. In 2002, the Green Party campaigned against the amendment to the Nice Treaty as having no legal basis, failing to preclude NATO membership, and lacking any mention of a UN mandate for crisis management missions (Boyle, *Dáil Debates* 554: 400–401). Five years later, the Green Party (2007a: 32) pledged to 'remain committed to protecting Irish neutrality from any further moves towards an EU Common Defence Policy or any strengthening of the Common Foreign and Security Policy' and would seek a referendum to define neutrality in the Constitution (2007a: 32). But whereas the Sinn Féin 2007 election manifesto and guide to the Lisbon Treaty showed a consistent support for positive neutrality, by comparison, after having entered into coalition government, the Green Party moved towards a more limited concept of neutrality and maintained official silence on the Lisbon Treaty (after a party membership vote of 63 percent in favour of the treaty failed to reach the required two-thirds majority to formally support the treaty). The Green Party information pack on the Lisbon Treaty (Green Party, 2007b: 5) acknowledged that it 'commits the EU to creating a common defence policy' and allows a military 'inner core' of states to 'deepen defence and military cooperation'.

What explains this shift from resistance to ESDP and protection of positive neutrality to a *de facto* endorsement of EU common defence policy in the Lisbon Treaty referendum? Is it due to 'Europeanization' or an internal party decision to stay in coalition government? The 'supranational relations' influence through membership of the European Green Party (EGP), the exclusive partner to the Green Group in the European Parliament, may have played a role (Laffan & Langan, 2005: 11). The EGP Committee (2007: 3) took a position in favour of the Lisbon Treaty, including its provisions on structured cooperation in defence. In the movement from opposition to coalition government, the influence of collective decision-making in cabinet has meant that the Green Party in Ireland has had to adhere to aspects of policy that go against major issue preferences (Müller-Rommel, 2002: 10–11; Bolleyer & Panke, 2009). The party may escape punishment from their traditional supporters at the polls for this neutrality/ESDP policy shift because party affiliations are not strongly linked to voters' attitudes to neutrality (Devine, 2006: 271).

Conclusion

In the Maastricht, Amsterdam, Nice and Lisbon referendums, Irish neutrality has consistently emerged as the first or second substantive policy reason behind the public's No votes. Although the government parties can be understood as engaging in a two-level game between the neutrality-supportive Irish public and the European Council demands for a common security and defence policy, the wider question of the dynamics driving the elite-public cleavage remains. Hooghe (2003) explains that elite preferences for the Europeanization of policies (such as foreign, security and defence policies) reflects a functionalist logic and desire for economies of scale, to achieve their goal of a European Union capable of governing a large, competitive market and projecting political muscle. Citizens, however, are more in favour of 'a caring European Union, which protects them from the vagaries of capitalist markets' and support different aspects of European integration, for example social, cohesion and environmental policies (Hooghe, 2003: 17–18). These different agendas illustrate the wider context in which the local dynamics of Ireland's postcolonial history and the Irish public's adherence to the values embodied in neutrality combine to produce a resistance to Europeanization in the sphere of foreign, security and defence policy.

This article has considered the ways in which Irish political parties have attempted to negotiate this two-level tension, as it is exemplified in the debate about Irish neutrality and European common security. A general trend whereby most Irish political parties have moved from support for 'positive'/'active' Irish neutrality to a limited 'military' concept that allows the development of European Security and Defence Policy is clearly discernible. Fianna Fáil copper-fastened its move away from neutrality to embrace a European common defence in the 1970s, Fine Gael converted in the 1980s, Labour took the same steps in the 1990s and the Green Party approximated the move in the 2000s. Presently, the only parliamentary party left supporting Irish neutrality is Sinn Féin. It remains to be seen whether this party will continue to resist the effects of Europeanization that have characterized the most significant movements across the 'Irish neutrality–EU CSDP' policy dimensions in the Irish party system.

In sum, the politicization of Irish neutrality and EU common security and defence policy have effected important party political changes in Ireland. Individual parties have, to differing degrees, modified their positions on both issues. Programmatic change has been especially apparent when judged in terms of evolving party discourse. Such change has been influenced by a combination of domestic and EU influences. Participation in government appears to be an important stimulant for party political change on neutrality and European security and defence policies. Party competition, particularly during referendum campaigns, is similarly significant in prompting modification in party positions. Other forces also important include domestic electoral objectives and agendas. The development of Irish party political attitudes towards neutrality and the evolution of the EU's foreign, security and defence policies have interacted in intricate ways with domestic party political agendas to produce a form of substantive Europeanization through subtle and muted discursive practices.

Notes

The author gratefully acknowledges postdoctoral research funding from the Irish Research Council for the Humanities and Social Sciences (IRCHSS).

References

Ahern, B. (1998) Address to the Institute of European Affairs, Dublin, 3 March 1998, available at: www.gov.ie/taoiseach/press/Archives/1998/3-3-98.htm (accessed March 2002).

Ahern, B. (1999) Verbatim, Opening Address at the European Movement National Conference on Partnership for Peace, Burlington Hotel, Dublin, 29 November.
Ahern, B. (2000) Speech at Fianna Fáil Ardfheis, Royal Dublin Society, Dublin, 4 March 2000.
Barroso, J.M.D. (2007) *The European Union after the Lisbon Treaty* President of the European Commission SPEECH/07/793 delivered at the 4th Joint Parliamentary meeting on the Future of Europe, Brussels, 4 December 2007, available at: http://europa.eu/rapid/pressReleasesAction.do?reference=SPEECH/07/793&format=HTML&aged=0&language=EN&guiLanguage=en (accessed February 2009).
Bolleyer, N. & Panke, D. (2009) The Irish Green Party: an unhappy marriage?, *Irish Political Studies*, 24(4), pp. 543–557.
Coghlan, D. (1992) Margin in favour of Maastricht is dramatically narrowed, poll finds, *Irish Times*, 10 June.
Curley, D. (1995) The makers of myths, *Irish Times*, 28 April.
Deighton, A. (2002) The European Security and Defence Policy, *Journal of Common Market Studies*, 40(4), pp. 719–741.
Department of Foreign Affairs (DFA) (2007) *Agreed Programme for Government Progress Report April 2007*, Dublin, available at: http://193.178.1.117/attached_files/RTF%20files/ForeignAffairs Progress07.rtf (accessed 20 July 2008).
Department of Foreign Affairs (DFA) (2008) *Post Lisbon Treaty Referendum Research Findings September 2008* (Dublin: Stationary Office).
Devine, K. (2006) *Public Opinion and Irish Neutrality: A Theoretical and Empirical Test of the 'Rational Public' Hypothesis*, Unpublished PhD Dissertation, University of Dublin, Trinity College.
Devine, K. (2008) Stretching the IR theoretical spectrum on Irish neutrality: a critical social constructivist framework, *International Political Science Review*, 29(4), pp. 461–488.
European Green Party Committee (2007) *EGP Committee Position Paper on the Lisbon Treaty*, available at: www.europeangreens.org/cms/default/dokbin/211/211081.egp_committee_position_on_the_ lisbon_tre@en.pdf (accessed July 2008).
Everts, P. (2000) Public opinion after the Cold War: a paradigm shift, in: B. L. Nacos, R. Y. Shapiro & P. Isernia (Eds) *Decisionmaking in a Glass House: Mass Media, Public Opinion and American and European Foreign Policy in the 21st Century*, pp. 177–194 (New York: Rowman and Littlefield).
Fanning, R. (1996) Neutrality, identity and security: the example of Ireland, in: W. Bauwens, A. Clesse & O. Knudsen (Eds) *Small States and the Security Challenge in the New Europe*, pp. 137–149 (London and Washington, DC: Brassey's).
Fine Gael (2000) *Beyond Neutrality*, available at: www.finegael.com/policydocs/beyondneutrality.htm (accessed July 2000).
Fine Gael (2007) *General Election Manifesto*, available at: www.finegael.ie/uploads/docs/ FG_Manifesto_07.pdf (accessed August 2008).
FitzGerald, G. (1988) Irish neutrality, *European Affairs*, 28, pp. 23–29.
FitzGerald, G. (1995) Military neutrality immoral, despite virtuous Irish claims, *Irish Times*, 14–15 April.
FitzGerald, G. (1996) Neutrality concept retains potency yet is ambiguous, *Irish Times*, 19 October.
Franklin, M., Marsh, M. & McLaren, L. (1994) Uncorking the bottle: popular opposition to European unification in the wake of Maastricht, *Journal of Common Market Studies*, 32(4), pp. 455–472.
Gilland, K. (2001) Ireland and the international use of force, in: P. Everts & P. Isernia (Eds) *Public Opinion and the International Use of Force*, pp. 141–162 (London: Routledge).
Government of Ireland (1996) *White Paper on Foreign Policy* (Dublin: Stationery Office).
Green Party (1997) *General Election Manifesto*, available at: http://www.michaelpidgeon.com/manifestos/party/gp/Green%20Party%20GE%201977.pdf
Green Party (2007a) *General Election Manifesto*, available at: www.greenparty.ie/en/about/ party_archives/election_2007/manifesto_2007/manifesto (accessed July 2008).
Green Party (2007b) *The European Reform Treaty Information Pack*, available at: www.greenparty.ie/ en/policies/eu_reform_treaty (accessed July 2008).

Hakovirta, H. (1988) *East–West Conflict and European Neutrality* (Oxford: Clarendon Press).
Hederman, M. (1983) *The Road To Europe: Irish Attitudes 1948–61* (Dublin: Institute of Public Administration).
Hooghe, L. (2003) Europe divided? Elites vs. public opinion on European integration, *Political Science Series* 88 (Reihe Politikwissenschaft: Institute for Advanced Studies, Vienna), available at: http://aei.pitt.edu/531/02/pw_88.pdf (accessed February 2009).
Hummer, W. (2006) The new EU – a 'military pact'? Solidarity–neutrality–Irish clause, in: G. Hauser & F. Kernic (Eds) *European Security in Transition*, pp. 63–72 (Aldershot: Ashgate).
Jones, J. (1987) 39 percent undecided about their voting intentions on the SEA, *Irish Times*, 20 May.
Jupp, R. (2002) Key to Treaty result, *The Star*, 16 October.
Karsh, E. (1988) *Neutrality and Small States* (London: Routledge).
Keatinge, P. (1973) *The Formulation of Irish Foreign Policy* (Dublin: Institute of Public Administration).
Keatinge, P. (1984) *A Singular Stance: Irish Neutrality in the 1980s* (Dublin: Institute of Public Administration).
Keatinge, P. (1996) *European Security: Ireland's Choices* (Dublin: Institute of European Affairs).
Kennedy, F. & Sinnott, R. (2007) Irish public opinion toward European integration, *Irish Political Studies*, 22(1), pp. 61–80.
Keogh, D. (1997) The diplomacy of 'dignified calm': an analysis of Ireland's application for membership of the EEC, 1961–1963, *Chronicon*, 1(4), pp. 1–68, available at: http://www.ucc.ie/chronicon/keogh.htm (accessed February 2008).
Ladrech, R. (2002) Europeanization and political parties: towards a framework for analysis, *Party Politics*, 8(4), pp. 389–403.
Laffan, B & Langan, A. (2005) Securing a 'yes': from Nice I to Nice II, *Notre Europe*, Policy Paper No. 13.
Maillot, A. (2009) Sinn Féin's approach to the EU: still more 'critical' than 'engaged'?, *Irish Political Studies*, 24(4), pp. 559–574.
Mair, P. (2000) The limited impact of Europe on national party systems, *West European Politics*, 23(4), pp. 27–51.
Marsh, M. (1992) *Irish Public Opinion on Neutrality and the European Union* (Dublin: Institute of European Affairs).
McSweeney, B. (1988) The European neutrals and the European Community, *Journal of Peace Research*, 25(3), pp. 205–211.
Moxon-Browne, E. (1999) The Europeanisation of political parties: the case of the Irish Labour Party, paper presented at the 6th International Conference of the European Community Studies Association, Pittsburgh, PA, USA, available at: http://aei.pitt.edu/2341/01/002324_1.pdf (accessed September 2008).
Müller-Rommel, F. (2002) The lifespan and the political performance of Green Parties in Western Europe, *Environmental Politics*, 11(1), pp. 1–16.
O'Dea, W. (2008) O'Dea confirms Lisbon Treaty will not change Ireland's neutrality policy, Fianna Fáil press release, Dublin, 29 April 2008.
O'Mahony, J. (2009) Ireland's EU referendum experience, *Irish Political Studies*, 24(4), pp. 429–446.
Page, B. & Shapiro, R. (1992) *The Rational Public* (Chicago: Chicago University Press).
Putnam, R. (1988) Diplomacy and domestic politics: the logic of two-level games, *International Organization*, 42(3), pp. 427–460.
Quinlan, S. (2009) The Lisbon Treaty referendum 2008, *Irish Political Studies*, 24(1), pp. 107–121.
Roche, D. (2002) *Comments on Report of Convention Defence WG ('Barnier Report')* Department of Foreign Affairs Press Release, Dublin, 19 December 2002, available at: www.dfa.ie/home/index/aspx?id=26152 (accessed October 2007).
Salmon, T.C. (1989) *Unneutral Ireland* (Oxford: Clarendon).
Sinn Féin (2004) *Positive Neutrality in Action: Towards the Achievement of Human Security*, 28 May, available at: www.sinnfein.ie/news/detail/4934 (accessed July 2008).

Sinn Féin (2007) *General Election Manifesto,* available at: www.sinnfein.ie/elections/manifesto/49 (accessed July 2008).

Sinnott, R. (1998a) *Post-Amsterdam Referendum Survey* (Dublin: Lansdowne Market Research & The Referendum Commission).

Sinnott, R. (1998b) EU treaty still widely viewed as irrelevant, *Irish Times,* 16 May.

Sinnott, R. (2001) *Attitudes and Behaviour of the Irish Electorate in the Referendum on the Treaty of Nice* (Dublin: European Commission Representation in Ireland).

Tonra, B. (1996) The internal dissenter (II): Ireland, in: S. Stavridis & C. Hill (Eds) *Domestic Sources of Foreign Policy: Western European Reactions to the Falklands Conflict,* pp. 132–150 (Oxford: Berg).

Treaty of Lisbon (2007) *Official Journal of the European Union C306,* 50, 17 December.

Fianna Fáil: Tenacious Localism, Tenuous Europeanism

KATY HAYWARD* & JONATHAN FALLON**
*Queen's University Belfast, Northern Ireland, UK; **EPS Consulting, Ireland

ABSTRACT *Fianna Fáil is a party used to government, authority and influence in the domestic sphere. This has been to a large part secured by the vitality and strength of its local organization. The party has, in contrast, struggled to find its place in the sphere of European politics. Its main successes in the EU arena have arisen from its experience as Ireland's governing party. This is reflected in the fact that the pro-Europeanism that exists within the party is pivoted on the belief that its leadership will defend national interests and negotiate good deals for Ireland in Brussels. These two 'fundamentals' in party support – localism and power – were thrown into doubt by the results of the 2008 Lisbon referendum and the 2009 European and local elections. This article draws on original, qualitative interviews with Fianna Fáil MEPs and party members across Ireland conducted in the wake of these election results. Using Ladrech's (2002) model as an outline, it reveals the ways in which the party's localism has delimited the effects of Europeanization. Furthermore, it argues that the crisis faced by the Fianna Fáil government in late 2009 represented the culmination of local/ central and national/European tensions within the party and beyond its control.*

Introduction

Fianna Fáil is one of the pre-eminent electoral and governmental machines in any European democracy (Carty, 2008). Yet, whilst it appeared able to weather most storms in Irish political life (see Girvin & Murphy, 2008), the party has been rather less steadfast in the context of European Union politics and debate. Indeed, be it chance or inevitability, the tenuous nature of Fianna Fáil's Europeanism was a critical factor in an event that marked the beginning of the spiral of decline in the party's fortunes just a year after winning a third consecutive general election in 2007. The result of the Lisbon referendum of June 2008 (see Quinlan, 2009) was inexorably connected to the failure of the party's pro-European campaign to convince many of its own supporters. Despite having 'led the way' for Ireland in Europe since negotiations for European Economic Community (EEC) accession 40 years earlier, Fianna Fáil's fragile and circumscribed 'European' programme, organization, and networks (identified as crucial by Ladrech, 2002) were exposed by the 2008 referendum . This article examines the root causes and manifestations of this restricted Europeanization. In particular, it identifies the tenacious localism of the party – which has been credited with turning localism 'into a craft' (Walsh, 1986) – as of critical importance in limiting the effects of Europeanization within the party. It is no coincidence that the major crises faced by the party in late 2009 occurred simultaneously in its internal local/central and its external national/European relationships of trust.

Programmatic Pragmatism: Fianna Fáil's Redline on European 'Interference'

The party programmes of Fianna Fáil defy categorization in typical ideological or left/right terms. Pragmatism is considered a guiding principle and selling point in the party: people can trust it to take the decisions necessary for national interest on any subject at any time (as seen in Devine's (2009) analysis of the party's approach to 'Partnership for Peace'). This is reflected in the limited Europeanization of its party programmes. Fianna Fáil's presentation of the EU traditionally emphasized the benefits for the Irish economy – an argument that fitted well with its programmatic pragmatism. Fianna Fáil has tended to perform better in general elections where campaigns have focused on economic (rather than social or moral) issues, as was the case in 1987 and 1997. Economic growth came to be both Fianna Fáil's core achievement *and* its core electoral promise:

> In 1997 we promised the people a new era of prosperity ... Under Fianna Fáil Ireland has been the world's most dynamic economy ... Our programme for the next five years is based on maintaining Ireland as a strong, dynamic economy and ensuring that we build lasting prosperity for all. (Fianna Fáil, 2002: 4)

The party programme thus came to depend on the claim that its experienced personnel are best positioned to handle the economy. This has had direct implications for Fianna Fáil's presentation of – and conditional support for – European integration. If EEC membership had been an economic necessity, participation in European Economic and Monetary Union (EMU) was sold as an economic *opportunity* for the country. 'Europe' has been conceived in Fianna Fáil's party programmes largely in terms of what it can offer Ireland, rather than in the ideological/idealizing way pro-integrationists might see it (cf. Reidy, 2009). It is possible to detect this even in the avowedly pro-European arguments put forward by Fianna Fáil, in which the EU takes something of a backseat, as 'facilitator' or 'market', for Ireland's innovative economic success. See, for example, the extract from a speech by Dick Roche (2008) as Minister of State for European Affairs prior to the first Lisbon referendum:

> Our membership of the EU has been a key attraction for US multinational companies locating in Ireland. For years, Ireland has promoted itself as providing a gateway to Europe and to its 480 million citizens. The best way to keep

Ireland as a fore [sic] for FDI [Foreign Direct Investment] from the US or elsewhere is to keep the positive image of Ireland as the gateway to the EU.

It is no coincidence that the rare but notorious public clashes between Fianna Fáil ministers and their counterparts in the Council, the Commission and the European Central Bank have centred on the management of the Irish economy. The potential for tension was illustrated most infamously in early 2001 when Fianna Fáil's Minister for Finance, Charlie McCreevy, received a reprimand from the EU for implementing an over-inflationary budget. Not only was McCreevy unrepentant, he was publicly supported by cabinet colleagues and the Taoiseach, who agreed that the Commission's warnings 'did not make a whole lot of sense'.[1] Fianna Fáil was annoyed at what it saw as EU interference in its economic policies, and this tension no doubt had a trickle-down effect on public opinion and, thereby, on the first referendum on the Nice Treaty held some three months later. McCreevy was one of the first to welcome the No result as 'a remarkably healthy development', Willie O'Dea applauded the 'healthy euroscepticism' within Fianna Fáil that it represented, Éamon Ó Cuív admitted he had voted No himself based on his own experience of 'scary moments' in Brussels, and Síle de Valera interpreted the vote as a clear message that 'people are against further integration' in the EU (Hayward, 2002; *Irish Examiner*, 18 June 2001). Such comments from sitting ministers undermined the government's credibility and indicated a growing schism within the party on the subject of European integration. The row (hastily glossed over in time for the second Nice Treaty referendum) revealed two crucial points. First, tension between local/national (specifically rural/urban) interests was becoming an increasingly 'public' problem within Fianna Fáil. Secondly, the party as a whole would not countenance overt EU 'interference' in national decision-making, particularly not in the economic arena.

Following global financial turmoil in 2008, Fianna Fáil had to rapidly retrace its steps – at least as far as reasserting the importance of the EU as an economic environment for Ireland. The necessity of this 'about-turn' was made all the more urgent by the prospect of the second Lisbon referendum, as these extracts from speeches around the time of the referendum announcement by the Minister for Foreign Affairs and Taoiseach demonstrate:

> We have derived particular benefit from the creation of the European single market and from participation in the euro, which has been especially important in the recent global economic crisis. (Martin, 2009)

> The European Union is central to our future. It is the platform for much of our prosperity. And it is essential for very many of our jobs. (Cowen, 2009a)

Nevertheless, the ability to wield power and make decisions over the Irish economy remains the most important tenet of Fianna Fáil's self-image and electoral credibility. It is possible to surmise that Fianna Fáil would be the party that would suffer the worst electoral consequences should the Irish government lose the ability to set tax rates, instigate broad economic policies or plot its own path for measures to support the Irish economy. Little wonder, then, at Fianna Fáil's opposition to the creation of an EU with strong fiscal policies and tax-raising powers. Indeed, even with regard to day-to-day EU policy-making, the party has promoted the impression that compliance is secondary to its protection of the competitive health of the Irish economy.[2] Fianna Fáil's economic 'redline' on EU competency – and the effects it has had on the cohesion of the party's EU message – indicates the limited scope for positive Europeanization in the party programme.

Maintaining National Organizational Structures: Evidence from MEP Experience

While much has changed in the sphere of Irish domestic politics in recent years, Fianna Fáil still relies heavily on an only-slightly modified version of its original organization structures (see Mockler, 1994). The Fianna Fáil party organization comprises 3000 cumainn (the basic unit of the party stretching into every locality of the country) and approximately 65,000 members.[3] The 'organigram' in Figure 1 illustrates that Fianna Fáil members act within an organization that is primarily designed to deal with national politics and local issues.

The 'European' dimension effectively constitutes an add-on to this architecture, feeding into several strands of the party and not sitting neatly at any particular level. The four regional constituencies that form the basis of European elections (Dublin, Leinster, Munster and Connaught-Ulster) only gain significant meaning for the organization of Fianna Fáil when party members gather at regionally-organized conventions to select Member of European Parliament (MEP) candidates. Even at that stage, the selection of candidates can be closely tied to the size and significance of the individuals' home county within the region or to their national profile beyond it. The 'regional' level is a fairly notional concept even for MEPs; activity in the party is not generally organized on the basis of those four 'European' constituency regions and there is little opportunity for MEPs to speak as political actors at this regional level. This situation was summarized by one Fianna Fáil MEP in an interview with an author of this paper:

> While I would receive a huge amount of representations from the public, most still come from my own county and the further you go from there, the less likely a person seems to be to contact me. Organized campaigns and lobbying is [sic] different of course. But, for the individual, there does seem to be a perception that they [sic] are not sure what help I can be, and indeed *a lot of representations relate to purely national issues.*[4]

The quandary of the position of MEPs in Fianna Fáil, and the fact that their role as currently practiced could not adequately address any 'democratic deficit', is thus neatly illustrated: their constituency appeal barely reaches beyond the borders of their local county council and the tasks citizens approach them with are often

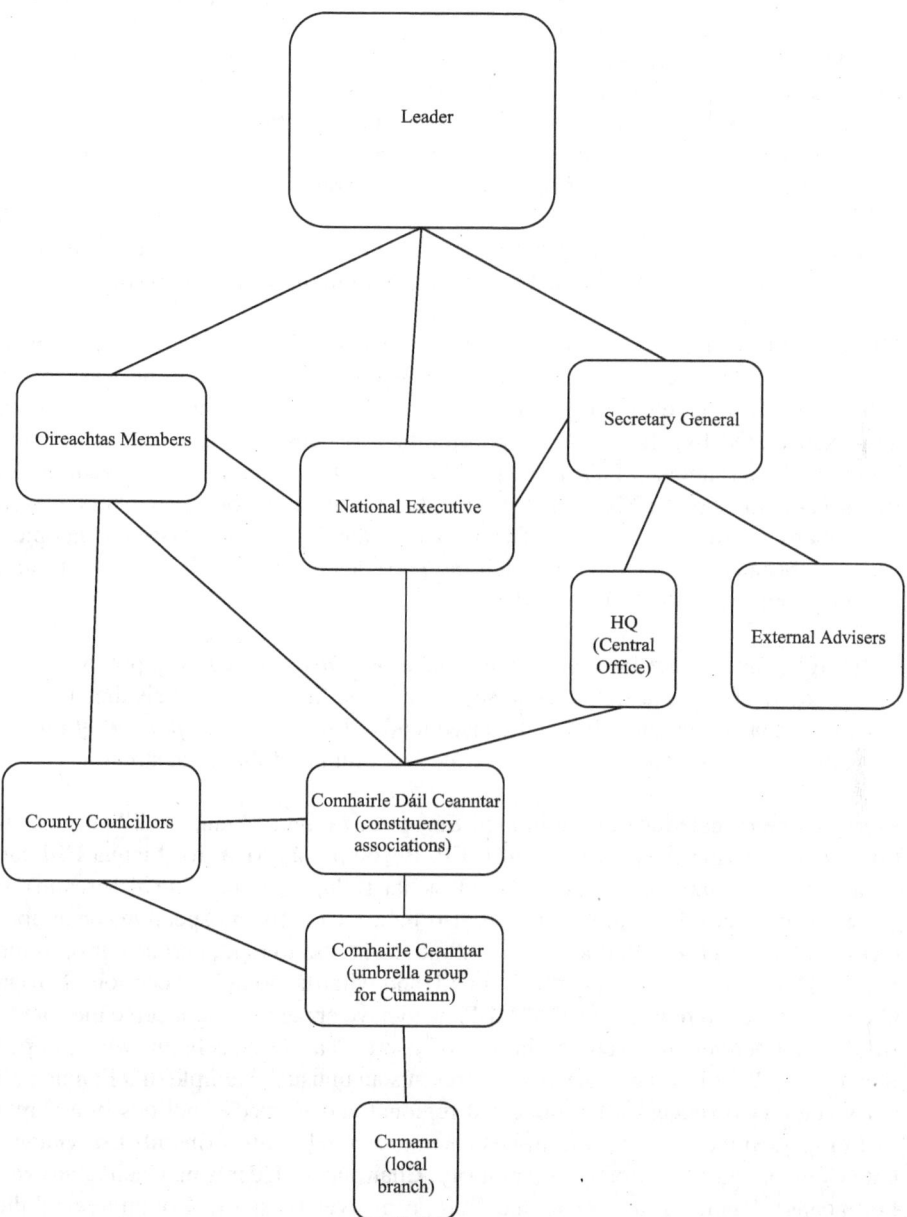

Figure 1. Organization of Fianna Fáil (organigram by Jonathan Fallon).

outside their remit and power. The mismatch between the principle and practice of representative democracy for MEPs is further aggravated by the fact that the work they do actually perform at the European level gains them little credit or authority within their party, let alone their regional constituency.

Indeed, MEPs in Fianna Fáil can feel 'somewhere out there with the Senators' in terms of their influence within the party and bemoan the lack of opportunity for them to shape policy at the all-important national level:

> It would be fair to say that as MEPs we don't have a huge amount of input in national policy. There is no real mechanism within the party [to do so].

The fact that Fianna Fáil MEPs have a certain degree of autonomy in the European Parliament is not necessarily a sign of their prestige within the party but perhaps an indication of low levels of party interest in EU affairs. This exacerbates, and is in turn exacerbated by, the limited 'opportunities to publicize our work within the [European] Parliament'. This is in part because of the nature of proceedings in Brussels or Strasbourg; MEPs' achievements arise mainly from their 'work within committees or groups' – the type of work which 'tend[s] to be dismissed by people'. It is also because of the way in which the party leadership publicizes activity and accomplishments in the European Parliament:

> [party] members are far more likely to hear a *Minister* discussing policy and legislative changes at EU level at, say, something like the Ard Fheis than they are to hear it from an MEP ... [Consequently] I think *a large portion of our work is misunderstood or not appreciated* by ordinary folk in the street.

More can be revealed about the limited Europeanization of Fianna Fáil's organization by considering the party-typical MEP. Becoming an MEP for Fianna Fáil can be a way for former or existing TDs (Teachta Dála, member of Dáil Éireann) to close-out their political career.[5] It can also be a means for prospective (or temporarily unseated) TDs to find a stepping stone for access to (and, perhaps, promotion within) Dáil Éireann.[6] Bearing this in mind, and with the notable exception of Brian Crowley, there are few Fianna Fáil MEPs who have appeared to conceive the role of MEP as an active career choice in and of itself. Seán Ó Neachtain, who stepped down at the 2009 European election, represents an unusual example of a Fianna Fáil party actor who successfully connected regional and European politics in a career that by-passed the national forum. His role in regional politics (member of Galway City Council and West Regional Authority, Chairman of Údarás na Gaeltachta) was his means of gaining access to the European level (first the Committee of the Regions, later the European Parliament). His role as MEP only became possible because Ó Neachtain substituted for Pat 'the Cope' Gallagher after the latter left the European Parliament to take up the seat (and ministerial position) he had regained in the Dáil in 2002. Yet, in the European election two years later, Ó Neachtain, given his lack of a political profile or ambition at the national level, was still not the party central office's preferred candidate. He only won the nomination due to the popular support of Fianna Fáil members at the regional convention in a contest 'billed as a battle between Fianna Fáil "grassroots" and the "might" of the party's national executive' (*Irish Times*, 1 March 2004). Such tension between the local and the central actors within Fianna Fáil has had consequences for the limited Europeanization of the structures and power-play in the party's organization.

Party Competition: The Liability of Localism

European Elections

The majority of elections to the European Parliament have been held on the same day as other elections in Ireland. On the five occasions (out of a possible seven) that this has occurred (the local elections of 1979, 1999, 2004 and 2009, and the general election of 1989), Fianna Fáil has performed less well in terms of seat return in comparison with the stand-alone European elections of 1984 and 1994 (see Figure 2). The party typically loses about 12 percent of its first-preference electoral support in elections for the European Parliament compared to votes in a general election (Laffan & O'Mahony, 2008: 100). The slight gains in seat numbers made by Fianna Fáil in 1984 (from the position of opposition) and 1994 (against a difficult background in government) were at the expense of fringe or independent candidates.

The weaker performance of Fianna Fáil when European elections are held on the same day as local/general elections reveals a downside of the party's localism. The party's grassroots become far more exercised by local or national elections

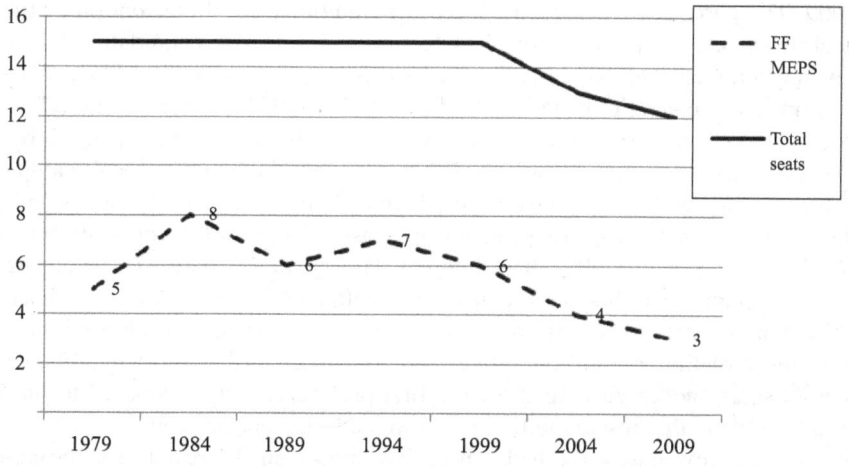

Figure 2. Number of Fianna Fáil MEPs.
Source: European Parliament Office in Ireland.

and candidates than European ones. In 1999, for example, a weary director of elections in one county reported that it was almost impossible to get canvassers out to meet the European Parliament candidates when they visited because potential councillors simply saw 'no votes in it'. He also reported that a few days before polling he distributed a number of posters on behalf of the European candidates, only to discover on polling day that at least one local election candidate had cut up the posters, and used them as backing board for his own election posters (Fianna Fáil, 1999). Posters have also been the medium of party-government/ local-European tensions in referendums in Ireland. The unofficial strategy to 'make Lisbon local' in 2008, for example, was most evident in the use of Lisbon referendum posters to promote potential candidates for the local elections the following year. This plan backfired in both the referendum (in part because so few of these party actors were willing to actively canvass for a Yes vote) and the elections (in small part because voters were turned off by the cynical personality-based publicity of the campaigns). Another illustration of the primacy of the 'local' is the way in which debates between candidates for the European Parliament become embroiled in highly localized issues, with even the birthplaces of candidates becoming legitimate targets for party 'point-scoring'. Thus, while holding local and European elections on the same day might encourage more party supporters to turn out to vote in the first place, it does not necessarily bring 'Europe' closer to home in party political debate. Neither does it offset the potential influence that more diligent canvassing on 'European' matters could have on floating voters.

Tension between the centralizing power of party headquarters and local politics in Fianna Fáil has been growing since the 1970s (Marsh, 2005: 174). This reached a new height of intervention and discord in the local elections of June 2009. The party central office replaced the traditional local convention as the key decision-maker (and venue) for the selection of local party candidates. The policy severely harmed the morale and image of the party at what was already a difficult time. For example, negative headlines such as 'FF election "disarray" as two go it alone' (*Meath Chronicle*, 19 March 2009) and 'I was shafted by FF' (*Nenagh Guardian*, 28 February 2009) plagued the party's local campaigns. Moreover, a number of non-selected Fianna Fáil councillors stood as independents and regained their seats at the expense of the party's official candidates (*Irish Times*, 9 June 2009). The internal damage to the party was worsened by the perception that this intervention by central office represented a disenfranchisement of the power of local party members. To add insult to injury, the judgement of the central committee may have been badly mistaken; Fianna Fáil lost 84 seats and seven percent of the first preference vote compared to the 2004 results. Given the inseparability of local and 'European' campaigns (as noted above), this row may have had a negative impact on the results for the party in the European elections on the same day (see Figure 3). Fianna Fáil's share of the first preference vote for MEPs in June 2009 was 24 percent, a decline of over five per cent from 2004.

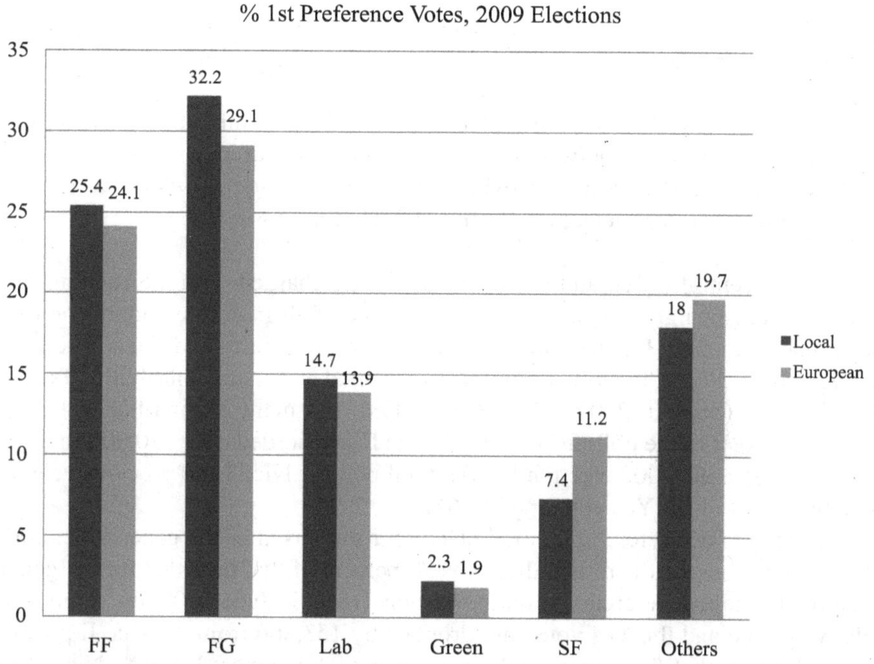

Figure 3. Percentage of first preference votes won by parties in local and European elections, June 2009.
Source: RTÉ (www.rte.ie/news/elections).

One party member interviewed for this article described the situation after the 2009 election results thus:

> Party morale has taken a big hit ... There is a lot of disaffection within the party at the moment. Headquarters are very unpopular, more so than was the case in the past ... people may fade out if they don't see change. I think a lot of Fianna Fáil members themselves stayed away from the polls in protest at their own party; this will have to be addressed, and a lot will depend on how it is handled.

The scale of this challenge was further amplified two months after the 2009 elections, with the resignation of TDs from the party whip in protest at the effects of government policy on their local constituency. Against this background, the second referendum on Lisbon (in October 2009) became a test of the authority of the Fianna Fáil leadership not only over the country but over its own party. Given the record of previous European referendums in Ireland, the party faced a great challenge in merely getting its supporters out to vote.

European Referendums

At a rally for the Lisbon Treaty referendum in Cork, Taoiseach Brian Cowen (2008) restated the principle and the power of his party's pro-Europeanism:

> Fianna Fáil has always been and will always be committed to a vision of Ireland as a positive, outward-looking and modern European nation ... Our party and its supporters have provided the core of the support which has delivered ratification for each amendment to the Union's basic law.

Fianna Fáil central office and party leadership are charged with the running of its referendum campaigns. In government at the time of all Irish referendums on European treaties to date, Fianna Fáil has had great responsibility and mixed success in this regard. In Nice I, the low turnout was identified as a main contributing factor to the No result (Sinnott, 2001; O'Brennan, 2003), and many Fianna Fáil voters had failed to make it to the polling stations. Fianna Fáil recorded over 770,000 first preference votes in the 2002 election but the total poll for Nice I the previous year was only 997,826 (with a Yes vote of 453,461).

The second Nice referendum took place four months after the general election in 2002 and turnout for the referendum was 77 percent of that recorded for the general election. In the first referendum on the Lisbon Treaty in June 2008, the turnout was relatively high and the Yes vote only dropped by 153,866 from its Nice II position, thus indicating that there was no dramatic loss of Yes voters between Nice II and Lisbon I. But Millward Brown IMS (2008) research findings on Lisbon I suggest that traditional supporters of the three main parties constituted only approximately 60 percent of those who voted in Lisbon I. In the 2007 election, 858,593 people cast a first preference in favour of Fianna Fáil and yet the total Yes vote in Lisbon I was only 752,451. Even setting aside the matter of *how* their supporters vote (although Millward Brown IMS (2008) research suggested their voters were the most 'disciplined' in terms of following the party line), Fianna Fáil – as with the other main parties – clearly has some difficulty in persuading its supporters to vote at all in European referendums.

Party–Government Relations: Conditional Pro-Europeanism of the Grassroots

Trust in EU Extends Only as Far as Confidence in Fianna Fáil Government

Opinion poll evidence suggests that voters perceive Fianna Fáil to be pro-integrationist (Marsh *et al.*, 2008: 50). Among Fianna Fáil party supporters, support for European integration remains apparently strong in comparison to those of other parties. According to exit polls from the European and local elections in June 2009, those who cast their first preference vote for a Fianna Fáil candidate were most likely to say they intend to vote Yes (65 percent) and least likely to state an intention to vote No (18 percent) in the Lisbon II referendum (Lansdowne, 2009). But what are the foundations of pro-Europeanism within the party and how deep and stable are they? This section addresses these questions on the basis of qualitative interviews with a significant number (n = 83) of members of the Fianna Fáil party from across the country in the wake of the June 2009 elections. The main point to be drawn from analysis of these interviews is that party members' positive view of EU membership has been dependent on the role of the party in shaping and mediating this relationship.

> The EU is hugely important to Ireland. Fianna Fáil led Ireland into the EU and has always been at the forefront of our involvement.[7]

According to members of the party interviewed for this article, the experience of EU membership for Ireland as a whole has been mediated through the leadership provided by Fianna Fáil governments. In members' opinion, the benefits of European integration for Ireland have been won by Fianna Fáil leaders' aptitude and the risks of European integration have been averted by their tenacity:

> Europe has brought us many benefits, but you have to be fair: countries like France and Germany didn't do it out of the goodness of their hearts. Several Fianna Fáil leaders had to battle hard to win those concessions. From getting cohesion policy adopted to negotiating the deals under Haughey, Reynolds and Ahern, *it has always fallen to Fianna Fáil to ensure a fair deal for Ireland.*

Analysis of party members' discourse on EU membership reveals that their pro-Europeanism is conditional.

> I think Europe has been good – you have to have a certain amount of trust in these things – but *I wouldn't say it has been all good.* I don't think they understand Ireland and more than once a Taoiseach or Ministers have had to set them straight.

General acknowledgement of the benefits of EU membership is permeated by a clear strain of cynicism about the motivation and trustworthiness of fellow member-states. The rhetoric of partnership and relationship that features in party elite discourse on Ireland (cf. Hayward, 2009) is, therefore, not loudly echoed at the grassroots. Indeed, our interview data would imply that party members' wariness of the project of European integration only slightly trails their general support for it:

> *If they were allowed, too many of the bigger countries would run rough shod over the likes of Ireland.* They have become a bit fond of dictating what's right and wrong, about what the government does here. And they haven't been that great at minding their own ship ... I think *they spent too much time trying to dictate to national governments and not enough managing Europe itself.*

Another party member went so far as to express scepticism about the actual importance of European integration when the record of the party on meeting national needs is compared to that of the EU:

> *I don't know if Europe matters that much at all.* From recessions to booms they don't seem to have any impact in saving us or helping us; there's always a reason they can't do something. I mean, they are good in terms of funding we received and all that; but in terms of policy, when you really need it, *I don't think we can rely on them.* If we come out of this recession, no more than the last one, it will be down to our own government and hard work.

The effects of such conditional pro-Europeanism were most evident in the first referendum on the Lisbon Treaty.

Voting Motivations in Lisbon I

From our interviews of party members, we gather that the guiding logic for voting Yes in Lisbon I was national, i.e. trust in Fianna Fáil, and the guiding logic for voting No was 'European', i.e. distrust of the EU. The comments below from one 'Yes' voting party member reveal the remarkable power that Fianna Fáil has over some members in terms of giving a symbolic lead rather than substantial reason in support of an EU Treaty.

> I voted Yes in Lisbon [I] and of course I'll do the same again. People talk a lot of nonsense on these things. I don't read treaties or anything like it, how would I know what they are talking about? But I also don't ask the Doctor if I can read my file when I go to the hospital, I have to presume he knows what he's doing … When people are paid to do a job, you trust them. And if I didn't trust the politicians in Fianna Fáil, then I wouldn't be voting for them in the first place would I?

Dedication to Fianna Fáil is quite distinct in the minds of some party members from their personal attitude towards the EU. This is seen in the justification given by some for planning to vote Yes in Lisbon II in support of the party. In the case of one member, this was despite not bothering to vote in Lisbon I because it did not seem important or relevant to local experience:

> I will vote Yes in Lisbon II. I didn't vote the last time. To be honest, I was just too busy and, unlike the local elections, *I don't think we will see or hear too much from Lisbon around these parts once it's done.* I don't think we should be having referenda on these issues at all.

It is also the case for a member who voted No in Lisbon I as a form of protest to the EU:

> I will vote Yes next time, I voted No the last time [Lisbon I]. *I voted No because I was annoyed at Europe.* I think Bertie Ahern negotiated a very good treaty in Dublin and when the French voted No they went back and changed things in

Lisbon. I don't like that; I don't think they would do it for us. I think they should have stuck with Bertie's constitution and, anyway, it's about time we had a treaty from Ireland instead of all these foreign places!

Given this attitude of some in the party, it is possible to predict that (precluding a major error of judgement by either the party leadership or the EU), the more vehement the criticisms of the government and the more vulnerable its position in the run-up to Lisbon II, the more keen Fianna Fáil members will be to support a Yes campaign. Just as the EU has been presented by Fianna Fáil leaders as necessary for the well-being of the Irish nation-state (see Hayward, 2009), so they may rely upon a Yes vote for the European treaty being seen by their supporters as vital for the health of the party.

Relations Beyond the National Party System: Extracting a Deal for Ireland

High Profile Negotiators

One consequence of the electoral dominance of Fianna Fáil since accession to the EEC has been that the party frontbench can claim much greater experience of working at a supra-national and intergovernmental level than most of its political opponents. The EU provided Fianna Fáil leaders with a rare opportunity (as representatives of a relatively small state) to play the role of international statesmen. This has reinforced Fianna Fáil's self-image as the strongest and most experienced party in the state, claiming an 'unmatched tradition' in foreign affairs (Fianna Fáil, 2007: 8). Certainly the skills demonstrated by Ireland's Taoisigh, ministers, and Commissioners (the majority of whom were Fianna Fáil politicians) in European-level negotiations gained the respect of their EU colleagues and were instrumental in ensuring that Ireland gained from such monumental processes as Economic and Monetary Union (Brennan, 2008; Laffan and O'Mahony, 2008: 76). Fianna Fáil has consciously tried to turn the good reputation it has built 'behind closed doors' in Brussels into a public dividend back in Ireland. This has been intrinsic to the pro-Europeanism of its own party members, as one boasted in an interview for this article:

> Experience counts in negotiations. *Fianna Fáil Ministers* have always had that and, therefore, have been capable of extracting a deal at European level; they *understand how these things work.*

Furthermore, party members also view the skills of Fianna Fáil leaders at the EU level as having made Ireland's experience of the EU a positive one and, therefore, as an electoral asset: 'The single greatest achievement in Europe was that of Albert Reynolds in bringing home the bacon when the country needed it.' The apparent confidence of Fianna Fáil government leaders when negotiating in Brussels contrasts somewhat with the awkwardness of the party in the sphere of the European Parliament.

Shifting Allegiances in Europe

> Everybody wants Fianna Fáil. We're a big party, we've been in government a long time, and we're seen as good operators at European level. So everybody wants us, but not everybody can have us. I think that we as a party can bring great things to any group that we're in. (Crowley, 2009)

Despite Brian Crowley's grandiose statement, Fianna Fáil has proven to be a difficult party to match-make in the European party political sphere. McElroy and Benoit's (2007) analysis of the European Parliament political groupings indirectly explains some of the causes of Fianna Fáil's discomfort therein. They describe the structure of political groupings in the European Parliament as being based upon two dimensions: left/right and EU/national. Fianna Fáil does not fit neatly into any of these spheres. First, it does not want to be labelled as a party of either the left *or* right. Secondly, it is a pro-European party but yet it values the principle of national sovereignty (and its own national control) above all else. Fianna Fáil's membership of the Union for Europe of the Nations (UEN) grouping was grounded in the fact that it crosses the left/right divide and that it opposes federal union. However, Fianna Fáil's (2002: 19) vision of 'the European Union of Nation States' is articulated as a positive, pro-European argument by the party and not (as was the case for some UEN members) as a rallying-cry for Euroscepticism. This difference was the primary justification given by Taoiseach Brian Cowen (2009b, emphasis added) when he confirmed Fianna Fáil's plan to leave the UEN after the 2009 elections to move to the European Liberal, Democratic and Reform Party (ELDR), which is part of the Alliance of Liberals and Democrats for Europe (ALDE) grouping:

> This is a time when parties who support Europe from all parts of the Union must work more closely together. They must make sure that the Parliament works well and stands *against the radical Eurosceptic agenda*. Given the changing role of the Parliament and the new structures of its groups, Fianna Fáil has no alternative but to reconsider current arrangements. We need to strengthen our work with others who share our basic approach while *insisting on the right to vote in accordance with the views of the people we represent*.

This plan, however, generated reported criticism from none other than Fianna Fáil's most electorally popular MEP who suggested it would have negative effects on the party's ability to 'deliver policy at a European level' (Crowley, 2009). As noted above, the unapologetically 'European' focus of Crowley's political and career objectives sets him apart from his party colleagues. His rise to the position of leader of the UEN grouping in the European Parliament was, as he notes, an achievement and advantage for the party itself (Crowley, 2009). Consequently, the legacy of the debate as to where Fianna Fáil belongs in Europe may linger *within* the party itself. Crowley was replaced as head of the party delegation to the European Parliament in June 2009 by the re-elected Pat 'the Cope' Gallagher.[8]

Although Fianna Fáil would struggle to define itself as a liberal party, its move into the ELDR party and, thereby, the ALDE grouping is one of the most significant examples of Fianna Fáil's recognition of the potential benefits of having the right connections in the European Parliament. The move was sought by the party leadership in the belief that it would enable the party to become more engaged and proactive in the EU. Plus, of course, it hopes to avoid being constrained any longer by the sheer embarrassment felt by association with some UEN colleagues (not least those who stood for the Libertas party in the 2009 European elections). The party sees opportunities to develop within the ALDE the type of cooperative relationships with other parties that it has enviously watched Fine Gael make much of in the European People's Party. The biggest adjustment will be faced, of course, by Fianna Fáil's MEPs. One interviewed on this subject for this paper hinted at the risks of gaining collective strength at the expense of individual (or party) influence:

> Joining the ALDE grouping will bring benefits for Fianna Fáil in terms of our network and influence undoubtedly. Size of groupings does matter in Europe, but you don't want to be subsumed into a massive grouping, where your own views disappear or it is impossible to have an effect on group policy.

The challenge faced by Fianna Fáil MEPs will be made all the greater by the increased level of interest that the national executive will take in the building of relationships in the European Parliament, at least in the short-term. In the longer term, this move may allow Fianna Fáil to feel less isolated in the European Parliament and therefore more willing to engage in debate on matters concerning the future EU, which can only be positive for Ireland in general. Nevertheless, the fundamental outlook of Fianna Fáil towards the EU remains unaltered and non-negotiable, as one MEP confirmed in an interview:

> *We have not been keen to simply follow the lead of others in Europe.* Obviously we support Europe and it has been good for Ireland, but in terms of the long term future *there are many divergent views on what Europe should become*, we certainly do not envisage a centralized federal state or the giving up of our independence.

Conclusion: The Prospects for Fianna Fáil's 'Euro-Positivism'

> Fianna Fáil is deeply committed to the European Union and the great ideals which it represents ... At a time of unprecedented crisis both here and internationally, we believe that Ireland should remain true to its Euro-positive tradition. (Cowen, in Fianna Fáil, 2009: 4)

The welfare of the Irish nation-state and the fortunes of Fianna Fáil are inseparable in the party's conception of Ireland's EU membership. The second referendum on the Lisbon Treaty was viewed by Fianna Fáil members as a test: a test of their leader Brian Cowen, a test of the party's own internal machine, a test of their voter discipline and loyalty, and most of all a simple test of electoral strength. A very different Fianna Fáil campaigning machine was consequently activated for the second Lisbon referendum. This was not, however, a consequence of the Europeanization of the party but rather a vital survival instinct. Somewhat ironically, although local/central tensions in the party increased under Brian Cowen's leadership (despite his remarkable marshalling of grassroots support in past elections (Fallon, 2009)), the urgent issue of power slipping away from the party became the primary rationale for members to canvass and vote in the second Lisbon referendum – something that few were prepared to do in Lisbon I. 'Europe' became an immediate, motivating concern largely because the future of the party was at stake; background opinion on European integration remained secondary. This is evident in the reasoning expressed by one party member (interviewed in July 2009) on pressure on Fianna Fáil for a successful Yes campaign in Lisbon II:

> I think the next Lisbon referendum must be won for Ireland's sake. It's also an important vote for Fianna Fáil. It's time we all stopped the messing and realized that, whatever about mistakes, Fianna Fáil has done a lot more good for this country than any other party ... We need to fight this referendum as a party and ... show some of those that have been dancing about since last June [2008, Lisbon I] that this party is far from finished.

According to this view, voting Yes is in Ireland's interests, not necessarily because the Lisbon Treaty is worth implementing but mainly because a No vote would irreparably damage Fianna Fáil.

But, following Cowen's call (above) for Ireland to 'remain true to its Euro-positive tradition' (a phrase, in its novelty, slightly more circumspect than 'pro-European'), what are the long-term prospects for Fianna Fáil's 'Euro-positivism'? We have shown that the foundations of support for European integration within the body of Fianna Fáil appear to descend no deeper than the well of members' faith in the party leadership. This has two serious implications, neither of which bode well for the future of the party's relationship with the EU. First, as internal party debates after Nice I and Lisbon I revealed, if party leaders become more critical of the European Union, party members may quickly follow suit. The rationale behind this was summed up by one party member interviewed:

> Well, to be honest, *I'll keep supporting Europe as long as it's what the party leadership thinks is right.* If I didn't trust them, I wouldn't be in the party. But I'd have reservations [on the EU]. *And if the party ever decided to go against Europe, I wouldn't have a problem with supporting them on it.*

The results of the 2009 local and European elections indicate that support for Fianna Fáil is shrinking towards reliance on a rural support base; such a development would have significant consequences for the party's approach to the EU. The small farmer – who feels both dependence on and distrust towards the EU – would be a tricky constituent for Fianna Fáil to please with regard to European policy. The renegotiations of the Common Agricultural Policy, the EU's nitrates directive, and the fiasco of the Rural Environmental Protection Scheme, for example, could become touchstone issues in *national* debates. This has been a challenge that Fianna Fáil has faced before, when in opposition and in closer reliance on the rural voter, and it resulted in more overt public criticism by the party of the European Commission, particularly on agricultural spending.[9] It is notable that already, in contrast to the presentation of other policy areas, the 2009 European election manifesto presents Fianna Fáil's role in defending Irish agricultural interests in the EU as a 'fight'.[10] This relates to the second core feature (and cause) of the tenuous Europeanism of Fianna Fáil, namely that it has become conditional on the party's perceived capacity to keep the EU's influence 'in check'. If this confidence suffers a critical blow, either by the unpopular actions of the party leadership or by the decay of its power, it may have a domino-effect on the precarious pro-Europeanism of the party's grassroots. In the predicament faced by Fianna Fáil, nearly forty years after Ireland's first referendum on European integration, the intrinsic connections between local, national and European politics are becoming unavoidably apparent at last.

Acknowledgements

The authors wish to thank the anonymous referees, and Mary C. Murphy and Eoin O'Malley for their helpful advice on previous drafts of this paper.

Notes

1. 'European Commission continues criticism of McCreevy's Budget', 2 February 2001, and 'EU Finance Ministers endorse budgetary reprimand', 12 Feburary 2001, available at: www.rte.ie/news/2001/0212/eu.html; 'Taoiseach backs McCreevy's stance on Budget', 2 February 2001, available at: www.rte.ie/news/2001/0202/eu.html (accessed August 2009).
2. For example: 'We will implement this initiative [on manufacture and use of chemicals] as a matter of priority *in a way which does not impact on the competitiveness of our economy*' (Fianna Fáil, 2007: 64, emphasis added).
3. Based on information in Fianna Fáil (2006) plus registered cumainn and membership lists provided to Jonathan Fallon by Fianna Fáil Party headquarters, May 2008.
4. All quotations in this paper expressing the opinion of MEPs are extracts from interviews with two sitting Fianna Fáil MEPs conducted (on the condition of anonymity) via telephone by Jonathan Fallon, 28 July and 31 July 2009. Emphases have been added.
5. For example, Gerry Collins (1994–2004), Gene FitzGerald (1984–1994), Jim Fitzsimons (1984–2004), Liam Hyland (1994–2004), Mark Killilea (1987–1999).
6. As was the case for, among others, Síle de Valera (1979–1984), Brian Lenihan (1973–1977), Tom Nolan (1973–1979) and, one who crossed back and forth between the roles of MEP and TD/Minister of State, Pat 'the Cope' Gallagher (1994–2002, 2009–).
7. All quotations in this article from party members are extracts from telephone and face-to-face interviews with 83 members of the Fianna Fáil party from across all 26 counties conducted (on the condition of anonymity) by Jonathan Fallon, 8 June–31 July 2009. Emphases have been added.

8. In a twist of fate, Gallagher's return to the European Parliament (following his loss of a ministerial position in Cowen's government and Ó Neachtain's resignation as MEP in 2009) necessitated a by-election in Donegal South West which posed the prospect of a minority government for Brian Cowen following resignations from the party whip in Summer 2009.
9. For examples, see *Dáil Debates* volumes 352 'EC Farm Spending' (18 October 1984), 358 'EC Agricultural Price Settlement' (21 May 1985), and 467 'Compensation for Beef Farmers' (25 June 1996).
10. 'We will, as we have always done, fight to ensure that the interests of Irish farmers, rural communities and the Irish food sector are fully protected' (Fianna Fáil, 2009: 20).

References

Brennan, P. (2008) *Behind Closed Doors: The EU Negotiations that Shaped Modern Ireland* (Dublin: Blackhall Publishing).
Carty, R.K. (2008) Fianna Fáil and Irish party competition, in: M. Gallagher & M. Marsh (Eds) *How Ireland Voted 2007: The Full Story of Ireland's General Election*, pp. 218–231 (Basingstoke: Palgrave).
Cowen, B. (2008) Speech by the Taoiseach at the Fianna Fáil Europe Rally, Cork, 21 April 2008, available at: http://ja-jp.facebook.com/note.php?note_id=11891216181 (accessed August 2009).
Cowen, B. (2009a) Statement by the Taoiseach at the EU Council, Brussels, 19 June 2009, available at: http://www.taoiseach.gov.ie/eng/Government_Press_Office/Taoiseach's_Speeches_2009/European_Council_18_19_June_2009_Statement_by_the_Taoiseach,_Brian_Cowen_T_D_.html (accessed October 2009).
Cowen, B. (2009b) Speech by the Taoiseach at the Official Opening of the 72nd Fianna Fáil Ard Fheis, Dublin, 22 February 2009, available at: http://www.fiannafail.ie/feature/entry/full-text-taoiseach-brian-cowen-at-the-official-opening-of-72nd-fianna-fail/ (accessed August 2009).
Crowley, B. (2009) UEN leader: 'nothing is decided yet' on Fianna Fáil's move to Liberals, *Euractiv* interview, 6 March 2009, available at: www.euractiv.com/en/eu-elections/uen-leader-decided-fianna-fil-move-liberals/article-180023# (accessed August 2009).
Devine, K. (2009) Irish political parties' attitudes towards neutrality and the evolution of the EU's foreign, security and defence policies, *Irish Political Studies*, 24(1), pp. 467–490.
Fallon, J. (2009) *Brian Cowen: In his Own Words* (Cork: Mercier Press).
Fianna Fáil (1999) Report of Director of Elections to Ballymahon Fianna Fáil Comhairle Ceantair (unpublished).
Fianna Fáil (2002) *Election Manifesto* (Dublin: Fianna Fáil), available at: www.irishtimes.com/focus/election_2002/parties/ffmanifesto.pdf (accessed October 2009).
Fianna Fáil (2006) *Corú agus Rialacha* [Constitution and Rules] (Dublin: Fianna Fáil).
Fianna Fáil (2007) *Now, the Next Steps: Election Manifesto* (Dublin: Fianna Fáil).
Fianna Fáil (2009) *Europe, We are Better Working Together: European Election Manifesto* (Dublin: Fianna Fáil).
Girvin, B. & Murphy, G. (Eds) (2008) Continuity, change and crisis in Ireland: new perspectives, research and interpretations, *Irish Political Studies*, 23(4), Special Issue.
Hayward, K. (2002) Not a Nice surprise: an analysis of the debate on the Nice Treaty in Ireland, *Irish Studies in International Affairs*, 13, pp. 167–186.
Hayward, K. (2009) *Irish Nationalism and European Integration: The Official Redefinition of the Island of Ireland* (Manchester: Manchester University Press).
Ladrech, R. (2002) Europeanization and political parties: towards a framework for analysis, *Party Politics*, 8(4), pp. 389–403.
Laffan, B. & O'Mahony, J. (2008) *Ireland and the European Union* (Basingstoke: Palgrave Macmillan).
Lansdowne Market Research (2009) European and Local Elections – Exit Poll, 5 June 2009, prepared for RTÉ and the *Sunday Independent*, available at: www.lansdownemarketresearch.ie/pdf/RTE%20Lansdowne%20Exit%20Polls%205th%20June%202009.pdf (accessed August 2009).

Marsh, M. (2005) Parties and society, in: J. Coakley & M. Gallagher (Eds) *Politics in the Republic of Ireland,* pp. 160–182 (London: Routledge).

Marsh, M., Sinnott, R., Garry, J. & Kennedy, F. (2008) *The Irish Voter: The Nature of Electoral Competition in the Republic of Ireland* (Manchester: Manchester University Press).

Martin, M. (2009) Minister for Foreign Affairs launches White Paper on Lisbon Treaty, 8 July 2009, Fianna Fáil Press Release, available at: www.dfa.ie/home/index.aspx?id=82342/ (accessed August 2009).

McElroy, G. & Benoit, K. (2007) Party groups and policy positions in the European parliament, *Party Politics,* 13(1), pp. 5–28.

Millward Brown IMS (2008) *Post Lisbon Treaty Referendum Research Findings* (Dublin: Department of Foreign Affairs)

Mockler, F. (1994) Organisational change in Fianna Fáil and Fine Gael, *Irish Political Studies,* 9(1), pp. 165–171.

O'Brennan, J. (2003) Ireland's return to 'normal' voting patterns on EU issues: the 2002 Nice Treaty referendum, *EPS: European Political Science,* 2(2), pp. 5–13.

Quinlan, S. (2009) The Lisbon Treaty Referendum 2008, *Irish Political Studies,* 24(1), pp. 107–121.

Reidy, T. (2009) Blissful union? Fine Gael and the European Union, *Irish Political Studies* 24(4), pp. 511–525.

Roche, D. (2008) Being at the heart of Europe is critical for FDI and for Irish Jobs, Press Release, 20 May 2008, available at: www.dickroche.com/article.php?sid=1086 (accessed August 2009).

Sinnott, R. (2001) *Attitudes and Behaviour of the Irish Electorate in the Referendum on the Treaty of Nice* (Dublin: European Commission Representation in Ireland).

Walsh, D. (1986) *The Party: Inside Fianna Fáil* (Dublin: Gill and Macmillan).

Blissful Union? Fine Gael and the European Union

THERESA REIDY
University College Cork, Ireland

ABSTRACT *Fine Gael presents itself as a model pro-EU party but as in so many areas of EU politics, it provides a case study of how the dichotomy of elite commitment and popular disillusionment is manifested and managed. This article will examine the Europeanization of Fine Gael using the Ladrech (2002) framework. It begins by outlining the elite level positions which drive Fine Gael involvement in EU politics and identifies the ways in which the party has used its membership of the European People's Party–European Democrats (EPP-ED) and European elections to further its political agenda and contribute indirectly to the development of public policy in Ireland. Attitudes to the EU, as displayed by ordinary party members, are also considered and serve to expose the dichotomy which exists between elites and lower level members. Europeanization, although evident, is not widespread and is invariably guided by wider domestic party objectives.*

Introduction

The tension between elite commitment and popular disillusionment is a constant theme in the analysis of EU politics. This article explores the Europeanization of Fine Gael using the Ladrech framework. Fine Gael presents itself as a model pro-EU party but, as in so many areas of EU politics, it provides something of a case study of how the dichotomy of elite commitment and popular disillusionment is manifested and managed.

 Fine Gael was formed in 1933 when Cumann na nGaedhael merged with two smaller parties. Since then, Fine Gael has been the second largest party in the state. It has had a number of periods in office, always as the lead partner in coalition governments. Many Irish political parties claim to be pro-European but Fine Gael narrowly secures the title of most pro-European (see Benoit and Laver, 2005; Laffan and O'Mahony, 2008). Fine Gael has had a conventional and warm relationship with Europe since Ireland first joined the European Economic Community (EEC) in 1973. The party was a long time advocate of EEC membership and campaigned to join in 1972. This support for the Community has persisted and grown over the nearly four decades of Irish membership. European enthusiasm is shared across the levels within the party but the party leadership have been central to driving and maintaining this agenda. In its interactions with Europe, Fine Gael has been very successful, winning the largest number of European Parliament seats in 2004 and again in 2009. Party personnel (John Bruton and Peter Sutherland) have won praise both within Ireland and Europe for their contribution to the European Union.

This article draws on the literature of Hix (2005), Ladrech (2002) and Mair (2002, 2004) to create a framework within which to consider Fine Gael's approach to EU politics since the 1970s. The Ladrech (2002) framework is used to evaluate Fine Gael's involvement in transnational party politics, participation in European institutions and the extent to which Europeanization can be identified in party policy. Mair (2002, 2004) and Hix (2005) provide useful structures by which the dynamics of party competition, electoral competition and party system change can be considered. The first section discusses the role of party elites in determining party attitudes towards the European Union. The Fine Gael approach to Europe is a top down one and this section demonstrates the impact of party leaders on the party's European policy. Subsequent sections are structured using the Hix, Mair and Ladrech literatures to examine different aspects of the Fine Gael position. Having opened with the party elites, the penultimate section will consider the attitudes of Fine Gael members to the European Union. It questions whether recent voting and opinion poll evidence may suggest diverging positions on EU politics between party elites and members. The article draws heavily on a series of semi-structured interviews with both elite and ordinary party members conducted over the period 2008–2009.

Party Elite Attitudes to Europe

Fine Gael claims to outshine Fianna Fáil on commitment and enthusiasm for the European project. During interviews, members of Fine Gael described their position on Europe as ideological whereas, they argued that Fianna Fáil is entirely pragmatic in their approach. While Fianna Fáil has occasionally lapsed in its allegiance to the EU, as seen in the first referendum on the Treaty of Nice, Fine Gael has been steady and constant in its approach to Europe under successive leaders (Laffan, 1991: 198). This support for Europe is a matter of some pride and is often referred to by the Fine Gael leadership. When speaking on Europe, Fine Gael leaders outline their commitment, telling their audience they are not willing to play party politics on European issues. In opposition, Fine Gael supports European Union (EU) policy initiatives and embarked on a nation wide campaign in support of the first Lisbon Treaty referendum. Similar pro-European campaigns were conducted at all previous European referendums. This is not unusual for a party in opposition and Crum (2007: 78) identifies this trend in many European countries among pro-integration parties.

During Ireland's early years in the EEC, Fine Gael was the lead partner in a coalition Government and Dr Garret FitzGerald, as Minister for Foreign Affairs, was the key link between the EEC and the Irish Government. FitzGerald, an enthusiastic Europeanist, laid the foundations for the party's longstanding orientation towards

Europe. He engineered the party's early involvement with the European People's Party-European Democrats (EPP-ED), an enduring relationship which has provided important opportunities for Fine Gael to outsmart and outmanoeuvre its main domestic rival, Fianna Fáil. FitzGerald's initial work encouraging the party to look to Europe had a defining influence on Fine Gael and his contribution resonates with party elites and members two decades after his departure from active politics.

FitzGerald set the tone for the party's policy on the EU but this position has been developed and enhanced under successive leaders. Two can be singled out: Alan Dukes and John Bruton. Dukes was a short-lived leader of the party but has always been a supporter of the European Community. Having worked in Brussels prior to entering politics, he became a key figure within Fine Gael on the European agenda and on leaving politics, pursued his interest in European affairs. Dukes has often spoken of his sense of Fine Gael as an outward-oriented party. He contrasts the party's position on Europe with that of Fianna Fáil, which he views as inward and at times isolationist in its approach. John Bruton, upon leaving the Irish political stage went on to assume high political office at European level, taking up the post of EU ambassador to the USA. During his period as Taoiseach, Bruton managed a successful Irish Presidency and has been heavily involved in the EPP-ED.

Party elites are the key driving force behind the pro-EU policy of Fine Gael. Opposition from the Catholic right of the party faded in the early years and since that period, the EU has not been a divisive issue within the party. The current position of the party displays path dependency from the early position on Europe taken by Garret FitzGerald. It is worth noting that Fine Gael has spent many terms in opposition and its involvement with the EU presents an opportunity for an involvement in policy-making which is largely absent at the domestic level during periods in opposition. In seeking to influence Irish policy, Fine Gael members admit, that on occasion, this is achieved more effectively through its EU channels. Fine Gael Members of the European Parliament (MEPs) argue that they can have a greater impact on Irish public policy through EU legislation than their fellow party members who are opposition Teachta Dalai (TDs) in Dáil Éireann.

It is not just at elite level within the party however, that Europe is given a high priority. Young Fine Gael (YFG) has tended to follow the senior party in its approach to the EU and has campaigned in favour of all major steps on the road to European integration. Occasionally, the youth wing has grabbed public attention with its slightly risqué advertising approach. A steamy poster campaign entitled 'yes yes yes to Europe' grabbed a few headlines for the Amsterdam Treaty campaign. A similar campaign was conducted more recently for the first Lisbon Treaty referendum (see Figure 1). Young Fine Gael members are also tied into the youth network of the EPP-ED. As members of the Youth of the European People's Party (YEPP), they make regular trips to visit European institutions, attend YEPP conferences and participate in their campaigns. All of these activities lead to greater awareness of the EU and political socialization on EU issues. According to members the interaction of Young Fine Gael with the EU is much greater than what would be experienced by members of Ógra Fianna Fáil.

Figure 1. Young Fine Gael, *Campaign for Europe* posters.
Source: Fine Gael HQ.

Fine Gael party leaders have been outspoken enthusiasts of the European Union. Their attitudes have had a significant influence on the way that Fine Gael manages its relationship with the EU and has sought to integrate itself within European institutions and trans-national federations. This has also translated into its communications with party members and the electorate more broadly. The Fine Gael position in Europe has been a top down one. This is not unique and Gallagher and Marsh (2004: 408) argue that Fine Gael has been top down in its approach to many aspects of policy and organization. The sustained enthusiasm of the Fine Gael leadership for nearly four decades is an important context for any analysis of Fine Gael as a Europeanized political party.

European Policy and Policy on Europe

Ladrech's (2002) framework begins with an examination of evidence of Europeanization in party programmes. Specifically, he is interested in the integration of European policy ideas into the policy programmes of national parties. Manifestos require political parties to provide explicit details on their policy positions, therefore they are a useful source of information on Europeanization in party programmes. There is evidence of a European dimension to policy amongst almost all Irish political parties. In fact, there is near consensus on issues such as monetary union, environmental protection and the Common Agricultural Policy (CAP) (Laffan and O'Mahony, 2008).

Fine Gael policy documents make regular reference to the role of the European Union in Irish policy making and EU issues receive some consideration in manifestos for national elections. A separate manifesto focusing on Europe is produced for the European Parliament elections. Benoit (2009) provides evidence from manifesto data that the EU is low on the agenda of all the pro-integration parties, although Fine Gael scores higher on EU mentions than Fianna Fáil in a couple of election years. The pro-integration agenda of Fine Gael is highlighted in the work, and evidence from an expert survey is used to underscore this.

Fine Gael has a spokesperson on European Affairs and many members of the senior party team claim an interest in EU issues and developments. However, it is important not to overstate the importance of the programmatic aspect of the Ladrech framework in the Irish case. Irish political competition has always been unusual because of the low impact of policy in political debate. While parties, and especially Fine Gael, have adopted a clear European line in their policy and evidence of Europeanization is present, Mair (1987) and others have argued that policy is of limited consequence in Irish politics. Poguntke *et al.* (2007) have also suggested that Europeanization may result in the creation of EU policy specialist elites within a party. Despite its emphasis on the EU, this development has not emerged in the case of Fine Gael.

The one policy area worthy of specific note is Irish neutrality. Irish neutrality has become a contentious issue, especially in European referendum campaigns (see Devine, 2009; O'Mahony, 2009). Fine Gael has deviated from the mainstream consensus on neutrality. The party has been influenced by the development of the European common foreign and defence policy. Fine Gael has proposed abandoning Irish neutrality and integrating into a European defence arrangement. This policy objective was most recently restated in its 2009 European election manifesto. Liam Cosgrave, Taoiseach during Ireland's early years in Europe, suggested that 'those participating in the new Europe must be prepared to assist, if necessary in its defence' (Ferriter, 2005: 686). This theme has emerged over the years and became official party policy when Gay Mitchell MEP, in his policy document *Beyond Neutrality* (Mitchell, 2000), advocated an examination of the Irish position but again in the context of developments at European level. In this policy document he argued:

> There is a clear momentum at European level towards a common defence and security arrangement. In the future, Ireland will have to decide if it will remain militarily unaligned, if it will join an EU common defence arrangement or join NATO ... Fine Gael advocates an EU defence entity.

Fine Gael is alone amongst Irish political parties in pursuing this discussion and there is a strong European influence to their policy discourse. However, this is a party elite attitude, and in their study of Fine Gael members, Gallagher and Marsh (2002) found that that this would not be a popular policy among ordinary party members. There is limited evidence of the Europeanization of party policy in some domestic policy areas. Neutrality however, is a particular policy area which demonstrates an increasingly sophisticated recognition by Fine Gael of the impact of the EU and the need to propose strategies for the future development of the polity. This feature of party policy development fits closely with the account of Europeanization as outlined by Ladrech (2002: 396).

Fine Gael within Europe

The second dimension to the Ladrech (2002) framework is organizational change. It is concerned with the affiliations of parties within European structures, the influence of the party delegations to European institutions and the monitoring of EU policy by party elites. Although Fianna Fáil has dominated Government over the last 70 years, Fine Gael has held office at a number of important junctures and as a result, has had interactions with all EU institutions. The party has had two European Commissioners and led the Presidency of the European Council on three occasions (1975, 1984 and 1996). As a member of the EPP-ED, it is also part of a large power bloc within the European Parliament. Its work within all of these realms has influenced, directly and indirectly, the extent to which it has been Europeanized.

Fine Gael personnel working within the European institutions have been commended for their work. For example, within the European Commission, former Fine Gael Commissioner Peter Sutherland was held in high regard for his part in negotiating complex trade agreements (Coogan, 2003: 403). Fine Gael Ministers have participated in the Council of Ministers and a number, from the 1970s, went on to win seats in the European Parliament. Tim Pat Coogan points to the admiration held for Foreign Ministers Peter Barry, James Dooge and Garret FitzGerald. According to Coogan (2003: 403), Fine Gael representatives in Europe were singled out as being 'somewhat more stylish' in the way they accomplished their work at European level, although Fianna Fáil were seen as effective.

Fine Gael-led Presidencies of the European Council have been overseen by former Taoisigh, Liam Cosgrave, Garret FitzGerald and John Bruton. John Bruton's Presidency received particular praise, although there is a general recognition that Irish presidencies have been very successful and well managed, whether led by Fine Gael or Fianna Fáil (cf. Quaglia and Moxon-Browne, 2006).

In its interactions with EU institutions, Fine Gael has pursued its pro-EU agenda. Selecting senior party personnel for European positions reveals the high priority which the party attaches to EU issues. However, in this, they are not significantly different to Fianna Fáil. It is Fine Gael's membership of the EPP-ED which has enabled it to play a more central role in EU politics, than it sometimes achieves at the domestic level.

The EPP-ED was first formed as a loose political grouping in 1976 but has evolved into a coherent organization with a centralized structure and clear policies. It has been one of the dominant groups in the Parliament and along with the Party of European Socialists holds over 60 percent of the seats in each Parliament. It remains the largest group in the European Parliament after the 2009 elections and its position of dominance was thought likely to secure the re-election of José Manuel Barroso for a second Commission in 2009. Indeed, members of the EPP-ED dominated in Barroso's 2004–2009 Commission, with nine European Commissioners drawn from EPP-ED parties.

Fine Gael's membership of the EPP-ED has been very significant. Fine Gael joined the EPP-ED prior to accession and this decisive decision briefly outsmarted Fianna Fáil. A key requirement for both parties was that they had to join different groupings in order to maintain the appearance of difference for domestic political competition. Unusually for Fine Gael, it was quick to seize the opportunity and joined the EPP-ED in advance of EU accession, leaving Fianna Fáil to join what has been described as an 'uneasy partnership', the Union for Europe of the Nations (UEN), a group formerly dominated by French Gaullists and in more recent years made up of French and Italian nationalist parties (Laffan and Tonra, 2005: 445).

There are practical advantages of membership of the EPP-ED for Fine Gael. They include secretarial and back-up services as well as the far more important consequence of ready access to the power structures within the European Parliament. Fine Gael's membership of the EPP-ED puts them at the heart of a large alliance which is broadly in favour of European integration and it is clearly a position which is comfortable for the party. The EPP-ED is federalist in its approach to the EU, and some Fine Gael MEPs do not fully support this position. They are not alone however, within the EPP-ED, as the grouping is comprised of centre and centre right parties from across the EU, accommodates a diversity of opinion on the future of the EU. The EPP-ED also has an extensive pan European network which MEPs, TDs and successive party leaders continue to engage with. The grouping holds a meeting of all its national party leaders in advance of European summits. This gives Fine Gael leaders direct access to European Heads of Government. Involvement with the EPP-ED has thus helped to sustain the elite commitment to the EU in Fine Gael. Such interactions provide party elites with incentives to extend their engagement with the EU and to maintain a pro-EU agenda. There is also a more subtle socialization effect on elites which is apparent from their long-term engagement with the EPP-ED. In contrast, Fianna Fáil, whilst a member of the UEN, found itself in a smaller grouping with members that often displayed ambivalence towards Europe, limiting the scope of its influence. Differences between Fianna Fáil and Fine Gael are probably always best seen as a matter of degree and this is equally true in relation to Europe. Both are pro-European but Fine Gael seems more committed than Fianna Fáil. Membership of the EPP-ED has been an important context within which this has been achieved.

The EPP-ED are currently the largest group in the European Parliament and since the 2009 European elections, Fine Gael has had four members in this 265 member bloc. Membership of the bloc is clearly important for the party's MEPs and it is a recurring theme in their public discourse. They place particular emphasis on the EPP-ED as a major driving force at European level and speaking before the first Lisbon Treaty referendum, current party leader, Enda Kenny, reinforced this point, advising his audience that 'the EPP-ED group is home to the Prime Ministers of fourteen EU member states and some would-be prime ministers' (speech in Adare, Co. Limerick, 21 April 2008).

Fine Gael MEPs argue that membership of the EPP-ED allows them to punch above their weight within the European Parliament, giving them access to networks across Europe, memberships of prominent committees within Parliament and the ability to draw on wide influence across Europe. There is evidence to support this view. Fine Gael MEP, Mark Clinton, was Vice President of the European Parliament from 1987 to 1989. Other Fine Gael MEPs have held the Vice Presidencies of various European Parliamentary committees and delegations (e.g. Avril Doyle – Committee on Fisheries; Mary Banotti – Committee on Youth, Culture and Sport; Richie Ryan – Committee on Budgets). There is a belief among the party's MEPs that they play a major role in EU policy-making and a sense that they achieve more as MEPs than they do as opposition TDs in Dáil Éireann. However, they share a common frustration in finding it difficult to communicate their work to an Irish electorate, hinting at poor media coverage and an electorate with little interest in European affairs.

As a party, Fine Gael has been active within the EPP-ED group at all levels and a significant proportion of Fine Gael members have attended meetings of the grouping (Gallagher and Marsh, 2002: 223). The party uses EPP-ED branding in its interactions with its own members and EPP-ED merchandise is distributed at party events. International members of the EPP-ED are also invited to speak at the party Ard Fheis. More controversially, Dr Angela Merkel, German Chancellor and fellow member of the EPP-ED group, endorsed Enda Kenny in the 2007 general election. Drawing on its broader role within European structures is an emerging theme in Fine Gael election campaigns. In seeking to position itself more effectively within the Irish electoral arena, Fine Gael has started to use its EU role. This has led to some rebranding as a Christian Democratic party. Merkel's endorsement provides evidence of the outward orientation of Fine Gael and was an opportunity to underline Fine Gael's position at the centre of European politics.

Fine Gael elected representatives have held senior positions within the EPP-ED and Enda Kenny is currently a Vice President. In the past, both Garret FitzGerald and John Bruton have played prominent roles within the group and have used the network to advance Irish policy positions in EU negotiations. As a small member state, Ireland has always depended on negotiating policy deals - relying on voting weight in the Council of Ministers is not an realistic or effective strategy for Ireland. Fine Gael has been able to use the EPP-ED network to build alliances and common policy positions with other states. All political parties work in this way but the greater size and influence of the EPP-ED gives Fine Gael optimum access to a powerful European network (Laffan and O'Mahony, 2008: 90–91).

Interestingly, EPP-ED membership is increasingly important for Fine Gael in terms of developing and strengthening its *domestic* identity. The party has drawn on its European credentials and allegiances to position itself within Irish electoral contests. The EPP-ED is a conservative and Christian Democratic coalition and Fine

Gael has increasingly used the Christian Democrat label within the domestic setting. In the 2007 general election, references to Christian Democracy and Fine Gael's membership of the EPP-ED were used to distinguish the party from Fianna Fáil. Relative to other Irish political parties in the Republic of Ireland, Fine Gael is unusual in explicitly using its European identity for the purposes of domestic branding. This arguably sets Fine Gael apart as a more Europeanized political party, and in the context of Ladrech's framework, organizational change is the category in which Fine Gael displays the strongest evidence of Europeanization. However, the usefulness of Europeanization for political parties must be queried in the context of evidence from the Irish National Election Study which suggests that voters' positions on the EU are only weakly related to their intention to vote for a political party (Marsh *et al.*, 2008: 51).

European Elections

There are two types of European elections, the first are elections to the European Parliament which take place every five years. The second election type are referendums on European issues and in Ireland, European referendums have become reasonably frequent since the Crotty judgement in 1987 (see O'Mahony, 2009). Fine Gael campaigns in both sets of elections. It has supported all EU referendums since 1973 and has competed in all elections to the European Parliament. Fine Gael has four sitting MEPs and 17 former MEPs and became the largest Irish political party in the European Parliament after the 2004 election. It retained this position at the 2009 elections.

Fine Gael has placed considerable importance on European elections, partly because it allows the party to emphasize electoral successes but also because of a genuine interest. An examination of the profile of Fine Gael candidates suggests that it is mid-level party personnel who contest European elections, with some notable senior exceptions. On election, most choose to remain in Europe and many have built successful political careers on the European stage, such as Mark Clinton, Avril Doyle, Gay Mitchell and Richie Ryan. For Fine Gael MEPs, the choice of staying in Europe is perhaps easier than for Fianna Fáil. Fine Gael has had only a small number of periods in office, since Ireland joined the EEC. For Fine Gael, the choice is often to remain in Europe or return to Ireland, to a party in opposition (notably, former Fine Gael MEP, Simon Coveney, returned to Irish politics, and opposition, in 2007).

Personality is a key aspect of political competition in Ireland and the calibre and profile of the candidates contesting European elections is therefore a symptom of the significance attached to the competition. Paddy Cooney, Mark Clinton and Richie Ryan all held ministerial office in Ireland before moving to the European Parliament. John Cushnahan had been leader of the Alliance Party in Northern Ireland before winning a Fine Gael seat in the European Parliament representing the Munster constituency. Former MEP Avril Doyle and current European Parliament (EP) representative, Gay Mitchell were both junior ministers. Fine Gael MEPs spend on average 7.35 years in the European Parliament with seven of the MEPs spending more than one term (author's own calculations).

European Parliament elections might be contested on European issues but the reality in many member states is that elections are used to punish the Government for their current performance, in the classic second order sense. Hix (2005) argues that in most member states party competition centres on the left–right economic dimension, however, in the European Union the central cleavage is between parties that favour further integration and those who wish to maintain the status quo or undo what has already been reached (Hix, 2005: 181). He devised a cross cutting model to explain party competition in EU politics and has concluded that the requirement for pro-integration parties on the left and the right of the spectrum to co-operate on European issues has effectively neutralized the opportunity for debate on Europe to emerge in the domestic context. In many countries, parties on both sides of the spectrum share similar views on Europe and only limited debate emerges as a result. This model is very useful in explaining the consensus that appears to exist on European issues between parties in Ireland.

Ireland, then, is one of the many countries with what has been termed a 'pro European cartel' (Hix, 2005: 185). This point has been made specifically in relation to Ireland by O'Mahony and Laffan (2008: 84–85). Elections on Europe are not fought along normal lines of party competition, a point made in April 2008 by former leader, Michael Noonan, in a speech on the Lisbon Treaty (Adare, Co. Limerick, 21 April, 2008). He told party members that support for the European Union was a key platform of the Fine Gael party but confidently assured party members that the wider European consensus was growing. The consensus that Noonan was speaking of related to the referendum on the Lisbon Treaty, but a similar context exists in elections to the European Parliament. Elections tend to be dominated by national issues with personality politics coming a close second. The third part of the Ladrech (2002) framework concerns patterns of party competition. In the Irish case, until recently only limited politicization of the EU had occurred because of the pro-European cartel. This may be changing and the defeat of the first Nice referendum, followed by the defeat of the first Lisbon referendum and the emergence of Libertas as an organized Euro-sceptic movement may be evidence of a drift towards a more politicized context. Specifically for Fine Gael, opinion poll evidence from the Lisbon Treaty demonstrated that only a bare majority of party members voted with the party in its position on the Lisbon Treaty (*Irish Times*, 25 July 2008). Libertas appeared to make a direct appeal to Euro-sceptic Fine Gael voters at the 2009 European Parliament elections, advocating policy positions with specific appeal for conservative rural voters. However, the Fine Gael share of the vote increased at the election and Libertas did not secure a seat. Voting behaviour at referendums has often broken party lines and the Lisbon Treaty alone cannot be interpreted as evidence of the emergence of a dissonance between party elites and party members.

Mair (2004: 28–38) points out that the party systems of European countries have been impervious to change and that the European Union has not led to a restructuring of domestic party competition. He argues that European elections have become a stage on which national parties rehearse the normal lines of party competition.

Table 1. Elections to the European Parliament

	Fianna Fáil %		Fine Gael %	
Election	Share of the vote	Seats won	Share of the vote	Seats won
1979	34.7	5	33.1	4
1984	39.2	8	32.2	6
1989	31.5	6	21.6	4
1994	35.0	7	24.3	4
1999	38.6	6	24.6	4
2004	29.5	4	27.8	5
2009	24.1	3	29.1	4

This analysis fits the Irish experience. The results of the elections to the European Parliament mirror to some degree elements of national outcomes. Fianna Fáil had always received a higher percentage share of the vote and Fine Gael only exceeded Fianna Fáil in seats won for the first time in 2004, as can be seen in Table 1. The sharp decline in Fianna Fáil support in 2009 must be considered in light of the national economic crisis. In line with Reif and Schmitt (1980) Irish European Parliament elections tend to be fought on domestic issues. There are some second order effects visible in the results with the main party in Government seeing its share of the vote drop on occasion, particularly true of the 2009 election.

It is difficult to explain the patterns of competition at European elections. In a cross national study, Ferrera and Weishaupt (2004) demonstrated that an important element of a party's success in European elections lies in whether they have a coherent policy on Europe, rather than whether they are pro- or anti-integration. This may help explain Fine Gael's success as it has the most clearly defined policy position on Europe relative to other pro-European parties in the Republic of Ireland. European elections have been marked by candidate-centred politics (Marsh, 1996, 2000) and Fine Gael has bought into this as strongly as other parties, quite strikingly so at the European Parliament elections in 2004 and again in 2009. We see Fine Gael choose high profile candidates, often from outside the party, and that these candidates do well. But it is also true that the party's candidates do well when the party is popular, as in 2009. Second order effects are important and must be considered in tandem with the domestic context. Fine Gael recovered very strongly in the 2004 local and European elections after a devastating national election in 2002. Marsh (1998) demonstrates that European elections often have an anti-government swing which benefits opposition parties.

Up to 2009, a European cleavage had not emerged in Ireland and although Fine Gael has positioned itself as a pro-European party, campaigning for votes on this basis, it has not cornered this niche exclusively. In the context of the Ladrech framework, the implication is that there has only been limited Europeanization of domestic political competition. Partly a consequence of the domestic political context within which European elections take place, Fine Gael MEPs also believe they face difficulties in conveying the significance of the work undertaken by the party in Europe because of media and general public disinterest. An inability to communicate with the electorate on aspects of EU policy was a key complaint voiced by MEPs during interviews.

The Membership

The discussion to this point has focused on a macro examination of Fine Gael in the European Union. It has addressed how party elites deal with EU questions, work on policy and define themselves in terms of the party's EU position. It is clear that Fine Gael, at least at the elite level, is committed to the EU: it is a key party priority and receives a considerable attention. This section considers the rank and file members of the party and determines how much their attitudes to the EU mirror those of the party elite. Fine Gael is one of the few Irish parties where there has been a substantive investigation of the party membership. In a detailed examination of party members, Marsh and Gallagher (2002) draw a number of conclusions in relation to the attitudes of Fine Gael party members to the European Union. They found that 38 percent of Fine Gael members favoured further European integration while 31 percent believed that Europe had gone far enough or too far (Marsh and Gallagher, 2002: 158). This presents a picture of an evenly divided party membership. Further analysis of the survey allowed the authors to demonstrate that occupation, location and education were all indicators of attitudes towards Europe. Surprisingly, they indicated that urban members were more pro-European than rural ones, despite the fact that a significant proportion of Fine Gael's rural base are from the farming community, long identified as major beneficiaries of EU membership (Coogan, 2003; Lee, 1989). Party members who had participated in a meeting of the EPP-ED were likely to have the most pro-European profile, underlining the socialization effect of such interactions or that this is a self-selecting group.

Murphy and Puirséil (2008) identify a top-down approach to EU membership in Fine Gael from the early 1970s. They cite interviews with discontented party members who harboured misgivings about the amount of information on EEC entry being disseminated before accession. They point to enthusiastic senior members of the party as the driving force behind the Fine Gael position and conclude that in all likelihood the majority of Fine Gael voters supported entry to the EEC. This may be true, but in recent years, there appears to have been some slippage in enthusiasm for Europe among ordinary members of the party. Interviews with party members at Fine Gael events before the first Lisbon Treaty referendum suggest that low levels of knowledge are a major problem. Members were unsure about aspects of EU decision making and this was more likely to make them hesitant in their support.[1]

Survey evidence taken in the run up to the first Lisbon Treaty referendum confirms the picture of a divided membership (*Sunday Business Post*, Red C Poll, 25 May 2008). Farmers were initially the most positive in their support for the European Union but this position has been eroded, particularly since the Fischler

CAP reforms. Successive surveys have reiterated this point. As farmers make up a significant proportion of Fine Gael members, the growing ambivalence of Fine Gael members is apparent. This may present a potential difficulty for the Fine Gael leadership in time, if a serious gap opens between elite and party member attitudes to the EU.

Conclusion

Fine Gael is a pro-European political party, probably the most pro-European of all political parties in the Republic of Ireland. This position is driven by successive party leaders who have supported European integration, for both ideological and entirely pragmatic economic and political reasons. The approach has filtered through the party and party members are broadly supportive of the policy, although not as supportive as party elites. Fine Gael's public commitment to Europe has been widely communicated and Benoit and Laver (2005: 93–94) also present evidence of Fine Gael scoring highly in their expert survey in relation to EU strengthening and enlargement.

Fine Gael's pro European orientation is elite driven. Dr Garret FitzGerald was an influential figure in this respect. He defined and developed the party's early position on the EU, and crucially was succeeded by two dedicated Europeanists, Alan Dukes and John Bruton. The continuity afforded by like-minded party leadership on the EU has led to path dependency in the party's position on European matters. The pro-European orientation has been further reinforced by the party's involvement with the EPP-ED. The grouping has had a strong EU socialization effect on party elites, members of YFG and ordinary party members who have participated in EU activities with the EPP-ED. Furthermore, despite a history of long periods in opposition at the domestic level and the limits this imposes on direct involvement in decision making, Fine Gael MEPs and party elites are conscious of having impacted on Irish policy through EU channels. This provides an incentive for Fine Gael to engage more directly with EU institutions and activities – Fianna Fáil, as the dominant party of government, does not have the same opportunities. Finally, many Fine Gael members claim a more outward-oriented view of politics than their Fianna Fáil counterparts and explain their pro-EU policies on this basis.

It is clear that Fine Gael party elites see Europe as a core aspect of party identity and EU politics as a major feature of their contribution to Irish politics. Since 2002 there are indications that the party is using its European identity more prominently in electoral contests. The difficulty with this is that voters in general are not likely to consider a party's position on Europe in their decision-making and probably more seriously for Fine Gael, ordinary party members are not as interested in EU politics as Fine Gael elected representatives are. Furthermore, survey evidence indicates that the traditional farming support base of Fine Gael is increasingly disillusioned with the EU. The last minute decision by the Irish Farmers' Association (IFA) to support the first Lisbon referendum is further evidence of farmers' disaffection with Europe. As farming supports under the CAP decline, it is likely that this disaffection may increase and pose a major challenge for Fine Gael. In effect, the Europeanization of Fine Gael, although evident, is not widespread and is invariably guided by wider domestic party objectives.

Perhaps the most important judgement that can be made of Fine Gael in Europe is that it is one of the few areas in Irish politics where it has outmanoeuvred its main rival Fianna Fáil. In joining the EPP-ED, Fine Gael positioned itself within a significant EU power bloc, placing itself at the heart of a pan-European movement. Fine Gael MEPs have exploited this by securing senior positions in the European Parliament and achieving policy inputs in vital areas of Irish national interest (including CAP). Fine Gael Taoisigh and party leaders have also been able to use this network to further Irish policy priorities. In many of the Ladrech categories therefore, the Fine Gael party displays some evidence of Europeanization, although this should not disguise the complex nature of the phenomenon (Ladrech, 2002: 396). The Europeanization of the party is not reflected, to the same degree, in the behaviour of voters and ordinary party members. In effect, the nature of Fine Gael Europeanization is focused at elite party levels where many senior party figures are somewhat uncritical in their engagement with Europe. This may be the case because they are satisfied with their position, but it may also derive from an unquestioning approach. Some Fine Gael MEPs feel unable to criticize the EU overtly because they see their role as champions of the European project. As the party electorate becomes increasingly 'Euro-questioning' however, this may present future policy and electoral challenges for one of Ireland's most pro-European parties and it may potentially undermine the extent to which Europeanization of the party remains a feature of its long-term evolution.

Acknowledgements

An earlier version of this article was presented at the workshop *Party Politics and the EU on the Island of Ireland* at the Institute for European Affairs, 28 April 2008. The author is grateful to the participants at that conference for their comments on an earlier draft. She is also indebted to the many members of Fine Gael, MEPs, Parliamentary Party members, and members who gave generously of their time for the interviews for this piece.

Notes

1. This was not a scientific survey so only general impressions can be observed.

References

Benoit, K. (2009) Irish political parties and policy stances on European integration, *Irish Political Studies*, 24(4), pp. 447–466.

Benoit, K. & Laver, M. (2005) Mapping the Irish policy space: voter and policy spaces in preferential elections, *Economic and Social Review*, 36(2), pp. 83–107.

Coogan, T.P. (2003) *Ireland in the Twentieth Century* (London: Hutchinson).

Crum, B. (2007) Party stances in the referendums on the EU Constitution: causes and consequences of competition and collusion, *European Union Politics,* 8(1), pp. 61–82.
Devine, K. (2009) Irish political parties' attitudes towards neutrality and the evolution of the EU's foreign, security and defence policies, *Irish Political Studies,* 24(4), pp. 467–490.
Ferrera, F. & Weishaupt, J.T. (2004) Get your act together: party performance in European Parliament elections, *European Union Politics,* 5(3), pp. 283–306.
Ferriter, D. (2005) *The Transformation of Ireland 1900–2000* (London: Profile Books).
Fine Gael (1997, 2002, 2004, 2007) *Election Manifestos* (Dublin: Fine Gael).
Fine Gael (2002) *21st Century Fine Gael: Report of the Strategy Review Group* (Dublin: Fine Gael).
Gallagher, M. & Marsh, M. (2002) *Days of Blue Loyalty: The Politics of Membership of the Fine Gael Party* (Dublin: PSAI Press).
Gallagher, M. & Marsh, M. (2004) Party membership in Ireland: the members of Fine Gael, *Party Politics,* 10(4), pp. 407–425.
Hix, S. (2005) *The Political System of the European Union* (London: Palgrave Macmillan).
Ladrech, R. (2002) Europeanization and political parties: towards a framework for analysis, *Party Politics,* 8(4), pp. 389–403.
Laffan, B. (1991) The political process, in: P. Keatinge *et al., Ireland and EC Membership Evaluated,* pp. 197–208 (London: Pinter).
Laffan, B. & O'Mahony, J. (2008) *Ireland and the European Union* (Basingstoke: Palgrave Macmillan).
Laffan, B. & Tonra, B. (2005) Europe and the international dimension, in: J. Coakley & M. Gallagher (Eds) *Politics in the Republic of Ireland,* pp. 430–461 (London: Routledge, in association with PSAI Press).
Lee, J.J. (1989) *Ireland 1912–1985* (Cambridge: Cambridge University Press).
Mair, P. (1987) *The Changing Irish Party System: Organisation, Ideology and Electoral Competition* (London: Francis Pinter).
Mair, P. (2000) The limited impact of Europe on national party systems, *West European Politics,* 23(4), pp. 27–51.
Mair, P. (2004) The Europeanization dimension, *Journal of European Policy,* 11(2), pp. 337–348.
Marsh, M. (1996) Ireland: an electorate with its mind on lower things, in: C. van der Eijk & M.N. Franklin (Eds) *Choosing Europe? The European Electorate and National Political Processes,* pp. 166–185 (Ann Arbor: University of Michigan Press).
Marsh, M. (1998) Testing the second-order election model after four European elections, *British Journal of Political Science,* 28, pp. 591–607.
Marsh, M. (2000) Candidate centred but party wrapped: campaigning in Ireland under STV, in: S. Bowler & B. Grofman (Eds) *Elections in Australia, Ireland and Malta under the Single Transferable Vote,* pp. 114–130 (Flint, MI: Michigan University Press).
Marsh, M., Sinnott, R., Garry, J. & Kennedy, F. (2008) *The Irish Voter, the Nature of Electoral Competition in the Republic of Ireland* (Manchester: Manchester University Press).
Mitchell, G. (2000) *Beyond Neutrality* (Dublin: Fine Gael).
Murphy, G. & Puirséil, N. (2008) 'Is it a new Allowance?' Irish entry to the EEC and popular opinion, *Irish Political Studies,* 23(4), pp. 533–554.
O'Mahony, J. (2009) Ireland's EU referendum experience, *Irish Political Studies,* 24(4), pp. 429–446.
Poguntke, T., Aylott, N., Carter, E., Ladrech, R. & Luther, K.R. (2007) *The Europeanization of National Political Parties* (London: Routledge).
Quaglia, L. & Moxon-Browne, E. (2006) What makes a good EU presidency? Italy and Ireland compared, *Journal of Common Market Studies,* 44(2), pp. 377–395.
Reif, K. & Schmitt, H. (1980) Nine second-order national elections; a conceptual framework for the analysis of European election results, *European Journal of Political Research,* 8(1), pp. 3–44.

The Irish Labour Party: The Advantages, Disadvantages and Irrelevance of Europeanization?

MICHAEL HOLMES
Liverpool Hope University, UK

ABSTRACT *This article seeks to develop an understanding of the parameters of Europeanization when applied to political parties, and aims to modify and enhance some of the existing approaches. It does so on the basis of a case study examination of the Irish Labour Party, which, it is argued, provides an excellent example of the Europeanization of a political party, as well as bringing to light certain interesting additional features relating to this phenomenon. Examination of the Labour Party suggests that some aspects of Europeanization are more powerful than others and can even act as catalysts for further, deeper Europeanization. It also demonstrates that Europeanization not only directly affects actors such as political parties but it can also have an indirect impact through their subsequent activity.*

Introduction

The Irish Labour Party is a slightly odd creature. Throughout Western Europe in the period from 1945, social democracy was an immensely influential ideology and social democratic parties were amongst the most significant political actors. They enjoyed great electoral success and dominated government in many countries; even where they did not succeed in becoming the main party of government, they were clearly the primary opposition party.

But this did not happen in Ireland. Instead, the Labour Party has been permanently stuck in a rut behind the two large parties, Fianna Fáil and Fine Gael. One leading party adviser described 'its natural place as a mudguard for some other, bigger party' (Finlay, 1998: 158), while Mair (1987: 57, 58; Mair and Weeks, 2005: 142) refers to 'Labour's unfortunate position' and 'Labour's debility' and talks of how the party 'persistently takes third place'. Gallagher's (1982: 24, 255) analysis emphasized that 'the most unusual feature of the Irish left is simply its weakness', and suggested that 'Labour has come nowhere near overturning the established political order', while Puirséil (2007: 311) concluded that 'offering little and delivering less, Labour received the support that it deserved'. The Irish Labour Party is one of the poorest performing social democratic parties in Western Europe, and its electoral performance also lags well behind that of its sister parties in many eastern European countries.

From this point of view, the prospect of European Union membership was both a significant challenge and an enticing opportunity for the Labour Party. The opportunity lay in the possibility of strengthening the party by allying it clearly with its much stronger social democratic partners elsewhere in the Union. As one analyst put it, 'the engine of European social democracy has a much better chance of helping to pull the weak carriage of Irish Labour' (Keogh, 1990: 254). The challenge was whether such an overt social democratic identity would be a help or a hindrance to the party domestically. After all, Labour had long feared being tarred with any sort of left-wing brush in the very conservative world of Irish politics.

Despite initial qualms, the Labour Party eventually embraced participation in the European Union, and indeed emerged as a leading advocate of deeper Irish engagement with the EU. This article will examine the extent to which the Irish Labour Party could be said to have undergone Europeanization. Of course, this depends somewhat on the definition of Europeanization that is adopted. Most of the recent work on the subject has concentrated on Europeanization as a phenomenon related to European integration and the European Union – indeed, this is the primary approach of this special issue. In this context, the dominant framework for the analysis of the Europeanization of political parties is that put forward by Ladrech (2002) and Poguntke *et al.* (2007). The first half of this article will evaluate how the Labour Party fits these approaches, and will argue that the Labour Party is a perfect example of this form of Europeanization.

It can be said, however, that this approach to the Europeanization of parties has one important flaw. Parties can undergo textbook Europeanization and yet there can be no discernible signs that this has any wider political effect. Indeed, there is another way of perceiving the Europeanization of parties. This focuses not on the changes undertaken by individual parties, but on the impact such changes have had on patterns of party competition. Mair's (2000) analysis of the Europeanization of party systems argues that the main feature is the lack of any such impact. Party systems have not been changed as a result of states acceding to the EU. The second half of this article illustrates how this applies in the case of the Labour Party. The change in party policy in relation to the EU has had no discernible effect in relation to Labour's electoral performance.

This is further illustrated by an examination of the Labour Party's position on the Treaty of Lisbon. This provides a perfect illustration of the quandaries faced by the party. Although it campaigned for a Yes vote in both referendums, it failed to enthuse many of its members and supporters. But again, it is very unlikely that this will have any long-term significance for the party. The Irish Labour Party might be highly Europeanized, and its supporters remain less so, but these contrasting views on the EU seem to have very little impact on the party's performance in national politics.

The Europeanization of the Labour Party

Programmatic Change

A number of analyses have taken programmatic change to be an indicator of the Europeanization of political parties. In some cases, this has meant focusing on whether a party is for or against integration and, in particular, interpreting the decision to move from an anti- to a pro-European position as the key sign of Europeanization (see, for example, Daniels, 1998). This approach applies in only a limited number of cases, so Ladrech's (2002) approach to programmatic change goes further, taking into account broader programmatic and policy change.

However, both approaches are valid in relation to the Irish Labour Party. The most clear-cut and dramatic indicator of policy shift is in relation to the party's overall attitude about European integration. In the 1972 referendum, Labour led the opposition to membership; by 1992, they were supporting a Yes vote in the Treaty on European Union; and by 2002, they were one of the leaders in advocating approval of the Treaty of Nice (Holmes, 2006). Thus, there is a clear change of policy on European integration.

It is worth bearing in mind that Labour's initial opposition to membership was not a blanket refusal to countenance any dealings between Ireland and the European Economic Community (EEC). During the first half of the 1960s, the party itself characterized its approach as more of a 'wait-and-see' policy rather than immediate rejection, and although that stance hardened into a position where Labour led the No campaign in the 1972 referendum, nonetheless there were a number of pro-European voices in the party. Indeed, the official party position in 1972 was that Ireland was not yet ready for full membership, with Labour calling instead for associate membership to give the country a longer period of adaptation.

By the same measure, it should not be thought that the subsequent shift to a more pro-European position was uncontested. The policy change was clear and quick – as soon as the 1972 referendum result was known, party leader Brendan Corish immediately accepted the decision. But there was still a distinct lack of enthusiasm – Corish described Labour's task as being 'to minimise the disadvantages of membership and to transform the Common Market, if possible, into a more democratic and humane organisation' (see Holmes, 2006: 100–101). The party was unable to agree a position on the 1987 Single European Act (SEA) referendum, and at subsequent referendums, leading party members have expressed their reservations – for example, Michael D. Higgins and Emmet Stagg with the Treaty on European Union, and John Rogers and Fergus Finlay with the Treaty of Nice (Holmes, 2006: 145, 178–179). Other party members have been influential activists in No campaigns – notably, Roger Cole of the Peace and Neutrality Alliance.

But even acknowledging these caveats, the trajectory of the party's European policy from opposition to support is clear and unmistakable. Thus, at an initial level, Labour meets this test of Europeanization. And this analysis of programmatic change can be taken further. It is not just in terms of the overall attitude towards Europe that party policy has changed. It can also be demonstrated by looking at selected areas of economic and social policy. The Labour Party has increasingly couched its demands in such areas in terms of building in an EU dimension.

In some policy areas, this is simple common sense. For example, throughout the first 25 years of Irish membership, financial support from regional funds and from the Common Agricultural Policy meant that the party had to factor these sources of funding into its stances. Similarly, the party was supportive of the financial supports available from the EU through its regional and social programmes. Indeed, during Labour's participation in coalition with Fianna Fáil in 1992–1994, the Labour Party Minister of State Eithne FitzGerald earned the sobriquet 'Minister for Eight Billion', as she was seen to be in charge of the additional structural aid granted to Ireland as part of the Maastricht settlement.

But Labour's policy support for European integration has gone further than this. They have also used support for EU policies as a justification for altering other policies. This included key economic policies. Perhaps most notably, Labour came out in support of participation in the European Monetary System (EMS), the single market programme and Economic and Monetary Union (EMU) (Holmes, 2006: 209). The EMU programme came to fruition when Labour's Ruairí Quinn was Minister for Finance, and he was fully committed to ensuring that Ireland would achieve the convergence criteria set down for participation in the single currency, even at the expense of traditional Labour objectives. This was despite the fact that he was aware that there were criticisms in the party that 'their Labour Finance Minister was too strict in controlling expenditure' (Quinn, 2005: 362 – and glance, too, at his self-caricature in the illustrations in the same book, as 'Ruairi Quinntin Tarantino' bursting into the cabinet room cursing 'make those *+!¬ cuts you overspending *@+!.+*!@s!').

Thus, overall there is clear evidence to support the contention that Labour's policies have undergone a significant change as a result of EU membership. Ladrech's initial formulation perhaps lays less emphasis on being pro- or anti-EU, in order to accommodate a wider range of parties. But the Irish Labour Party's transition from opposition to support is certainly one clear marker of its transformation. And this is buttressed by the wider policy adjustments that have taken place, neatly corroborating this part of Ladrech's thesis.

Organizational Adaptation

Ladrech's second criterion for Europeanization concerns the degree of organizational adaptation a party undergoes. Here, there is another clear-cut change in the Labour Party, at least at a superficial level. Indeed, prior to the first moves towards accession, Labour had virtually no organizational framework for engaging with any form of international affairs. Up to the late 1960s, the party was insular and isolated. Brendan Halligan (2000: 19), the party's General Secretary at this time, has noted critically how 'it simply was not serious politics to be consorting with continentals; far better to be in Bruree than in Brussels'.

However, this altered rapidly once Ireland had joined. Labour's first ever International Secretary was appointed in 1974, and this was a prelude to creating internal party committees to deal with international matters. A European Affairs Committee was established in 1975, followed by an International Affairs Committee in 1978, and these two subsequently merged in 1980 under the latter title (Brown, 1980: 93). In 1993, a further organizational innovation was introduced, with the party's Members of European Parliament (MEPs) being incorporated into the Parliamentary Labour Party. This allows them to feed into party discussions in a more regularized fashion, and thus to contribute to policy formation more effectively.

The new committees have helped Labour develop a more consistent response to international and European events. But it does not mean that these committees have become very powerful or influential in the party. Nor does it mean that the organizational adaptation has resulted in very extensive change within the party. Thus, while the changes have undoubtedly taken place, whether they have any great significance for the party is another matter. Therefore, it is necessary to treat this evidence of Europeanization with a degree of caution.

Nor has the inclusion of MEPs in the parliamentary party been quite as important as it might have. The Labour Party has contested all European Parliament (EP) elections (see Table 1), but on only two occasions has it managed to win more than a single seat. In 1979, it won more than a quarter of the available seats on fractionally more than a seventh of the vote, and in 2009 it picked up exactly a quarter of the seats on slightly less than a seventh of the vote. And of course, the inclusion of one individual in the parliamentary party is more easily accomplished than trying to absorb a larger European Parliament faction.

Nonetheless, despite these reservations the Labour Party clearly exhibits the kind of organizational adaptation predicted by Ladrech. Indeed, it is possible to extend the argument further in two ways. First of all, members of the Labour Party were central to the adoption of an organizational reform at a European level. In 1995 and 1996, Ruairi Quinn and Dick Spring enabled the establishment of coordination meetings amongst representatives of EU social democratic parties in advance of meetings of Ecofin, the Union's Council of Economic and Finance Ministers (Lightfoot, 2005: 44). This was a prelude to the adoption of similar organizational structures by the Party of European Socialists (PES) across all of the Council agendas.

Table 1. The Labour Party and European Parliament elections

	Votes %	Seats
1979	14.5	4
1984	8.4	0
1989	9.5	1
1994	11.0	1
1999	8.7	1
2004	10.6	1
2009	13.9	3

Source: Coakley and Gallagher (2005: 469); Holmes (2009).

Secondly, the party has become a leading advocate of organizational change of Irish political structures in order to allow more effective discussion of European issues. It has called for enhanced procedures by which the Dáil scrutinizes EU legislation, particularly through reform of the Dáil's committee structures to allow for better debate on European issues. And it also played a crucial role in the introduction of the National Forum on Europe in the wake of the initial rejection of the Treaty of Nice referendum. The establishment of such a forum had been a key part of Labour's European policies in the run-up to the referendum, and when the treaty was rejected, the government latched on to this idea as a means of trying to extricate itself from the impasse.

It can thus be argued that Labour has gone beyond its own organizational adaptation to become a source of demands for organizational reform in two other directions: amongst their social democratic colleagues in Europe, and at the level of Irish political procedures. Thus, there is a kind of spill-over of Europeanization, from the internal party environment to both the national and the European political environments.

Party Competition

Ladrech's third feature of Europeanization concerns patterns of party competition. He suggests that Europeanization can lead to parties seeking to broaden their appeal to new groups of voters on the basis of their European policies. This was undoubtedly one of the motivations behind the party's decision to oppose membership in the 1972 referendum. With the two leading parties calling for a Yes vote, and with Labour making a determined attempt to go it alone at the time, the referendum offered the party the opportunity to mark out its own identity.

However, the outcome was a conclusive indication that Europe did not offer an easy route to new votes. In other states, notably Denmark, the result of the membership referendum was sufficiently close to encourage No campaigners to keep going and to offer them the prospect of a significant constituency of voters. But in Ireland, the decisive nature of the result in 1972 meant that had Labour not changed policy, it would have been risking ongoing marginalization.

The Labour Party's constant predicament has been how to expand its vote beyond low double figures, around 10–15 percent. From that point of view, opposition to the EU is not seen as a means of drawing in a lot of new voters but of further restricting the party's longer-term potential. Labour's decision to abandon its opposition to the Community in the immediate wake of the 1972 referendum was undoubtedly connected with a concern that if it did not change tack, it risked long-term marginalization in Irish politics. Unlike countries like Denmark and the UK, where there had been large numbers of No voters in membership referendums, only 17 percent had voted No in Ireland in 1972. This meant that there was no sizeable residual constituency opposed to membership.

The same calculation did not apply for other, smaller, parties. Parties such as the Workers' Party in the 1980s, the Greens in the 1990s and Sinn Féin from the late

1990s onwards have been prominent campaigners against successive EU treaties and saw some increase in their vote share. However, these votes are still firmly in single-figure territory (the Workers' Party grew from 1.7 percent in 1977 and 1981 to a general election high of 5 percent in 1989; the Greens had crept up to 4.7 percent in the 2007 general election; even Sinn Féin's recent dramatic rise has seen them reach just below 7 percent in 2007). As Mair (2000: 35) argued in his analysis of the Europeanization of party systems, such change is mostly a case of habitual anti-system parties latching on to the EU as one more aspect of the system to be opposed.

But at a general level the evidence is that European issues are simply not of much relevance to voters at all. EU issues do not feature prominently in general elections. Indeed, even in European elections, the constant reproach is that discussion of Europe is lost behind national, regional and local concerns. This is hardly a story that is unique to Ireland, but it undoubtedly helps to explain why this dimension of Europeanization does not feature strongly for the Labour Party.

A second way of interpreting the impact of Europeanization on party competition is in relation to Labour's eligibility as a coalition partner. There is very little evidence of this being an important factor. Labour's European policies have never damaged its credibility as a potential coalition partner for other parties in the Irish system. This was shown most dramatically in 1973, the year after the membership referendum where Labour had led the No campaign. A general election resulted in the incumbent Fianna Fáil government being defeated by a coalition made up of Fine Gael and the Labour Party. Fine Gael had been a strong advocate of Irish membership, but this did not create any serious obstacle to collaboration between the two parties. Although the initial negotiations between the two parties were slow, nonetheless they were able to agree a full, if short, programme for government in advance of the election.

It might be argued that Labour's opposition to membership did carry a penalty in terms of its participation in government in another way. With the 1973 coalition, Fine Gael's Garret FitzGerald (1991: 294) has noted that certain ministries with a large EU responsibility, notably that of Foreign Affairs, 'could not credibly have been allocated to the Labour Party' so soon after the referendum. However, this overlooks the fact that Labour had never previously held nor even sought such ministerial portfolios. It was not until 1992, when Labour under Dick Spring's leadership went into coalition with Fianna Fáil, that Labour took charge of some of the key EU-related ministries, with Spring himself becoming Minister for Foreign Affairs (see Holmes, 1998: 174–175). Even then, that decision was met with some bafflement within the party, with one senior party official commenting that it was 'more than a little perplexing for Labour in that the Department of Foreign Affairs was new territory for us and not associated with our areas of traditional concerns' (Kavanagh, 2001: 31).

Party–Government Relations

Ladrech's fourth feature of Europeanization relates to party-government relations. There has always been a tension for parties created by participation in government.

Although it is usually necessary to be in office in order to be able to bring about change, at the same time the exigencies of office-holding can constrain ideological or programmatic commitments. This tension has been exacerbated by the way in which the European Union does its business. On the one hand, the powers and capacities of governments have been enhanced, since it is they who participate in the core decision-making bodies in the EU (the Council of Ministers and the European Council). On the other hand, institutions of governmental scrutiny and oversight have been weakened. National parliaments are less effective at supervising EU policies for a variety of reasons, and the European Parliament has not made up that deficit.

Participating in government has been a particularly strong motivating factor in persuading Labour politicians to adopt a more pro-EU position. It is very evident in a number of instances. During Michael O'Leary's time as Minister for Labour in the 1970s, he was 'extremely fortunate in that the political climate in 1973, following Ireland's membership of the Common Market, strongly favoured progressive legislation' (Desmond, 2000: 58). Dick Spring as Minister for Foreign Affairs and Ruairí Quinn as Minister for Finance in the 1990s played important roles in Ireland's relations with the EU, particularly in relation to EMU and the Treaty of Amsterdam (Holmes, 2006: 155). And Proinsias De Rossa (then a member of Democratic Left, though he was later to join Labour) played a significant role in relation to developing the Social Charter when he was Minister for Social Welfare in the 1990s (Holmes, 2006: 156).

In each case, close involvement with EU affairs contributed to an appreciation of the extent to which the EU could be a vehicle for progressive change and the delivery of Labour policies. Of course, there is a need to be a little bit cautious. There is inevitably a tendency for those who put themselves forward for EU-related posts and responsibilities to be already interested in and potentially sympathetic to the ideals of European integration. But the change in statements and positions is noteworthy. Some of the most pro-European activists in the party are ones who have served in government and risen to very senior positions in the party (of the four listed above, three served as party leader).

This has implications for wider relations in the party. Opinion polls show that Labour members and supporters are generally and consistently less enthusiastic about Europe than the party leadership (see Table 2). Although the party officially supported ratification of the Treaties of Maastricht, Amsterdam and Nice, there were Labour members who campaigned against each of those treaties, and on almost every occasion Labour supporters were less likely to have voted in favour than supporters of other pro-EU parties. The one thing that prevents this becoming a more serious source of difficulty for the party is that ordinary members and supporters tend not to rate EU issues as being all that important. It is an issue when it comes to European referendums, but otherwise does not feature as a significant factor for the party.

Transnational Party Networks

Ladrech's fifth feature relates to engagement in transnational party networks, and again there is very straightforward evidence of Labour's transformation. Up to the

Table 2. Voting intentions on various European treaties, by party support

	National total (%)		Labour supporters (%)	
	Yes	No	Yes	No
SEA	40	21	13	36
TEU	49	28	47	33
Ams.	43	18	46	19
Nice I	45	28	50	36
Nice II	42	29	38	35

Note: This takes the final opinion poll prior to each referendum.
Source: Holmes (2006: 132, 148, 162, 180, 187).

mid-1960s, Labour eschewed virtually all international contacts, and it was not until 1967 that the party joined the Socialist International. This isolation existed for a variety of reasons, ranging from the penurious finances of the party to the desire to avoid being associated with any taint of a left-wing ideology.

Membership of the Socialist International opened doors for the party into a number of other frameworks. In particular, it meant that Labour had a ready-made party family to adhere to when it took its place in the European Parliament after accession. And as the Parliament and its party groups have evolved, Labour's ties have inevitably deepened. Labour joined what was then a Liaison Bureau of the Socialist International for parties from EEC member-states. In 1974, the Bureau evolved into the Confederation of Socialist Parties, which 'saw itself as a regional association, though distinctly not as a substructure, of the Socialist International' (Pridham & Pridham, 1981: 113). In 1992, the Confederation in turn became the Party of European Socialists (see Hix, 1996).

Participation in the PES has meant a growing range of common, shared activities. As Cole (2001: 26) argues, 'the number of contact points between socialist politicians has increased exponentially over the past decade', particularly as a result of the work of the PES. The member parties negotiate common manifestos for European Parliament elections, even if these tend to be rather tepid and bland; there are regular meetings for international secretaries, party leaders, MEPs, national parliamentarians, youth members; there are regular conferences.

The Parliament itself also provides a forum for trans-national engagement by the party. Hix and Lord (1997) measure the Europeanization of parties by their willingness to participate in European elections and in the European Parliament. This is of limited analytical use, simply because there are hardly any parties that do not meet these criteria – parties by their very nature abhor the political vacuum of abstention. But while the fact that Labour was prepared to engage in European Parliament elections and to take the seats it won does not tell us a great deal, its choice of partner in the Parliament does provide another indication of the extent of Europeanization of the Labour Party. The Party of European Socialists has generally been regarded as a consistently pro-integration and pro-European Union party federation. And as Hix (2005: 190) notes, 'there has been a strengthening of group cohesion' in the Parliament, with the PES demonstrating a consistently very high level of cohesion.

For the Labour Party, the Parliament and the Party of European Socialists have become increasingly important focuses of activity. However, this has had a knock-on effect on other links, and it can be argued that European Parliament-related commitments have begun to take over from other international networks. For example, the Socialist International is now a much less significant forum for Labour as for most social democratic parties, simply because it does not have the spare resources to maintain extensive links with the Socialist International as well as the PES. Thus, although there is ample evidence of further Europeanization, it has also led to the weakening of other forms of transnational links.

The Impact of Europeanization

In overall terms, there is thus consistent evidence across virtually all of the five criteria for Europeanization set out by Ladrech in the case of the Irish Labour Party. However, the extent to which this has had any impact on the party's wider fortunes is open to debate. In the period since Irish membership of the EU, Labour has experienced European successes (for instance, the four European Parliament seats won in 1979) and failures (like the loss of all four seats in 1984). It has also experienced national political successes (such as the surge in votes in the 1992 election) and failures (for example, the collapse of the party's vote in 1997). However, these successes and failures do not really correlate with each other. The European and national political spheres do not interact to any substantial degree, so despite the party's Europeanization, the EU does not really seem to matter too much.

This is also evident in terms of the attitudes of the party's own politicians. In one noteworthy period, a succession of Labour Party members clearly decided to place a national political career above a European one. The 1979 European Parliament elections were the prelude to a remarkable period of musical chairs on the part of the Labour Party. They had won four seats, but over the course of the five-year parliamentary term, 11 different people held those seats. And the main reason for the MEPs to resign their seats was the lure of national political office. One (Michael O'Leary) became party leader and subsequently Tánaiste and a government minister; two others (Liam Kavanagh and Frank Cluskey) were also appointed government ministers; two more (Eileen Desmond and Seamus Pattison) were appointed ministers of state; and one (John O'Connell) accepted the post of Ceann Cómhairle (Holmes, 2006: 54). It is clear where their priorities lay.

Since then, attitudes towards European Parliament seats and other European political offices have become less mercenary. While Barry Desmond, a one-time deputy leader and government minister, also resigned as MEP, it was in order to take up a position in the European Court of Auditors. However, it should also be noted that this came towards the end of his career, so that Europe was more a very comfortable retirement home rather than the primary focus of his political life. But in 2009, Proinsias De Rossa won his fourth term of office in the European Parliament, having previously won seats in 1989 (for the Workers' Party) and in 1999 and 2004 (for Labour).

Labour and the Lisbon Treaty

A further good indication of the limits to Europeanization of the Labour Party is provided by the first referendum on the Treaty of Lisbon in June 2008 (see Quinlan, 2009). The party supported the treaty from the outset – indeed, it could even be argued that their support goes back even further, as the decision to support the treaty was made a month before the final document was signed by the EU heads of government in December 2007. Labour's support for Lisbon was to be expected both because of the party's general support for European integration since the 1990s and because of its support for the Treaty of Lisbon's precursor, the failed European Constitutional Treaty. The Labour MEP, Proinsias de Rossa, had been an active member of the Convention on the Future of Europe, which had fed into the Constitutional Treaty.

The main party document on Lisbon was clear-cut, stating 'Labour supports Ireland's full participation in the European Union' and 'Labour supports the Lisbon Reform Treaty' (Labour Party, 2008). It argued that Lisbon made the EU more democratic, more socially progressive and more effective, and the party paid particular attention to the fact that the treaty would make the Charter of Fundamental Rights legally binding. Former Labour leader Ruairí Quinn, chairman of the Alliance for Europe, argued that Lisbon was very beneficial for ordinary workers. 'By voting 'Yes' we will be giving unprecedented protection to Irish workers by enshrining the Charter of Fundamental Rights into EU law' (Ruairí Quinn, in the *Irish Times*, 6 May 2008).

As in previous referendums, there was an acknowledgement that neither the EU nor the treaty was perfect. The party document accepted that 'none of this is to suggest that the European Union is as democratic as it should be, nor as effective as it should be in protecting the well-being of all our citizens'. But the overall evaluation was that Lisbon would mean 'a Europe that is better able to meet the challenges facing us in today's globalising world' (Labour Party, 2008).

Labour's pro-treaty position seemed to have widespread support in the party. Unlike previous referendums, which had featured at least some fairly high profile dissenting voices in the party, there was hardly any disagreement on this occasion. Some members of Labour Youth indicated their opposition to the party's stance, and one of them set up a Bebo network page called 'Labour Against Lisbon' (*Irish Times*, 16 May 2008). And Labour's Colette Connolly was amongst a group of Galway councillors who issued a joint call for a No vote (*Irish Times*, 26 May 2008). But generally, party members toed the line.

Two problems emerged for the party during the campaign. First, Labour was criticized for not campaigning with sufficient enthusiasm. A particular bone of contention was the main poster produced by the party. It featured a large photo of party leader Eamon Gilmore and a big party slogan, but the message 'Yes to Europe, Proud to be Irish' was printed in far smaller type, easily overlooked. Towards the end of the campaign, Labour responded to these criticisms by issuing a redesigned poster with a more prominent 'Yes' call, but the feeling was that the party had been much more concerned with promoting itself with the 2009 local elections in mind.

But a more significant problem began to emerge as opinion polls were conducted. It became apparent that the public might not support the treaty, and enthusiasm for Lisbon was weakest amongst demographic groups that included working class voters and Labour Party supporters. The Labour Party position on Europe was simply not chiming with the concerns of its core constituency. The outcome of the referendum was a No vote, and poll data suggests that working class and Labour supporters voted preponderantly against the treaty.

In the aftermath of the referendum, Labour sought to distance itself from the defeat. The party was critical of a Fianna Fáil proposal to set up an Oireachtas committee to examine options for how to proceed. Party leader Éamon Gilmore also refused to attend a round-table meeting with French President Nicolas Sarkozy, who visited Ireland in July after France had taken over the presidency of the Council. Sarkozy met with representatives of both sides of the referendum campaign, but Gilmore argued that the meeting was pointless as it would simply be going over the ground of the Lisbon debate. 'That debate is over and the referendum has delivered a result' (Eamon Gilmore, in the *Irish Times*, 19 July 2008).

However, while the party seemed to be arguing that the result should be taken as conclusive and that there should not be a second referendum, the position was a little more nuanced than that. Gilmore was careful not to completely preclude another referendum, arguing that while Labour would not support another vote on an unaltered treaty, they might support one on a significantly altered treaty or on the broader issue of Ireland's relationship with Europe. By the end of the summer, the party was already indicating its support for an alternative referendum of some sort, and when the government announced in July 2009 it was to hold a second referendum, Labour at once declared it 'fully supports a Yes vote again' (Labour Party, 2009).

Gap between Party Elite and Supporters on EU

The Lisbon campaign encapsulates Labour's relationship with European integration. The support for the European Union and for further, deeper integration is plainly evident. However, the extent to which this support translates into effective action is open to some doubt. Interest in and enthusiasm for European issues is the preserve of a small minority, and does not percolate more widely through the party. And there are clear problems in getting this to extend beyond the confines of the party to its supporters.

Indeed, the first referendum highlighted a marked reluctance on the part of Labour supporters to follow the party's line on Lisbon. As Table 3 shows, Labour

Table 3. Voting patterns in the first Treaty of Lisbon referendum, by party support

	Voted yes %	Voted no %
FF supporters	63	37
FG supporters	62	48
Labour supporters	39	61
Green supporters	47	53
SF supporters	12	88

Source: Millward Brown/IMS (2008: 6).

supporters were far less likely to have voted Yes in the first Lisbon referendum than supporters of almost all other Dáil parties. There are two possible explanations for this. One is that in supporting the EU, Labour is being pulled away from the policy positions that some people feel it 'ought' to occupy as a left-wing party. Certainly, a number of tiny left-wing parties and groups had no qualms about campaigning unequivocally for a 'No' vote, including the Socialist Party, the Workers' Party and the People Before Profit Alliance. In addition, two trade unions came out in favour of a 'No' vote, citing in particular the European Court of Justice rulings in the Laval and Ruppert cases as evidence of the dominance of right-wing policies in the EU (see Holmes, 2008).

However, it would be wrong to declare the Irish 'No' vote to be a left-wing rebellion. The second explanation is simply that people took advantage of the referendum to give 'the establishment' a kicking. Who or what constitutes 'the establishment' is always very hard to determine, but it is clear that Labour was being included in this instance. Partly, it reflects growing disillusionment with parties and the political process in general. The outcome of the Lisbon referendums is unlikely to matter very much to the Labour Party. There is no evidence that voters followed up their 'No' vote in 2008 by flocking away from the parties that had called for a 'Yes'. This was illustrated perfectly within a year of the first Lisbon referendum. The 2009 European Parliament elections gave Labour a clear success. Campaigning on a solidly pro-EU platform, the party gained its second-best share of the vote in a European Parliament election, and won three seats. But the elections were also a clear success for the Socialist Party, which won a seat in the Dublin constituency. Thus, the two winners from the election were the pro-EU left (Labour) and the anti-EU left (the Socialists). This demonstrates how tricky it is to try to draw inferences about attitudes to Europe from electoral behaviour. The European political sphere remains remarkably self-contained, and does not consistently affect how parties perform in the national arena.

Conclusion

The Europeanization of political parties can be taken in two ways. One approach, that developed by Ladrech, deals with the organizational and programmatic adaptation of parties. It concentrates on how they respond to the demands of the European Union as a political and policy-making system. On the basis of the evidence presented here, the Irish Labour Party clearly fits into most, if not all, of the features of the Ladrech model, and can be argued to have experienced significant Europeanization at the organizational and programmatic levels. It has undergone organizational transformation, it has developed its transnational linkages and it has adapted its policies – all as a direct result of Ireland's membership of the EU and the consequent demands on the party. In terms of party competition and participation in government, the desire to be in government has perhaps been strengthened by the fact that this is such an important conduit into the EU system.

However, this is not the only way of understanding the term Europeanization. It can also be taken to refer to the 'progressive emergence of a bundle of common norms of action' (Mény, Muller & Quermonne, 1996: 8) – the diffusion of common practices and values across borders in Europe, particularly with reference to societies shifting towards some form of European modal position (Featherstone, 2003: 7).

The Labour Party desperately needed this form of Europeanization. Had Ireland moved much closer to the European norm, with a powerful and influential social democratic party at the core of the party system, Labour stood to benefit hugely. But the conclusion must be that Labour's aspirations have been disappointed. There is no evidence that participation in the EU has led to a greater degree of left–right polarity in Irish politics, much less that Labour has been able to expand its place in the Irish party system as a consequence of Europeanization. In the first sense of the word, Labour is undoubtedly more Europeanized. But in a wider sense, the conclusion might have to be 'so what?'

Acknowledgements

This paper is derived from a version presented at the Annual Conference of University Association for Contemporary European Studies (UACES) in Zagreb in September 2005 under the title 'Europeanization and political parties: developing an understanding of the European-national political domains'. The author would like to acknowledge the support provided by the British Academy towards attending that conference.

References

Brown, T. (1980) Internationalism and international politics: the external links of the Labour Party, *Irish Studies in International Affairs*, 1(2), pp. 74–94.
Coakley, J. & Gallagher, M. (2005) Electoral data, in: J. Coakley & M. Gallagher (Eds) *Politics in the Republic of Ireland*, pp. 465–472 (London and New York: Routledge in association with the PSAI Press).
Cole, A. (2001) National and partisan contexts of Europeanization: the case of the French Socialists, *Journal of Common Market Studies*, 39(1), pp. 15–36.
Daniels, P. (1998) From hostility to 'constructive engagement': the Europeanization of the Labour Party, *West European Politics*, 21(1), pp. 72–96.

Desmond, B. (2000) *Finally and In Conclusion: A Political Memoir* (Dublin: New Island Books).
Featherstone, K. (2003) Introduction: in the name of 'Europe', in: K. Featherstone & C.M. Radaelli (Eds) *The Politics if Europeanization*, pp. 3–26 (Oxford: Oxford University Press).
Finlay, F. (1998) *Snakes and Ladders* (Dublin: New Island books).
FitzGerald, G. (1991) *All in a Life: An Autobiography* (Dublin: Gill and Macmillan).
Gallagher, M. (1982) *The Irish Labour Party in Transition, 1957–82* (Manchester and Dublin: Manchester University Press and Gill and Macmillan)
Halligan, B. (2000) What difference did it make? Setting the scene, in: R. O'Donnell (Ed.) *Europe: The Irish Experience*, pp. 18–31 (Dublin: Institute of European Affairs).
Hix, S. (1996) The transnational party federations, in: J. Gaffney (Ed.) *Political Parties and the European Union*, pp. 308–331 (London: Routledge).
Hix, S. (2005) *The Political System of the European Union*, 2nd ed. (Basingstoke: Palgrave Macmillan).
Hix, S. & Lord, C. (1997) *Political Parties in the European Union* (Basingstoke: Macmillan).
Holmes, M. (1998) *Political Parties and European Integration: The Policies and Attitudes of Left-Wing Irish Parliamentary Parties, 1960–1997*, PhD thesis, University College Dublin.
Holmes, M. (2006) *The Irish Labour Party and the European Union* (Lewiston and Lampeter: Edwin Mellen Press).
Holmes, M. (2009) The European Parliament election in Ireland, 5 June 2009, European Election Briefing No. 35, EPERN.
Kavanagh, R. (2001) *Spring, Summer and Fall: The Rise and Fall of the Labour Party, 1986–1999* (Dublin: Blackwater Press).
Keogh, D. (1990) *Ireland and Europe, 1919–1989: A Diplomatic and Political History* (Cork and Dublin: Hibernian University Press).
Labour Party (2008) Yes to the Lisbon Reform Treaty – for a better Europe (Dublin: The Labour Party), available at: http://www.labour.ie/lisbonreformtreaty/whyyes/ (accessed July 2009).
Labour Party (2009) Yes to Europe – Labour for Europe, available at: http://labourforeurope.ie/blog/archive/2009/07/17/yes-to-europe/ (accessed July 2009).
Ladrech, R. (2002) Europeanization and political parties: towards a framework for analysis, *Party Politics*, 8(4), pp. 389–403.
Lightfoot, S. (2005) *Europeanizing Social Democracy? The Rise of the Party of European Socialists* (London and New York: Routledge).
Mair, P. (1987) *The Changing Irish Party System: Organization, Ideology and Electoral Competition* (London: Pinter).
Mair, P. (2000) The limited impact of Europe on national party systems, *West European Politics*, 23(4), pp. 27–51.
Mair, P. & Weeks, L. (2005) The party system, in: J. Coakley & M. Gallagher (Eds) *Politics in the Republic of Ireland*, pp. 135–159 (London and New York: Routledge in association with the PSAI Press).
Mény, Y., Muller, P. & Quermonne, J-L. (Eds) (1996) *Adjusting to Europe: The Impact of the European Union on National Institutions and Policies* (London: Routledge).
Millward Brown/IMS (2008) *Post-Lisbon Treaty Referendum: Research Findings, September 2008* (Dublin: Millward Brown/IMS).
Poguntke, T., Aylott, N., Carter, E., Ladrech, R. & Luther, K.R. (Eds) (2007) *The Europeanization of National Political Parties: Power and Organizational Adaptation* (London and New York: Routledge).
Pridham, G. & Pridham, P. (1981) *Transnational Party Cooperation and European Integration: The Process towards Direct Elections* (London: George Allen and Unwin).
Puirséil, N. (2007) *The Irish Labour Party, 1922–1973* (Dublin: University College Dublin Press).
Quinlan, S. (2009) The Lisbon Treaty Referendum 2008, *Irish Political Studies* 24(1), pp. 107–121.
Quinn, R. (2005) *Straight Left: A Journey in Politics* (Dublin: Hodder Headline Ireland).

The Irish Green Party and Europe: An Unhappy Marriage?

NICOLE BOLLEYER* & DIANA PANKE**
*University of Exeter, UK; **University College Dublin, Ireland

ABSTRACT *To what extent is the Irish Green Party affected by the presence of an additional, European arena next to the domestic one? The answer is twofold. Organizationally, the Irish Green Party drew on the experience and support of the pan-European Green Party Federation and more developed Green parties in other countries. The European arena also provided a platform for electoral success and thereby an important route to resources used to professionalize the organization. Programmatically, and despite the above, the positioning of the Green Party towards European integration has always been ambivalent. European environmental law is more demanding than national law and environmental problems often ask for international solutions which, theoretically, should be welcomed by the party. Yet their fight for direct citizen participation makes them wary of shifting power to a polity whose democratic credentials are contested. While the Green Party originally opposed Europe, they have become more differentiated and constructive over time, pushing for democratization whilst simultaneously viewing the EU as an arena in which desired policies are generated. Having entered government at a national level in 2007, its closer involvement in EU decision-making should reinforce this trend.*

Introduction: The Europeanization of Eurosceptic Parties

The extent to which national parties are affected by European integration is an on-going debate. Regularly national elites try to maintain a consensus and exclude European Union (EU) issues from electoral competition on the national level. Active opposition to EU integration tends to be the domain of new parties, both on the left and the right. These new parties often have more electoral success outside the national arena, be it on the European, regional or local levels. This finding raises questions as to how these parties use the European arena as an opportunity to pursue their primary goals – regardless of their critical attitudes towards European integration – and how far this engagement triggers organizational and programmatic change. This question will be addressed by studying the evolution of the Irish Green Party which, despite the steadily growing literature on new left and Green parties, is rarely included in comparative studies. It is a particularly interesting case because of its (until recently) sustained anti-European stance. Despite its history as a genuine opposition party, it entered national government with the pro-European Fianna Fáil and the Progressive Democrats[1] in 2007 which coincided with an increasing openness towards European integration.

But how does the Europeanization of political parties manifest itself? Existing literature expects an increasing organizational centralization, professionalization, as well as the growing relevance of EU experts in a political party in response to Europeanization pressures. Also, a moderation of EU-critical stands is expected (e.g. Bomberg, 2002; Ladrech, 2002; Poguntke et al., 2007a, 2007b). What complicates analyses considerably is that Europeanization is only one potential trigger for these types of changes – especially when studying new parties which, in their formative years, are very weakly institutionalized. Taking over legislative office, not to mention executive office, can push parties towards professionalization, more centralized decision-making and more moderate policy positions (Burchell, 2001; Pedahzur & Brichta, 2002; Heinisch, 2003; Bolleyer, 2008). Thus, we are likely to find alternative, 'domestic' and 'European' explanations for the same structural and programmatic outcomes (Poguntke et al., 2007b: 15–16). With this methodological challenge in mind, the following study assesses the organizational and programmatic development of the Irish Green Party.

The Organizational Development of the Irish Greens

In a party's formative years, change tends to be reflected in *organization-building* rather than the *adaptation of a pre-existing organization*. Facing scarce resources, new parties are likely to draw on domestic as well as European resources to build up their infrastructure. This is particularly plausible with respect to the Irish Green Party which initially found more electoral support at the European level than at either the national or local level (Boyle, 2006: 19). In analysing party-building and adaptation, local, national and European elections form windows of opportunity, especially for a little-known and under-resourced party. The multiplicity of arenas increases potential access to urgently-needed resources, be they secretarial support, elected representatives' salaries (which, if donated, can be used to finance the party), or media access. Success in one of these arenas, even if it is considered to be of 'secondary' relevance compared to national parliament (by the public, the party or both) can be used to strengthen the party; congruously, failure can create negative feedback. Thus, it is crucial to consider the domestic and EU level as separate but interlinked arenas. If national rationales dominate the party's organizational development, internal changes should be triggered in the domestic realm, while successes (or failures) at the EU level should play less of a role.

The Initial Years: Protest Against and Learning from Europe

To analyse the organizational responses of the Green Party, we draw on existing case study literature and refer to primary material issued by the party (i.e. statutes and party publications) as well as to interview material.[2]

The Green Party was founded in 1981. It contested its first (*de facto*) election in 1982, but its candidates went forward technically as independents prior to 1984, the year the party formally registered candidates (Whiteman, 1990: 51–53). In 1985 it experienced its first electoral success when a Green candidate was elected to the Killarney Urban District Council (Mc Cluskey, 1992: 16). Nonetheless, the party's resistance to becoming a conventional party was still pronounced, finding expression in a major reorganization in 1983/84 which produced 'Comhaontas Glas/Green Alliance', an alliance of largely autonomous Green groups each of which developed its own structures and policies (Boyle, 2006: 207). This reform shifted the party away from a more centralized decision-making style (initially to meet the requirements of formal party registration) and satisfied more radical groups within the party (e.g. the Rathmines Radicals and the Green Action Now Group (GANG)) which were still very influential at the time.

The Greens were deeply suspicious of Ireland's EU membership. Opposition to the EU as a polity, however, has never implied that the party refused to use resources associated with EU membership. Their emphasis on environmental problems presses Green activists to take an international perspective on policy problems whose solutions often presuppose transnational cooperation. Correspondingly, the first constitutive meeting of the founders of the Ecology Party of Ireland, 3 December 1981, referred in its agenda to the European Green Party manifesto as the accepted basis from which the party's own policy has been derived. While it was the intention to form an explicitly Irish-based organization, the pan-European Greens provided a major orientation. The British Ecology Party and Green parties entering parliaments in, for example, Belgium, also provided important examples for the Irish Green Party. Indeed, the first official Irish Green Party document, 'The Reckoning', was a reprint of a document the British Ecology Party used in their 1981 general election (Boyle, 2006: 26, 35). Irrespective of whether the dominant coalition in the party preferred a more or less decentralized organization, Europe played a role in the organizational formation of the party. In more general terms, the empowerment of European institutions favours the formation and strengthening of pan-European party federations representing particular party families which, later on, can motivate the formation of new parties in the national realm. Such federations facilitate the transfer of knowledge between parties sharing an ideological affiliation across national settings. Throughout their history, the Irish Greens tried to learn from older and more developed Green parties, as seen in the regular visits of foreign Green activists (such as Petra Kelly from the German Greens).

Right from the start, we further observe the endeavour to engage in Green activities on a European scale such as the regular participation of the Irish Greens in the meetings of the European Co-ordination Committee of Green Parties. The links established with the European Federation of Green Parties were to prove a valuable resource of support for this 'party in the making'. Despite severe financial difficulties,[3] the party decided as early as 1983 to pay for a Green representative's trip to attend meetings in Brussels (Boyle, 2006: 33, 50) which indicates the considerable importance of European-wide organizational activities. The Green Party also decided to run in the 1984 European Parliament elections, in line with the pan-European approach being adopted by Greens of various national organizations across Europe pushing for the democratization of the then-EEC (Boyle, 2006: 53–54). While the Greens did not obtain a seat in the European Parliament, their participation represents one of their first experiences in conventional politics and one that was contentious at the time, when being called 'political' was still considered to be an insult in the party.[4]

Getting Established in Europe and at Home

After severe internal struggles within the party, another renaming (to 'Green Party/Comhaontas Glas') in 1988 indicated a final commitment to electoral politics. It followed a split from those radical groups which favoured a more decentralized party active primarily outside the electoral realm (Whiteman, 1990: 52). This step resolved a conflict between 'fundamentalists' and 'realists' in favour of the latter – an outcome in line with developments in a range of other Green parties in Europe. While some critical voices are still heard in the party today, the increasing electoral success of the party clearly reinforced the decision to get involved in professional politics. In 1989 the first was elected to the Dáil and this was followed in 1994 by the election of two Green Members of European Parliament (MEPs). In 1997 Trevo Sargent was joined by John Gormley, a second Green representative, and the two MEPs succeeded in holding their seats in 1999.

This strengthening was accompanied by the move towards an intra-organizational hierarchy. While the party had already shifted from pure consensus to majority decisions in the 1990s, one core step in 2001 was the selection of a formal leader (as well as a deputy leader and a secretary general). Such a proposal was long-resisted by strong internal opposition against the institutionalization of a leader able to restrict the activities of ordinary members. In the end a special convention in Kilkenny in 2001 elected Trevor Sargent, the second Green Teachta Dála (TD) to enter the Dáil, as the formal leader. This step initiated the creation of a power base rooted in the – however small – party in public office. Soon after his election in 1992, it became clear that Sargent (to a greater extent than Roger Garland (the first Green TD)) was driven by getting re-elected; for example, Sargent held constituency clinics and attempted to meet the needs of his constituents. A support team began to develop around him and his Fingal Green Group became the most effective political machine in the party (Boyle, 2006: 116). This development reflects a common organizational pattern in the established Irish political parties whose structures evolve around individual incumbents and are directed towards maintaining their personal support (Bolleyer, 2009) – a structure that notably conflicts with Green egalitarian ideals.

It was also Sargent (later Minister of State at the Department of Agriculture, Fisheries and Food) who, in his inaugural speech in the Dáil in 1992, publicly announced the Green Party's governmental ambitions. Government aspirations intensified over the years and were internally debated and most visible when Green ministers from Germany and Finland shared their experiences at party conventions (Boyle, 2006: 188). This occurred in a structural context in which the pressure to enter national government is particularly pronounced and associated with an interest in policy influence: policy-making power is monopolized by the executive, while the parliamentary channels for opposition influence are particularly weak (Bolleyer & Weeks, 2009).

To achieve this goal, the two TDs initiated organizational reforms indicating the linchpin position of the party in public office. Before the 2002 election a policy was adopted to target the strongest constituencies, indicating the party's increasing professionalization. Following the election of six Green TDs, the party could rely on extra resources such as a parliamentary group secretary, the leader's allowance as well as voluntary contributions of parts of TDs' salaries to the party organization, compensating for its rejection of corporate donations and its rather modest access to membership fees. After 2002, reform processes were most intense. They initiated the streamlining of decision-making processes to allow for faster decisions on behalf of party elites but which complicated communication with the grass-roots. A separate communications officer was appointed next to the existing press officer and the party started to organize its annual conference as a major event. In short, the party's growing parliamentary strength and its increasingly professionalized parliamentarians facilitated the Green Party's transformation into a serious candidate for government – both in size and personnel capacities.

Europeanization or Domestic Pressure?

While it has been argued that Europeanization can be a trigger for centralization and professionalization (i.e. Bomberg, 2002; Poguntke, 2007a, 2007b), there are no indications that this factor played a decisive or immediate role in the formalization of the leadership in 2001 or the internal reforms after 2002. The party elite was eager to run elections successfully – in whatever arena – which made the formal nomination of a leader as the party's public face a rational move. In terms of primary goals, the Green Party wanted to get into power in the national realm since electorally-salient issues are still decided there. Environmental issues were less crucial in rural Irish society than in other European countries, and the Greens became aware of this when experiencing initial electoral drawbacks. As a response, they started to focus on core issues such as tax policy that is decided 'at home'. The party created a Spokesperson for European Affairs only in 2004, when both MEPs failed to be re-elected, which is an indication of the limited priority of EU-related issues in the daily business of the party (in comparison, the first paid administrator was hired for the party's national office in 1997, as was the first appointed press officer).

Despite the party's strategic focus on the national arena, it is important to note that the organization profited from benefits linked to public office at both the national and European level. By 1994, the Green Party had two elected representatives in Dáil Éireann and two members of the European Parliament. Until the breakthrough of six Green TDs at the 2002 general election, the numbers of national and European office-holders was the same. Each additional seat won by the party was of tremendous importance in indicating its sustainability in Irish politics. The media described the entry of the Greens to the Dáil in 1989 as a mere 'accident' (Boyle, 2006). However, their presence in an additional electoral arena, namely Europe, was a means of fighting this impression.

In the European Parliament, the Greens showed considerable continuity: the same Green MEPs, Nuala Ahern and Patricia McKenna, were in office for a period of ten years (losing their seats in the 2004 elections). The two MEPs assured the party's presence on the European level and removed the national party from the need to deal with the EU. This situation, however, was portrayed by various interviewees less as a 'division of labour' than as a lack of interest by the national party. This was less affordable when the seats in the European Parliament were lost and, even more so, when the Greens entered government and their ministers started to participate in EU decision-making. What is interesting to note is that the MEPs' increasing familiarity with the EU over these 10 years did not shift their attitudes in more pro-European directions. In 2008, Patricia McKenna became active in the People's Movement, which successfully campaigned for the rejection of the Lisbon Treaty after a majority of party members had embraced the treaty in January that same year. Previous to 2004, positions on European treaties were strongly shaped by Green MEPs, the continuous presence of one strongly Euro-sceptic Green MEP is more likely to have supported EU-scepticism on the party level than having triggered any learning effects leading to a more pro-European stance.

In sum, the party's orientation has shifted away from protest to conventional political participation – a shift that found expression in a variety of organizational changes which produced greater professionalization and centralization in line with the literature on the evolution of new parties (e.g. Burchell, 2009; Deschouwer, 2008). While the party profited from Europe in terms of resources and expertise, its primary goal did not change as a consequence of Europeanization but was driven by shifting coalitions within the party: more radical groups left in protest when the party engaged in conventional politics, while party elites ambitious to access power in the national arena gained increasing significance and coined the evolution of the party organization.

Programmatic Changes

This section analyses the programmatic changes of the Green Party from the year when the Greens took up legislative office in Ireland (1989). In drawing on manifestos, speeches in the Dáil and secondary literature, we map the Green Party's stance towards local democracy and decentralization of power, the relevance of environmental policies relative to other issues, and the positions towards the European Community/European Union as articulated in the national arena, the focal point of the Green Party's strategic orientations.[5]

Winning a Dáil seat in the 1989 general election was the Green Party's first national electoral success. At that time, their manifesto and politics put a strong emphasis on environmental issues and on local democracy – the two programmatic cores of Green parties more generally (Girvin, 1990: 17; Whiteman, 1990: 52, 56; Garland, *Dáil Debates* 408, 14 May 1991). The Green Party put forward post-materialist positions, criticizing Irish society as being too oriented towards economic welfare (Garland, *Dáil Debates* 395, 14 February 1990). As a result of this mix of policies, the Irish Green Party's position towards European integration gained its ambivalent character. On the one hand, the EU engaged in environmental policy even before the Single European Act formerly transferred these competences to the European level in 1986. Since environmental problems often require international solutions and can be tackled more effectively on a higher level than the state, and since the EU was active in this field, one would expect a favourable Green Party position towards the EU. But, on the other hand, the Green Party's emphasis on local democracy and citizen participation still appeared to conflict with the shift of policy-making competences to Brussels. In line with the latter, the Green Party was against European integration, mainly due to fears about the centralization of competencies in a 'superstate' and the move of policy-making away from the local level (Bomberg, 2002: 34).

Between 1992 and 1997, the Green Party manifesto and policies were post-materialist and favoured ecological issues and local democracy, while opposing (growth of) the industrial system (Girvin, 1993: 15; Sargent, *Dáil Debates* 432, 9 June 1993). Aspirations of environmental protection ranked high on the agenda of the Green Party and encompassed an internationalist as well as a European element (Sargent, *Dáil Debates* 434, 15 October 1993 and 454, 8 June 1995). However, when realizing these issues' limited electoral relevance at home, the Green Party started to concentrate more and more on domestic issues. This included themes such as local democracy and materialist concerns such as child care and pensions. Issues, such as citizen participation, local democracy and post-materialist sketches of Irish society and economy became less important (Marks, Wilson & Ray, 2002: 587; Collins, 2003: 33; Sargent, *Dáil Debates* 843, 27 November 1997 and 502, 25 March 1999). Nonetheless, the incompatibility of the local democracy ideal with the nature of EU-governance still generated a rather sceptical position on European integration:

> there is growing disenchantment with the direction Europe is taking. The centralisation of power will lead to a power vacuum, leading in turn to an emergence of right wing groups and greater political instability. The democratic deficit has not been addressed and ordinary Europeans feel alienated from the decision making process. Many who voted for the EEC do not want a federal Europe. (Gormley, *Dáil Debates* 492, 23 June 1998)

Also in this period, the Greens frequently referred to the EU as a centralized 'superstate' (e.g. Gormley, *Dáil Debates* 489, 1 April 1998). When Ireland held the referendum on the Nice Treaty in 2001, the Green Party (as well as Sinn Féin) campaigned for a No vote (Murphy, 2003: 15) from which the party benefited domestically. At the second referendum on the Nice Treaty in October 2002, the party again campaigned for a No vote and benefited: an *Irish Times* TNS/MRBI poll showed that the party's public support had increased and in fact doubled since the general elections four months earlier (Boyle, 2006: 174).

Throughout 2002–2007, programmatic changes continued. Local democracy and post-materialism lost further importance, positions on subsidiarity and environmental protection became less relevant and the stance towards European integration increasingly positive (e.g. Gormley & Boyle, *Dáil Debates* 588, 7 July 2004; Cuffe, *Dáil Debates* 611, 29 November 2005 and 631, 8 February 2007; Ryan, *Dáil Debates* 611, 29 November 2005 and 625, 10 October 2006). The Green Party moved from Euroscepticism towards neutrality and eventually strong support (in particular concerning EU environmental legislation which the party portrayed increasingly positively, c.f. Green Party, 2004: 4). Reflecting this development, the debate became more fine-grained and focused on what type of European Union could be desirable:

> The question we must ask ourselves from the outset is, to what type of Europe do we aspire? I aspire to a Europe which is ecologically sustainable ... Likewise, we aspire to a Europe that is nuclear free ... I also aspire to a democratic Europe and a Europe that treats its citizens and states equally. (Gormley, *Dáil Debates* 572, 15 October 2003)

Furthermore, the Green Party developed a strong interest in democratizing the EU and made constructive proposals how this could be done (i.e. Gormley, *Dáil Debates* 558, 28 November 2002 and 582, 30 March 2004). Hence, the Green Party engaged increasingly in proposals for shaping EU policies instead of merely critiquing them, although the Greens still advocated subsidiarity and the primacy of the local level:

> The Green Party is always concerned when it sees power drifting upwards. One of the more important issues in a democracy is that the representatives of that democracy do their utmost to ensure that power is exercised at the lowest effective level. (Cuffe, *Dáil Debates* 631, 8 February 2007)

But now they conceded that some policies are better dealt with at the national level, others at the European level (Cuffe, *Dáil Debates* 631, 8 February 2007; Green Party, 2004: 4, 13; Green Party, 2007: 6–9, 33).

The manifesto for the 2007 Irish general election continued the line of programmatic changes that started in 1997, according to which the goals of participatory democracy, post-materialist societal values and, to some extent, even environmental protection lose relative importance, while references to the EU become increasingly positive (e.g. Budge *et al.*, 2001; Klingemann *et al.*, 2006). The manifesto downgrades environmental politics and even places local government at its very end.[6] On top of this, the Green Party explicitly committed itself to the EU. It proclaimed to be a pro-European party and a proud and active member of the European Greens, actively forging closer ties to its sister parties throughout Europe and at the European level (Green Party, 2007: 32). The support for the Constitutional Treaty and the opposition to a referendum correspond with the party's programmatic transformation.

National Manoeuvring, EU Influence or Both?

After 2002 the Green Party increased in size to six TDs.[7] Aspirations to government thereby became more realistic, giving the party a major push to change as evident in the organizational reforms laid out above. Programmatic changes are also likely to be driven by this motivation. The preparations for the Irish EU Presidency of 2004 created an additional boost of EU support among the main political parties since it considerably increased Irish involvement in EU affairs. This development facilitated the Green Party's programmatic reorientation, especially in the light of its intensifying aspiration to become an acceptable coalition partner.

Long-term changes in the party policy and programme, in particular in the field of local democracy slowly increased the compatibility of the Green Party's core policies and the implications of European integration. The Green Party put less emphasis on participatory democracy and local level issues relative to other aspects more crucial to the domestic electorate in an attempt to increase its support at home. The fact that EU membership requires the transfer and pooling of competencies at the European level, far away from the citizen, became therefore less critical for the party.

At the European level, major events do not coincide with the Green Party's programmatic shift which reinforces the role of domestic rationales. EC summits and intergovernmental conferences such as Maastricht, Amsterdam and Nice did not consistently provoke programmatic changes of the Green Party towards either stronger EU opposition or support. The Greens were relatively oblivious towards the Maastricht Treaty and the saliency of European issues did not increase, since the Green Party neither explicitly welcomed nor explicitly criticized the 1993 reforms of the European Union. By contrast, the Treaty of Amsterdam fostered Green Party opposition, although this was strengthened further during the debate about the Treaty of Nice in 2001 (Murphy, 2003: 15). Unlike these events, the European Convention and the intergovernmental conferences in 2003 and 2004 on the Constitutional Treaty went hand in hand with increasing numbers of positive statements by the Green Party towards the EU.

In 2003, the EU Convention on the Future of Europe was in the final stage of its deliberations on a future constitutional treaty for Europe. At this time, John Gormley, who participated in the European Convention, welcomed democratic elements in the draft Constitutional Treaty, expressed their strong support for achieving more democracy via the convention method (*Dáil Debates* 572: 974–977, 15 October 2003) and even went so far as to argue that a 'constitution for Europe is not only necessary but desirable' (Dáil Debates 610: 1579, 23 November 2005). Gormley was positive about the Convention's democratic deliberative potential and its aim of bringing Europe closer to the citizens (*Dáil Debates* 559, 17 December 2002 and 566, 8 May 2003). Although Gormley criticized specific aspects of the Constitutional Treaty (e.g. regarding the role of an elected EU president, see *Dáil Debates* 572, 15 October 2003), the deliberative procedures of the Convention, some outcomes (i.e., citizens' initiative, transparency of Council meetings, more democracy, fundamental rights) and inclusive ratification procedures fitted nicely with the direct democratic approach of the Green Party (*Dáil Debates* 610, 23 November 2003).

Shift towards Moderate Support for the EU

While domestic calculus clearly played its part in motivating the Green Party's programmatic reorientation, the European Convention helped to reduce the programmatic misfit between Green values and the EU. This development facilitated a programmatic shift from Euroscepticism towards moderate EU-support. Official support for the Lisbon Treaty by Green Party members in 2008 reinforces this interpretation. Over time, the Green Party shifted towards a more differentiated and more positive judgment of the EU. After 2003, the party hardly ever applied the old, simplistic frame of the EU as a centralized superstate thought to be incompatible with local democracy. Their criticisms became less fundamental and much more refined in subsequent years. Agreement with major goals put forward by the Convention made it easier for the Greens to take a much more constructive approach to European integration and reform. At the same time, the incremental down-grading of local democracy and citizen's participation in Green Party manifestos and policies since 1997 decreased the mismatch between Green core values and the EU. Aspirations of the Green Party to participate in government (intensified by the 2002 electoral success, and realized in 2007) and the pro-EU boost associated with the Irish Presidency in 2004 further motivated a shift towards a pro-EU stance.

Analysing the Dáil debates after the Green Party came into government, it is striking that party members hardly participated in debates on the European Union in general and the Lisbon Treaty in particular (see Quinlan, 2009). Green TDs did not endorse the institutional reform of the European Union and its associated procedural, policy-related changes contained in Lisbon. This is, however, not a consequence of governmental participation or the reflection of another programmatic shift, but in all likelihood a result of the membership poll on the Lisbon Treaty in January 2008 which produced 63 percent in favour of the treaty.[8] Interviewees explain this vote with reference to a generational change: younger Green members are more pragmatic and less sceptical towards Europe. Furthermore, the poll's result was welcomed at the elite level. Programmatically the party had moved towards a more pro-European position already but, more importantly, it by then governed with Fianna Fáil and the Progressive Democrats, two Europe-friendly parties.[9] It is most likely that the pro-EU effects of generational changes were reinforced by the decision to time a membership poll once in government. Yet while 63 percent support was a success for pro-European Greens, the two-thirds majority required by the party constitution to formulate and pass an official pro-European party policy was missed. Consequently, the Greens as a party could not officially participate in a pro-Lisbon campaign. So, while some Green activists as individuals (not as party representatives) campaigned against Lisbon, Green TDs and Senators favoured the Lisbon Treaty (De Búrca, 2008; Green Party, 2008), as one would expect given the government constellation. This makes all the more sense given that Green ministers by now regularly participate in EU decision-making.

Conclusions

As we have seen in the analysis, the European level provided access to resources for the Green Party but also an opportunity structure to gain political experience for its candidates. In a unitary system such as Ireland's, the EU level plays a similar role to that of the regional level in federal systems, which often functions as a 'stepping stone' for new parties eager to enter public office on the national level. This impact cannot be underestimated as the party suffered severely from a lack of resources before 1997. Until then funding provisions discriminated against minor parties (Murphy & Farrell, 2002: 227–229). Overall, the party's orientation has shifted away from protest to conventional political participation. This shift in its primary goal is, however, not a consequence of Europeanization but of strategic calculations in the national arena. This shift found expression in a variety of organizational changes which produced greater professionalization and centralization. Regarding the more general debate on the Europeanization of political parties, our analysis of the Europeanization of the Irish Green Party suggests that scholars need to look very carefully at 'rival' domestic pressures which might constitute major drives for developments which are otherwise read as 'European impacts'. This holds true at least for those parties which consider electoral success at the national level as their primary target, which is clearly the case for the Irish Greens as for most other parties in Europe.[10] And as long as European Parliament elections function as 'second order' elections, this orientation is likely to remain dominant, an interpretation supported by recent findings on the (rather limited) adaptation of national parties in Europe to Europeanization pressures (Ladrech, 2007; Poguntke et al., 2007b). The Greens' fate during the 2009 European Parliament elections substantiates this point. The party won only 1.9 percent of the first preference vote and did not secure a seat (the party also lost all 10 of its councillors in Greater Dublin in the local election contest which was held simultaneously). Both European and local election results are widely read as a punishment for the ruling Fianna Fáil–Green government.[11]

Europe itself did not change the party's goal orientation; it served as one means to achieve whatever goal was dominant at a given time and thus functioned as an opportunity structure. It can also be a source of vulnerability whenever voters use the EU as an outlet for their disappointments with national politics. Just to mention one example, we observe the introduction of a Spokesperson for European Affairs when the party lost its representation at the EU level in 2004, an event which forced the national party to deal with EU-related issues itself. This also came in a phase during which the party already considered itself as a potential coalition partner, a role which increases the necessity to deal with European matters much more than the opposition status. Both observations imply that this move was a functional and strategic response rather than the expression of a socialization process triggered by European influences.

Simultaneously, programmatic changes concerning societal values, citizens' participation as well as changes at the EU level affected the programmatic stance of the Irish Greens towards European integration. The European Convention strengthened participatory democratic values and resonated well with Green values. Also, the Green Party had incrementally downgraded direct democratic measures and post-materialist conceptions of society vis-à-vis other policies with greater domestic relevance in the last decade. This lessened the tension between the distant EU and the Green local democracy ideal and reduced the programmatic mismatch of the Irish Greens and European policies. Together these developments facilitated a programmatic shift of the Irish Green Party towards EU support in early 2003 which led to constructive proposals towards shaping European institutions and policies,[12] rather than generally opposing the EU as an undemocratic, centralized super-state. That the Convention moved the EU closer to Green ideals clearly added to this process. One Green Party official, in an interview with an author of this article, outlines the Green Party's current attitude towards the EU:

> We are comfortable with the EU level. It is an opportunity structure. The EU complements our domestic policy since EU policies have always been aligned to ours. (Green Party official I, face-to-face interview, Dublin, 2 April 2008)

This position is the result of a long-lasting process driven by strategic calculus most fundamentally directed towards assuring the survival of this new party – a calculus naturally shaped by domestic pressures. It is also the result of a learning process bringing the party and the EU closer together. Yet when it comes to new parties which still struggle to get established, domestic pressures naturally prevail since it is there that the major resources for political parties are still allocated. Accordingly, to understand the major rationale of organizational and programmatic change in new parties, we clearly should not ignore Europe, but neither should we overestimate its effects.

To conclude, the literature on the Europeanization of political parties expects a moderation of EU-critical stances over time (e.g. Bomberg, 2002; Ladrech, 2002): a hypothesis that our findings confirm in principle. At the same time, however, we have noted that the Greens and the EU moved towards each other – a finding which supports an 'interactive perspective' on Europeanization (Olsen, 2002) rather than a top-down process (driven by the European level) or a bottom-up process (exclusively driven by the domestic level). Since the foundation of the Green Party, the democratization of the EU has become a common demand articulated by many political parties (not only those with strong participatory traditions like the Greens). Accordingly, recent EU reforms, especially the EU Convention on the Future of Europe, have made it easier for the Green Party to accept European integration without causing overt conflict with their democratic ideals. Simultaneously, the Greens have become more pragmatic – prioritizing the policy gains that the EU can bring (e.g. in environmental policy) over an insistence on local democracy. This pragmatism was fuelled by the domestic need to broaden the party's profile in order to increase its electoral appeal. Arguably, even the party's original opposition to the EU was not solely ideological. As long as it was still playing the role of a principled opposition party, the electoral benefits of opposing EU treaties paid off. Once it attempted to become part of the established elite and entered government, a more moderate approach proved beneficial.

Acknowledgements

The authors are thankful for helpful suggestions of the editors and of the participants of the PSAI conference 'Party Politics and the EU' on 28 April 2008, Institute for International and European Affairs, Dublin. They also thank the Green Party office in Dublin which allowed them to access their archive and numerous interviewees. Parts of the research for this article have been conducted in the context of a project funded by the British Academy on the 'The Organisation of New Parties in Western Europe' run at the University of Exeter (October 2008–October 2009).

Notes

1. Note that the Progressive Democrats was officially dissolved as a party in July 2009.
2. Private, semi-structured interviews have been conducted in 2008 and 2009 with Green Party officials, TDs, party staff and experts (journalists and academics).
3. The capacity of the Greens to raise money was very limited. The party does not receive trade union or business donations, and private funding tends to be small scale and from collections or social events. Even this source of revenue can create internal difficulties, since local groups have been known to refuse to engage in fundraising methods if they consider them 'un-green', thus further restricting the potential to generate party income (Mc Cluskey, 1992: 38–39). This situation could only improve with electoral success.
4. For instance, some groups refused the label 'party' as part of the Green Alliance's official name.
5. While many analyses in party research draw on the data from the manifesto data project to trace programmatic change, we found it more insightful to refer to Dáil speeches as a major source to capture the public position-taking of the party over time. To back up this analysis, however, where possible, we refer to the manifesto data. It also shows that the Green Party became less Eurosceptic over time.
6. It covers 23 issues in its summary, starting with energy, transport, housing, child care, health, education, tax social welfare, crime, and road safety. Only then, is environmental protection listed (Green Party, 2007: 4–5).
7. While Trevor Sargent and John Gormley had been the only Green TDs in the legislative period starting in 1997, they were joined by Dan Boyle, Éamon Ryan, Ciarán Cuffe and Paul Gogarty in 2002.

8. See www.europeangreens.org/cms/default/dok/216/216162.63_of_irish_greens_vote_in_favour_of_eu, accessed July 2009.
9. For example, Senator de Búrca stated that: 'The result of today's Special Convention explodes the myth that the Green Party is anti-European. 63 percent of party members voted to support the Lisbon Treaty' (Green Party, 2008). John Gormley, Party Leader and Environment Minister, argued 'This is a historic day for the Green Party. I believe that our conception of, and approach to, Europe has been updated to reflect what our parliamentary party thinks, and what the majority of our councillors and members think. The large majority of Green Party members have endorsed the view of the Party's Leadership' (Green Party, 2008).
10. Exceptions might be those parties that are found by MEPs to push for more transparency in the EU, such as the 'Hans-Peter Martin's List – for genuine control and transparency in Brussels' which won one Austrian seat at the 2009 European Parliament elections, or parties which deliberately do not run at national elections such as the Eurosceptic Danish 'June Movement' which was dissolved after failing to win a seat at the 2009 elections.
11. Fianna Fáil gained just 23 percent of the first-preference vote in the June 2009 elections to the European Parliament.
12. For example, the 2007 manifesto even goes beyond environmental issues and states that the Greens seek to 'press for the EU's competition, state aid and public procurement policies to be adapted to include social and ecological factors' (Green Party, 2007: 33).

References

Bomberg, E. (2002) The Europeanization of Green parties: exploring the EU's impact, *West European Politics:* 25(3), pp. 29–50.

Bolleyer, N. (2008) The organisational costs of public office, in: K. Deschouwer (Ed.) *New Parties in Government, In Power for the First time*, pp. 17–41 (London: Routledge).

Bolleyer, N. (2009) Inside the cartel party: party organization in government and opposition, *Political Studies*, 57(3), pp. 559–579.

Bolleyer, N. & Weeks, L. (2009, forthcoming) The puzzle of non-party actors in party democracy: independents in Ireland, *Comparative European Politics*, 7(4), pp. 299–324.

Boyle, D. (2006) *A Journey to Change: 25 Years of the Green Party in Irish Politics* (Dublin: Nonsuch Publishing).

Budge, I., Klingemann, H.D., Volkens, A., Bara, J. & Tanebaum, E. (2001) *Mapping Policy Preferences. Estimates for Parties, Electors, and Governments 1945–1998* (Oxford: Oxford University Press).

Burchell, J. (2001) Evolving or conforming? Assessing organisational reform within European Green parties, *West European Politics*, 24(3), pp. 113–134.

Collins, S. (2003) Campaign strategies, in: M. Gallagher, M. Marsh & P. Mitchell (Eds) *How Ireland Voted 2002*, pp. 21–36 (New York: Palgrave).

De Burca, D. (2008) Green TDs and senators back EU Treaty 'yes' vote, Statement issued on 15 January 2008, available at: www.greenparty.ie/en/news/latest_news/green_tds_and_senators_back_eu_treaty_yes_vote (accessed July 2009).

Deschouwer, K. (Ed.) (2008) *New Parties in Government: In Power for the First Time* (London: Routledge).

Girvin, B. (1990) The campaign, in: M. Gallagher & R. Sinnott (Eds) *How Ireland Voted 1989*, pp. 5–22 (Galway: PSAI Press).

Girvin, B. (1993) The road to the election, in: M. Gallagher & M. Laver (Eds) *How Ireland Voted 1992*, pp. 1–20 (Galway: PSAI Press).

Green Party (2004) *Manifesto 2004: European and Local Elections* (Dublin: Green Party).

Green Party (2007) *Manifesto 2007: It's Time* (Dublin: Green Party).

Green Party (2008) Majority of Greens back Lisbon Treaty, Statement issued on 19 January 2008, available at: www.greenparty.ie/en/news/latest_news/majority_of_greens_back_lisbon_treaty (accessed July 2009).

Heinisch, R. (2003) Success in opposition – failure in government: explaining the performance of right-wing populist parties in public office, *West European Politics*, 26(3), pp. 91–130.

Klingemann, H.D., Volkens, A., Bara, J., Budge, I. & MacDonald, M. (2006) *Mapping Policy Preferences II. Estimates for Parties, Electors, and Governments in Eastern Europe, the European Union and the OECD, 1990–2003* (Oxford: Oxford University Press).

Ladrech, R. (2002) Europeanization and political parties: towards a framework for analysis, *Party Politics*, 8(4), pp. 389–403.

Ladrech, R. (2007) Europeanization and national party organization: limited but appropriate adaptation?, in: T. Poguntke, N. Aylott, E. Carter, R. Ladrech & K.R. Luther (Eds) *The Europeanization of National Political Parties: Power and Organizational Adaptation*, pp. 211–229 (London: Routledge).

Marks, G., Wilson, C.J. & Ray, L. (2002) National political parties and European integration, *American Journal of Political Science*, 46(3), pp. 585–594.

Mc Cluskey, F. (1992) Organisation as ends: Comhaontas Glas observed, Unpublished MA thesis, University College Dublin.

Murphy, G. (2003) The background to the election, in: M. Gallagher, M. Marsh & P. Mitchell (Eds) *How Ireland Voted 2002*, pp. 1–20 (New York: Palgrave).

Murphy, R. & Farrell, D. (2002) Party politics in Ireland: regularizing a volatile system, in: P. Webb, D. Farrell & I. Holliday (Eds) *Political Parties in Advanced Industrial Democracies*, pp. 217–247 (Oxford: Oxford University Press).

Olsen, J.P. (2002) The many faces of Europeanization, *Journal of Common Market Studies*, 40(5), pp. 921–950.

Pedahzur, A. & Brichta, A. (2002) The institutionalization of extreme right-wing charismatic parties: a paradox?, *Party Politics*, 8(1), pp. 31–49.

Poguntke, T., Aylott, N., Ladrech, R. & Luther, K.R. (2007a) The Europeanization of national party organisations: a conceptual analyis, *European Journal of Political Research*, 46(4), pp. 747–771.

Poguntke, T., Aylott, N., Carter, E., Ladrech, R. & Luther, K.R. (Eds) (2007b) *The Europeanization of National Political Parties: Power and Organizational Adaptation* (London: Routledge).

Quinlan, S. (2009) The Lisbon Treaty Referendum 2008, *Irish Political Studies*, 24(1), pp. 107–121.

Whiteman, D. (1990) The progress and potential of the Green Party in Ireland, *Irish Political Studies*, 1, pp. 45–58.

Sinn Féin's Approach to the EU: Still More 'Critical' than 'Engaged'?

AGNÈS MAILLOT
Dublin City University, Ireland

ABSTRACT *Sinn Féin's relationship with the European Union has changed significantly since the late 1990s. The party has moved from a position of outright opposition to European integration to one of 'critical engagement'. This has been embodied most clearly in its campaigning (and growing success) in European Parliament elections and referendums on European treaties. The degree to which this constitutes a process of Europeanization of the party is tempered, however, by the motivations for this shift in policy, which are closely related to the party's electoral and political strategies in both parts of Ireland. Moreover, the party's cautious engagement with the EU is predicated on a careful presentation of itself as a resolutely republican and left-wing party. The role it plays in European elections and referendums, therefore, is a self-consciously independent and oppositional one. The Europeanization of the party is clearly shaped by the motives, context and dynamics of the domestic arena as much as the European one. This is exemplified in the* de facto *prioritizing of the 'critical' over the 'engaged' elements in Sinn Féin's approach to European integration.*

Introduction

Sinn Féin has experienced what might be described as a process of partial Europeanization. The party has moved from a position of consistent opposition to Ireland's membership of the then European Economic Community (EEC) to one of critical acceptance of the European Union (EU) and a willingness to contest European elections and fight EU referendum campaigns. According to the criteria set out by Ladrech (2002), Sinn Féin's engagement with and acknowledgement of the EU has increased with reference to its political programmes and policies. The EU has also been a basis on which to compete with other parties in the Republic of Ireland, most notably in the context of the Nice I and II and Lisbon Treaty referendum campaigns. Furthermore, the party has nurtured formal links with other political parties outside of Ireland, through its alliance with the European United Left parliamentary group (Gauche unitaire européenne/Nordic Green Left, or GUE/NGL).

Sinn Féin's discourse and strategy regarding European affairs have experienced, as in many other areas, significant change in the past three decades. Outright opposition to what was termed 'the rich club' in the early 1970s has now been replaced with a pragmatic view of what the EU can contribute to Ireland in general and to the party in particular. There are still remnants of traditional republican rhetoric in the new discourse on EU membership, mostly on issues of neutrality and sovereignty which remain at the core of Sinn Féin's main objections to the European project. The party has developed this changed discourse in the context of an EU electoral strategy which has allowed it to increase its profile, north and south, and appeal to a particular electoral base. Sinn Féin's movement towards engagement with the EU is founded in recognition of the capacity of the EU as an arena and as an issue to offer electoral opportunities for the party.

This article analyses what prompted a change of attitude in Irish republican political strategy from unambiguous opposition to the EU towards what the party now labels 'critical engagement'.[1] This question is addressed by firstly examining what formed the basis for Sinn Féin's opposition to the then EEC. Then examination of Sinn Féin's electoral and campaigning records demonstrates how the party's discourse and strategies regarding the EU have evolved over time. Finally, this article will assess Sinn Féin's current engagement with the EU and suggest that it is based on a willingness to capitalize on the opportunities offered by politicizing the EU project.

The Traditional Roots of Sinn Féin's Opposition to European Integration

No to the Imperialist Club

Sinn Féin's predictions for the future of Ireland within a European Community were wholly negative. The party equated membership of the EEC with economic disaster and imperialist threat for the whole island from an early stage: 'Free State and British sponsored industries ... are being run down as a result of EEC directives and imperial economic penetration' (Sinn Féin, 1979). Its response was unique among Irish political parties and reflected its experience as a grassroots oppositional movement: it advocated (in the 1979 *Éire Nua* document, an update of the 1971 *Éire Nua, the Social and Economic Dimensions*) a campaign of economic resistance to counter the effects of European integration, calling on Irish people:

> pending Ireland's withdrawal from the EEC, to resist the implementation of any decrees or policies of the Common Market which would be detrimental to the best interests of our people or any section of it.

This call was reminiscent of Arthur Griffith's economic resistance campaign in the early twentieth century, which promoted a policy of 'buying Irish' in order to increase the chances of economic independence. Moreover, the anticipation here that Ireland would withdraw from the EEC echoes the expectation of territorial reunification in Article 3 of *Bunreacht na hÉireann* (the Irish Constitution), i.e. a matter of nationalist idealism rather than political realism. Such 'gesture' rhetoric served to keep Sinn Féin supporters aware of a purported connection between traditional Irish republicanism and opposition to the EEC. Although for the most part the party's energies were at that time channelled elsewhere, namely into local concerns arising from the conflict in Northern Ireland, keeping a political mantra on Irish national sovereignty consistent across Sinn Féin's domestic and foreign policy was a core party strategy.

Defending Neutrality and Sovereignty

Sinn Féin's early foreign policy was predicated upon a binary opposition made between rich countries – those belonging to the EEC, the North Atlantic Treaty Organization (NATO), the Warsaw Pact, to any alliance from which the party sought to distance itself at all costs – and poor, developing, non-aligned countries. Republicans argued that Ireland had stronger affinities with the latter than with the countries which constituted the then EEC. The early Sinn Féin policy document, *Éire Nua*, originally published in June 1971, contained a section devoted to the EEC, in which the party claimed that membership would entail the loss of sovereignty and economic disaster. This remained Sinn Féin's position for a number of years, and was restated in the updated policy document *Éire Nua: the Economic and Social Dimensions* (1979):

> We have more in common with the developing countries of the world (where two-thirds of the world's population live) than we have with the rich club of former colonial powers in the EEC.

To this was added the unswerving belief in neutrality and independence in Irish foreign policy,[2] which was deemed the only viable position for Ireland to take in the international arena for two reasons.

First, Irish neutrality was presented as a guarantee that Ireland would remain outside any military alliance, such as NATO. Such a policy position was considered to be in line with the aspirations of the First Dáil and the Second Dáil which had such significance for Sinn Féin's political legacy. Secondly, this was coupled with a strong stance on national sovereignty. Sinn Féin's interpretations of sovereignty were also historically-rooted, in this case on the 1919 Democratic Programme of the First Dáil Éireann and on Patrick Pearse's declaration that, 'the nation's sovereignty extends not only to all men and women of the nation, but to all its material possessions'. Pearse's declaration was quoted in the 1979 *Éire Nua* document as the cornerstone of Sinn Féin's policy on sovereignty. This party policy is twofold: 'Freedom denotes separation and sovereignty', and 'The national sovereignty implied in national freedom holds good both externally and internally, i.e. the sovereign rights of the nation are good as against all other nations and good as against all parts of the nation'.

Neutrality and sovereignty have remained consistent themes in Sinn Féin's discourse on foreign affairs and, therefore, on European integration. As Mary Lou McDonald, Sinn Féin's spokesperson on European Affairs and Member of European Parliament (MEP) from 2004 to 2009, elaborates in relation to the former:

> What's good about Irish neutrality is how we came to be neutral. It's our own experience as a nation and a people, of those who have been colonized, of those who have been oppressed, those who have suffered from imperialism. (Interview with author, Sinn Féin officer, Dublin, June 2003)

Seen through this prism, any concerted EU foreign policy is deemed dangerous: the EU rapid reaction force is described as an 'army designed for war', and leads to the cancellation of the prerequisite UN mandate for military operation. The Seville Declaration signed in the aftermath of the Nice I referendum, far from assuaging Sinn Féin's fears in this respect, consolidated them, as it was seen as mere 'political statements, not protocols' (*An Phoblacht*, 10 October 2002). Interestingly, research commissioned by the Irish Government after the Lisbon referendum to investigate the reasons for voting 'No' found that among the main concerns was the possibility of conscription into a European army (*Irish Times*, 10 September 2008). Although this is not contained in the treaty, it shows that the type of discourse that Sinn Féin presents on some issues reflects the concerns of some voters. Indeed, the party has always sought to be considered the guardian of principles which have traditionally been seen to be deeply cherished by the Irish people themselves.

The 'traditionalist' connection between Irish nationalism and independence and Sinn Féin's foreign policy, i.e. the integrity of the nation-state, is the centre point of the party's criticisms of the EU. For example, Alex Maskey (2003), Sinn Féin Member of the Legislative Assembly (MLA) and former Lord Mayor of Belfast, claimed that:

> like [Wolfe] Tone, we also value Irish sovereignty and independence and we say that the basis for democracy and the basis for peaceful co-operation and mutual respect between nations is the democratic nation-state. Sinn Féin believes that too much of our sovereignty has already been ceded to EU institutions.

This enabled the party to present itself as the only defender of Irish interests in that specific – and, to some voters, crucial – respect. But Sinn Féin's discourse on sovereignty – and the threat posed to it by European integration – was not without its irony, as pointed out by Frampton (2005: 237):

> Given, then, that republicans had typically viewed sovereignty in absolute terms (there was no question of them seeing the Southern state as some kind of 'semi-sovereign' entity), there was a perversity in the claim that joining the EEC would result in a loss of sovereignty.

Nevertheless, at this point, Sinn Féin's policy on the EEC was not anticipated to be a topic of detailed debate either inside or outside the party. The lines clearly and thickly drawn between Irish nationalism and opposition to the EEC by Sinn Féin were shaped far more by dogmatic republicanism than on the actuality of EEC membership. Indeed, other than in the notable documents mentioned above, the European dimension featured very little, if at all, in the party's motivating priorities. This was to change gradually during the 1980s, when 'Europe' started to become a central feature of Sinn Féin's political and electoral strategy.

Abandoning Abstentionism

For the first decade of Ireland's membership of the EEC, Sinn Féin was in no position to engage in the electoral process, for two key reasons. Firstly, the party did not believe in the usefulness of elections in general, not only because of its historical abstentionist principle, but also because it saw any election as flawed, in that it legitimized the partition of the island, and thus served as a distraction from the conflict, where the military strategy still took precedence. Secondly, it is doubtful whether the party had the necessary resources – be they in terms of finance or personnel – to actively campaign in any given election. Consequently, the party did not mount any significant campaign against the entry of Ireland into the Common Market in 1972, but contented itself with advocating a boycott of the accession referendum. Moreover, until 1985, Sinn Féin was an abstentionist party. This, in theory, did not affect the European Parliament, as this principle was only concerned with the Irish legislature on both sides of the border. In practice, nevertheless, abstentionism did have an effect on Sinn Féin's European strategy.

In 1979, a debate took place within the party about whether it should put candidates forward for the European Parliamentary elections, which were held for the first time on the basis of universal suffrage. The discussion emanated from the party's decision that same year to end abstentionism at local level. It was finally agreed to retain a form of abstentionism for the European Parliament, although the reasons for this were undoubtedly more practical – the incapacity of the party to put forward any candidates – than ideological. *An Phoblacht* (2 June 1979) did publish a list outlining the criticisms made of the EEC, which included the 'consolidation of European capitalism' and the creation of a 'mutual protection society for big business'. But as the two local and European elections were held on the same day, Sinn Féin's message was, at best, complex, at worst, contradictory: full participation in the former, boycott of the latter. Republicans themselves acknowledged the dilemma: 'This presents *An Phoblacht Republican News* with a headache on how best to present the Republican Movement's position' (*An Phoblacht*, 2 June 1979).

Following the success of the strategy consisting of 'borrowing electoral seats' used first by Bobby Sands in Fermanagh South-Tyrone, Sinn Féin decided in the early 1980s to contest European Parliament elections. The objective was probably not so much to have its candidates elected as to use the electoral process to maintain the level of local activism that it had already established in the 1982 Northern Ireland Assembly election and in the 1983 Westminster election. In other words, what was important was to ensure that the vote-winning momentum of the party was maintained. Participation in the 1984 European elections was therefore less an instance of Europeanization than a purposeful electoral strategy. The party focused specifically on the Northern Ireland constituency, given that Sinn Féin's electoral performance in the 1982 general election in the Republic of Ireland had been very poor (receiving two percent of the vote). Danny Morrison was nominated as the party's candidate for Northern Ireland in 1984. The expectations were inevitably high, given the good performance of the party in Northern Ireland during the previous Assembly and Westminster elections. The results, however, were somewhat disappointing. Morrison did not reach the 100,000 vote mark, which was seen as a symbolic threshold which the party had managed to cross in the 1983 Westminster elections (an increase of three percent on the Assembly elections of the previous year).

The disappointing result raised questions regarding the clarity of Sinn Féin's message. The party did not expect a vote for or against Europe, but rather, it followed its own internal logic (*An Phoblacht*, 21 June 1984):

> We fought the elections for a number of reasons. As part of a process to end the isolation of Republicans in that part of the country, to have a look at our own organisation, and to make it come into the real world.

Politically, the message was equally blurred (*An Phoblacht*, 21 June 1984):

> There are two aspects of the Sinn Féin vote which will be illustrated today: a protest vote by nationalists frustrated by decades of loyalist bigotry and discrimination, and a vote of confidence in Sinn Féin's principled stance on the national question.

This further illustrates how Sinn Féin's European electoral ambitions were grounded in the logic of domestic politics, and not in a genuine desire to engage, critically or otherwise, with the EEC. In any case, it is doubtful that the electorate made sense of the ambiguous message delivered by Sinn Féin during the electoral campaign. In addition to a failure by the party to explicitly clarify why voters should choose a party that did not believe in Europe, there was also the additional contradiction that would haunt the movement for the next decade, that of 'the armalite and the ballot box' (a phrase coined by Director of Publicity and later MEP candidate, Danny Morrison, at Sinn Féin's Ard Fheis in 1981). Morrison himself came to recognize the limits and tenuousness of this strategy shortly after the 1984 European elections he contested; in an interview with *Magill* magazine in 1984, he surmised, 'Perhaps it is not entirely possible to harmonise the relationship between armed struggle and electoral politics' (Morrison, 1984). In essence, the 1984 European election demonstrates little evidence of the Europeanization of Sinn Féin, rather it shows the limits of the party's electoral strategy, as a result of the difficulty of dissociating a vote for Sinn Féin policies from a vote for violence.

Towards Cautious, Critical Engagement

Electoral Fortunes in the European Parliament

While Sinn Féin's involvement in EU politics failed to convince the electorate in the 1980s, its share of the vote in European Parliament elections gradually increased thereafter, to reach a peak at the beginning of the twenty-first century both north and south (see Table 1 below). Although the results for Northern Ireland (where votes for all party candidates in European Parliament elections tend to be interpreted as a type of unofficial 'border poll') are noticeably different from results across the island, it is notable that it was only from 1999 onwards that Sinn Féin made inroads into the European arena both north and south. This is partly because of local facilitating issues (e.g. John Hume's retirement as MEP in Northern Ireland), but it also corresponds with a change in the party's wider electoral performance. The party's first breakthrough in the Republic of Ireland came during the 1997 general election to Dail Éireann and it became the largest nationalist party in Northern Ireland in the 2001 general election to Westminster. Rising electoral fortunes undoubtedly correlate with public support for Sinn Féin's engagement with the peace process. As Northern Ireland became less of an 'issue' for Sinn Féin, it was able to capitalize on nationalist concerns north and south about the course of European integration.

The election of two Sinn Féin MEPs in June 2004 (Mary Lou McDonald in the Dublin constituency and Bairbre de Brún in Northern Ireland) was undoubtedly a major boost for the party, as an all-island political force. This was the highest vote that the party had obtained in any single election (11.3 percent in the south, 26.3 percent in the north). Its electoral performance thus reached a pinnacle on issues not directly related to the status of Northern Ireland. This would seem to vindicate the

Table 1. Percentage share of first preference vote received by Sinn Féin in European elections

Year	Dublin	East (Leinster)	South (Munster)	North West (Connaught/ Ulster)	AVERAGE in south	N. Ireland
1984	5.17	4.32	3.74	6.81	*5.01*	13.35
1989	2.58	2.63	No candidate	4.06	*4.32 (in 3 constituencies)*	9.15
1994	2.95	2.49	1.42	5.99	*3.21*	9.86
1999	6.64	5.86	6.48	6.39	*6.34*	17.33
2004	14.32	8.68	6.74	15.5	*11.31*	26.31
2009	11.79	11.07	12.98	9.19	*11.25*	26.04
Average	*7.24*	*5.84*	*6.27 (5 elections)*	*7.99*	*(6.90)*	*17.00*

Source: Data from *Elections Ireland,* available at: http://electionsireland.org/results/europe/index.cfm (accessed July 2009).

party's efforts to carve a place for itself within Irish politics which is not solely related to the peace process. Europe is one such opportunity, and the 'enthusiasm' for European politics, if not for the whole of the EU project, might find its explanation partly in that phenomenon. The fact that one of the most prominent figures within the party happens to be the former Dublin MEP, Mary Lou McDonald, who is at her best when talking about European affairs, is an indication of how important EU politics have become for the party and how seriously they are taken at elite levels. This was evident at the turn of the century, when Sinn Féin saw an opportunity in the 'European' arena and began to dedicate more effort to elaborating a European policy of its own.

Entering the European Parliament afforded Sinn Féin the opportunity to further affirm its left-wing approach and to distance itself, albeit mildly, from the Irish nationalist label with which it has been traditionally identified. Sinn Féin MEPs joined the European United Left parliamentary group (GUE/NGL). Formed in 1986, the group had a total of 41 MEPs after the 2004 election, drawn from 17 political parties and 13 member states, including the French Communist Party, Partido Comunista Portugués, Izquierda Unida, Bloco de Esquerda, Partido Comunisti italiani and Die Linke. Its main policy concern includes sustainable development, which it interprets to mean the encouragement of investments which create quality jobs, and disarmament. More generally, it advocates:

> Equal sovereignty between the States, the sovereignty of people and nations, the duty of cooperation with regard to the resolution of problems and conflicts, the respect of international law and the UN constitute the fundamental pillars of this concept of foreign policy.[3]

The group's objectives are close, both in aspiration and in theory, to the literature that Sinn Féin produces on the EU.

The Development of Policy on the EU

The party's improved election results in 1999 were perhaps aided by the fact that, for the first time, Sinn Féin had published a joint north/south European electoral manifesto. This all-Ireland election manifesto laid the foundations for Sinn Féin's policy of 'critical engagement', which would from then on become the cornerstone of the party's approach to European affairs. The meaning of this expression could be taken to be the juxtaposition of pragmatism ('We recognize the European Union as a key terrain for political struggle and one which we can use to advance our republican aims') and caution ('We are keenly aware of the dangers for Ireland as more and more decisions regarding political, economic and military matters are ceded to the unaccountable structures of the European Union'; Sinn Féin, 1999). The increasing sophistication of Sinn Féin's European message is clear: it no longer wants to be seen as a Eurosceptic party, much less as anti-European, but is keen to maintain some distance from other parties on a number of key EU issues.

In the decade following the 1999 manifesto, the themes that formed the consistent basis to Sinn Féin's opposition to European integration can be categorized as: defence of 'positive' neutrality and sovereignty, more transparency and accountability in EU institutions (that is, combating the so-called democratic deficit), and a more 'social Europe'. This means, for example, that the party rejects the erosion of national sovereignty through the loss of the Irish European Commissioner in Brussels and the extension of Qualified Majority Voting in the Council of Ministers. It also condemns the threat to Irish neutrality it perceives in the development of Europe's common foreign, security and defence policies. The party's left-wing identity also plays a role here as it criticizes what it sees as the EU's move away from adherence to the principles of a 'social Europe'. Such issues form the basis on which Sinn Féin has developed its EU message in recent years. Yet, arguably, the impact of Sinn Féin's European policy has been felt less in the nuance or detail of its interpretation of 'critical engagement' than in attention-grabbing soundbites, which help reinforce the popular image of the party as 'critical' rather than 'engaged' with the EU: 'No to a two-tier European Union and a European superstate', as Adams succinctly put it after the first Lisbon referendum (*Irish Times*, 21 June 2008).

No Campaigns in Nice and Lisbon Treaty Referendums

Sinn Féin's opposition to European integration has been manifestly evident in its decision to vigorously, and on occasion, successfully, campaign for a No vote in the referendums on the Nice and Lisbon treaties. Although the final result of the referendums can by no means be attributed solely to the campaigns of the party, its role is not inconsequential. Broadly speaking, the Nice and Lisbon referendums afforded Sinn Féin the opportunity to gain visibility, and therefore a degree of credibility, in the Irish political arena, on European issues. In the case of Nice I and II, the campaigns came at a time when Sinn Féin was seeking to increase its share of the vote in the Republic of Ireland. The party was the only parliamentary party alongside the Green Party to oppose the treaty. This gave the party the opportunity to brand itself as a strong defender of neutrality, sovereignty and left-wing ideals. Nevertheless, as with other referendums, the stakes are complex, as the multitude of voices within the No camp are often contradictory and do not reflect the party's specific discourse on some issues. In the Nice referendums, for instance, Sinn Féin had to clarify that it was not the potential arrival of immigrants from new member-states that formed the basis of its opposition to further European enlargement (see O'Malley, 2008). Nonetheless, Fintan O'Toole's (*Irish Times*, 9 June 2001) summary of the No position in the first Nice referendum inadvertently reveals quite how broad Sinn Féin's EU policy is:

> For the Catholic right, it is a further step in the advance of a godless European superstate. For the old left and the Greens, it formalises the moves towards a

common defence and security policy that has long been under way. For nationalists, it is a further dilution of national sovereignty.

These arguments were also present in the debates surrounding the first referendum on the Lisbon Treaty in 2008. Sinn Féin fought this campaign under the slogan 'Ireland deserves better' – a phrase which emphasizes the prioritizing of national interests without precluding support for a different version of this EU treaty. The party made a head start in its campaign, launching it in February (four months in advance of the forecast referendum date), and distributed a total of 500,000 leaflets. The message was direct, simple and straightforward. The '10 reasons for voting No' were worded in clear and strong language, the tone being one of foreboding and menace, while maintaining a certain vagueness that reinforced the argument of a lack of transparency and of a potential conspiracy against the people (see Sinn Féin, 2008a). The document states, for instance, that the Lisbon Treaty 'gives 105 additional powers to the EU and removes the Irish government's right to stop legislation which is not in our interest in more than 60 of these areas' (Sinn Féin, 2008a).

It could be argued however, that Sinn Féin embarked on this campaign from a slightly impaired position. Most notably, its performance in the 2007 general election to Dáil Éireann was considered a disappointment. The party lost one of its five existing Dáil seats and failed to secure the election of its rising star, MEP and later vice-president, Mary Lou McDonald, to a seat in Dublin Central. Yet, despite this relative decline in performance in the national elections, Sinn Féin was the *only* party with representation in Dáil Éireann to campaign against the Lisbon Treaty in 2008 (due to the non-campaigning of the Green Party, see Bolleyer & Panke, 2009). It thus turned to its advantage what might otherwise have been seen as the further isolation of a party still somewhat shunned by its political colleagues. Sinn Féin thus conscientiously presented itself in the 2008 referendum as the *only* defender of a social Europe, as the *true* advocate of neutrality and as the party offering the *best* protection against the loss of power within the new proposed EU structures. Moreover, its self-assurance in acting in the 'European arena' had been bolstered by the results of Nice I (which indicated some public disillusionment with the EU) and by the election of its two MEPs in 2004.

Sinn Féin as a Vocal Critic of the EU (and Mainstream Parties)

In the 2008 referendum campaign, the party aimed to acquire the status that it had hoped to achieve during the 2007 Irish general election: that of a radical voice, a credible and perhaps unique opposition to what it calls the 'Establishment'. The No result undoubtedly gave Sinn Féin renewed confidence in its ability to make its voice heard. Sinn Fein's (2008b) counter proposal to the Lisbon Treaty, *A Better Deal,* published in the aftermath of the referendum results, is a document based on the actual articles of the Lisbon Treaty, but with some amendments and corrections. One interesting feature of the document is its use of the 'track changes' tool available on Word documents, which clearly gives the impression of Sinn Féin playing the role of a teacher handing back a corrected copy of a bad assignment to an average and misguided student (in this case the EU – the articles are taken from the Official Journal of the EU). For example, see the following annotations (the text in italics being Sinn Féin's proposals, and the text in brackets being what Sinn Féin would like to see erased from the treaty) (Sinn Féin, 2008b):

> The members of the Commission shall *be elected by their respective member state parliaments on the basis of* [be chosen on the grounds of] their general competence and European commitment [from persons whose independence is beyond doubt].

Whether the party actually believed that these suggestions, in this format, would be taken into account by other Irish political parties, not to mention the other 26 EU member states, in the redrafting of the treaty is uncertain. Most significantly, though, it is a sign of the increasing willingness and confidence of Sinn Féin to set out a detailed and specific European policy – despite being under little illusion as to the actual effects it might have at a European level or, indeed, in national policy-making. For example, Sinn Féin expressed scepticism at the remit of the Oireachtas Sub-Committee on Lisbon established in 2008, which was to 'broadly consider Ireland's membership of the Union and to examine our future engagement with the EU'. Mary Lou McDonald (2008) justified her party's criticisms of the sub-committee following the publication of its report:

> We made it clear from the outset that we would not collude in a process whose primary purpose was to lay the ground for a rerun of the Lisbon Treaty referendum. Regrettably the sub-committee report published today reflects precisely that [which] happened.

Indeed, Sinn Féin was critical by default of such efforts as were being made by the dominant, pro-EU, Yes campaigning parties as to how they were addressing the concerns of the Irish electorate about European integration. Sinn Féin's representative on the Oireachtas sub-committee, Senator Pearse Doherty (*An Phoblacht*, 27 November 2008), stated afterwards that the whole process had a foregone conclusion – thereby reaffirming the party's contention that the large political parties (and the EU in general) were not truly interested in public opinion:

> We were concerned from the outset that the purpose of the committee was to prepare the ground for a rerunning of the Lisbon Treaty and not, in fact, to tackle the issues raised by the people throughout the referendum campaign or indeed engage with them on the future of the EU and Ireland's role within it.

For its part, Sinn Féin launched its own report, *The Future of the EU and Ireland's Role in Shaping that Future,* in which it attempted to portray itself as both a strong political party, with 'insider' membership in national decision-making bodies (thereby distinguishing itself from the array of No campaigning groups), and as a forthright defender of people's interests (Sinn Féin, 2008c: 3):

> Sinn Féin submitted very detailed and wide ranging amendments to the report. Speaking in advance of the final session of the sub-committee Senator Pearse Doherty described the contents of the draft report as being out of step with the views of voters and not reflecting the very real concerns of the people in key issues of democracy, workers rights, public services, defence and neutrality.

Evidence of Europeanization?

Programmatic Change

There is some synergy between Sinn Féin's broad electoral strategy and its evolving position on the EU. Indeed, the modification of its policy on Europe meets the expectations for Europeanization as outlined by Ladrech (2002). The motivation for this change, however, is rooted in *national(ist)* party priorities. Campaigns on European issues are the only electoral opportunities that transcend the border. This is where Sinn Féin can really put to the test its all-Ireland party programmes, and for the 1999, 2004 and 2009 elections, the party put forward a single all-Ireland manifesto. There is also a noticeable overlap now between the party's national programmes and those it puts forward for the EU context, as seen in the prominence of expressions such as 'equality agenda' and 'all-Ireland agenda' in both national and European manifestos. This is arguably made possible by the fact that many changes in the relevant policy areas have been *led by the EU* rather than national parliaments: 'We have supported EU and other Europe-wide measures that promote and enhance human rights, equality and the all-Ireland agenda' (Sinn Féin, 2005: 2). Indeed, Sinn Féin has readily capitalized on what it believes EU membership could achieve for Ireland and, significantly, the goals of the party. It views the EU as an international platform for promoting what it terms the 'all-Ireland agenda', i.e. towards the reunification of Ireland, including the development of cross-border initiatives.[4] The 1999 Sinn Féin European manifesto stated that the EU was the 'key terrain for political struggle and to advance national independence and economic and social justice' (Sinn Féin, 1999). Furthermore, Bairbre de Brún (2006) has elaborated her belief that the EU can facilitate Irish unity in practical ways: 'As a demonstration of its stated objectives of peace, reconciliation and the removal of borders, the EU has a responsibility to assist the process of Irish reunification'.

Sinn Féin acknowledges the EU's contribution to the Northern Ireland peace process. The Peace I, II and III programmes brought considerable amounts of money to Northern Ireland (a total of 796 million for Peace II alone a further 267 million to be spent on Peace III between 2007 and 2013). Adams (2005) argued that securing Peace III funding could:

greatly assist the bedding down of the peace process. It would also assist in dealing with the legacy of the conflict in terms of tackling social and economic exclusion and discrimination, and building local and national reconciliation.

De Brún (2005) echoed this view when she stated that, 'Peace I and Peace II programmes have made an important contribution towards the process of conflict resolution and community development'. Within this, she sees Sinn Féin's role as one of ensuring that the British government were strongly committed to securing the funds – a notable case of the party's support for EU action in Northern Ireland relating to domestic political concerns. Sinn Féin is prepared to acknowledge the usefulness of the EU on some issues, and this has proved beneficial for the party machine. The party's slightly more nuanced approach to European integration came together with its heightened profile on EU issues in the political arena in Ireland, north and south.

Organizational Change

Sinn Féin's European message may be considered 'opportunistic', in that is has allowed the party to target new voters and reap electoral rewards. Key figures recognized the potential opportunities available to Sinn Féin in terms of increased visibility, profile and votes. It appears that the 'politicisation of the EU ... became a concern for party management' (Ladrech, 2002: 397). Within this process, Sinn Féin has rejected the label 'Eurosceptic', which it does not view as adequately or accurately capturing the character of its relationship with the EU. According to the analysis of Taggart and Szczerbiak (2002: 7), Sinn Féin would be a 'soft Eurosceptic' party, that is to say:

> there is NOT a principled objection to European integration or EU membership but [there are] concerns on one (or a number) of policy areas [which leads] to the expression of qualified opposition to the EU, or [where there is] a sense that 'national interest' is currently at odds with the EU's trajectory.

Why and how does the party maintain this 'qualified opposition' on an issue and in an arena that may reasonably be regarded as constituting a diversion of energies and personnel? It must be concluded that European integration has become central to Sinn Féin's overall electoral strategy, not least because it has enabled the party to demonstrate its relevance and interests far beyond Northern Ireland, and to consolidate its image as the defender of 'social' policies and the equality agenda. This strategy has proved fruitful in terms of increasing the party's vote-winning capacity at European elections, and in terms of heightening its profile during EU referendum campaigns.

European issues and the European arena provide a crucial potential platform and profile for Sinn Féin. The party's changed, yet consistently critical position on Europe, appeals to a specific voter constituency and has brought the party recognition from voters, other political parties and a broader range of parties across Europe. Mary Lou McDonald's public visibility and media appeal during European election and referendum campaigns served the party well and clearly reflects a strategic decision on the part of Sinn Féin to dedicate key party resources and personnel to its EU agenda. The selection of younger party candidates for the 2009 European elections is regarded by some as being part and parcel of a wider Sinn Féin strategy to 'reinvent republicanism' (see *Irish Times*, 26 May 2009). Paradoxically, the strategy of putting forward one particular personality, who is strongly identified with a particular issue, can also prove risky. McDonald's failure to secure a seat in the 2007 general election, and then the loss of her European Parliament seat in 2009 caused both real and symbolic damage to the party as a whole. The party is now reduced to one MEP, elected in Northern Ireland. Using the European electoral backdrop as an arena within which to broaden the party's general appeal across the island has not proven hazard-free.

Patterns of Party Competition

As Sinn Féin developed its EU policy and made shifts in its organization in order to capitalize on the opportunities offered through 'critical engagement' with Europe, it also reaped benefits in the arena of party competition – at least for the decade leading up to the June 2009 elections. The European Parliament election contest in Dublin in 2009 was more competitive than previously, not only because the constituency seat allocation was reduced from four to three seats, but also because one of Mary Lou McDonald's opponents was the Socialist Party candidate Joe Higgins, who shares with Sinn Féin a left-wing, anti-Lisbon discourse. According to former party General Secretary Robbie Smyth (*An Phoblacht*, 11 June 2009):

> The importance of the Sinn Féin vote in electing Joe Higgins to the last MEP seat cannot be underestimated and shows that there is a substantial core of left republican votes in the city, the potential development of which cannot be ignored in the coming months when it comes to broad based campaigns against a government obsessed with cut backs and penalising those who can least afford to pay for its failures.

What this analysis fails to suggest, however, is that Sinn Féin's left-wing discourse might not be sufficiently convincing for a critical percentage of the electorate who seem to prefer the more obvious and familiar left-wing discourse of a Socialist to that of a candidate whose party is still not, in spite of its best efforts, fully identified with left-wing politics. The assessment of Eoin Ó Broin (Sinn Féin's former Director of European Affairs) of the disappointing results for the party in both the European and local elections in the south outlines the depth of the challenge now facing Sinn Féin:

> My own experience from the canvass was that, while a significant section of the electorate were open to our message, we failed to 'close the deal' with

many. Why this was the case is a matter for discussion within the party. Issues of organisational capacity, access to and use of the media, and clarity and credibility of our policies and message will all be scrutinised. (*Irish Times*, 16 June 2009)

Sinn Fein's taken-for-granted equation of republicanism with left-wing ideology, as if both terms were interchangeable, might have some resonance within the circles of its traditional supporters but is not sufficient to convince the electorate at large. Sinn Féin has used the concept of 'Europe' to anchor its radical legacy and claim, as seen in Mary Lou McDonald's maiden speech in the European Parliament in July 2004: 'As Irish republicans, following in the tradition of Bobby Sands MP, we are committed to the politics of equality, justice and freedom' (*An Phoblacht*, 24 July 2004). However, the limitations of this strategy are evident when Sinn Féin is faced with a competing left-wing discourse.

Conclusion

Sinn Féin has effectively been transformed in recent times from an 'embryonic electoral force' to a modern and professional political party espousing a form of participatory politics built upon an egalitarian agenda (see Tonge, 2005: 117). The EU has brought increased legitimacy to a party that is constantly in search of political recognition. Moreover, the partial Europeanization of Sinn Féin has reaped partial rewards. Moving from an anti-EU position to one based on 'critical engagement', together with the strategic decision to contest European elections and fight EU referendum campaigns, allowed the party to bolster its appeal and profile, particularly in the south. Indeed, the party's domestic political strategy became so closely linked to its 'European' one (perhaps even Europeanized) that the disappointment of the 2009 southern electoral results for Sinn Féin instigated a process of introspective debate within the party. Sinn Féin's approach to the EU helped to distinguish it from other political parties, particularly in the south – perhaps too successfully. The party stands alone now as the only political party in the Republic of Ireland which openly and critically questions European integration. This has consequences far wider than merely inciting some (unfamiliar) apprehension within party ranks about the Lisbon II referendum campaign. The next steps in Sinn Féin's engagement with the EU will demonstrate the degree to which Europeanization is compatible with an independent, critical party political stance.

Notes

1. This expression is commonly found in Sinn Féin literature. Although it only appeared once in the 1999 manifesto ('Sinn Féin's position is one of engaging with the European Union and its institutions in a critical manner'), the phrase appears nine times in the 2004 manifesto, albeit in different forms (e.g. 'critical but constructive engagement', 'critical engagement', 'engaging critically') and is regularly used in press releases and public speeches.

2. The early *Éire Nua* (Sinn Féin, 1971: 4) document promised: 'An independent stand will be taken in foreign policy. Power blocs such as NATO and the EEC on the one hand and COMECON and the Warsaw Pact on the other will be avoided'. This position was reaffirmed in the updated version of this policy document (Sinn Féin, 1979).
3. Quote taken from the GUE/NGL website, available at: www.guengl.eu (accessed July 2009).
4. See www.irelandofequals.com/constituencies/5209 (accessed July 2009).

References

Adams, G. (2005) Call for continued EU support of the peace process, Sinn Féin Press Release, 5 October 2005, available at: www.sinnfein.ie/contents/5188 (accessed August 2009).

Bolleyer, N. & Panke, D. (2009) The Irish Green Party: an unhappy marriage?, *Irish Political Studies*, 24(4), pp. 543–557.

De Brún, B. (2005) Sinn Féin set to continue Peace III campaign, Sinn Féin and GUE/NGL Press Release, 18 July 2005, available at: www.sfguengl.com/news/entry/180 (accessed August 2009).

De Brún, B. (2006) European Union can bring about Irish unity, Sinn Féin and GUE/NGL Press Release, 20 October 2006, available at: www.sfguengl.com/news/entry/470 (accessed August 2009).

Frampton, M. (2005) Sinn Féin and the European arena: 'ourselves alone' or 'critical engagement'?, *Irish Studies in International Affairs*, 16, pp. 235–253.

Ladrech, R. (2002) Europeanisation and political parties: towards a framework for analysis, *Party Politics*, 8(4), pp. 389–403.

McDonald, M.L. (2008) Press Release on Launch of 'Majority View–Minority Report', Sinn Féin, available at: www.sinnfein.ie/contents/16464 (accessed August 2009).

Maskey, A. (2003) Speech delivered at the annual Wolfe Tone commemoration, Bodenstown, available at: www.sinnfein.ie/contents/15202 (accessed July 2009).

Morrison, D. (1984) Interview with Gene Kerrigan, *Magill Magazine*, September.

O'Malley, E. (2008) Why is there no Radical Right Party in Ireland? *West European Politics*, 31(5), pp. 960–977.

Sinn Féin (1971) *Éire Nua: The Social and Economic Programme of Sinn Féin* (Dublin: Sinn Féin).

Sinn Féin (1979) *Éire Nua: The Social, Economic and Political Dimensions* (Dublin: Sinn Féin), available at: http://cain.ulst.ac.uk/issues/politics/docs/sf/sinnfein79.htm (accessed June 2008).

Sinn Féin (1999) *European Parliament Election Manifesto* (Dublin: Sinn Féin), available at: www.sinnfein.ie/elections/manifesto/24 (accessed June 2008).

Sinn Féin (2005) *Ireland and the EU Constitution* (Dublin: Sinn Féin), available at: www.sinnfein.ie/pdf/EUConstitutionPamphlet.pdf (accessed June 2008).

Sinn Féin (2008a) *Ten Reasons to Vote No* (Dublin: Sinn Féin), available at: http://voteno2lisbon.wordpress.com/10-reasons-to-vote-no/ (accessed June 2008).

Sinn Féin (2008b) *A Better Deal – Sinn Féin Submission* (Dublin: Sinn Féin), available at: http://voteno2lisbon.wordpress.com/alternative-guide-to-the-lisbon-treaty/ (accessed June 2008).

Sinn Féin (2008c) *The Future of the EU and Ireland's Role in Shaping that Future* (Dublin: Sinn Féin), available at: www.sinnfein.ie/files/EUMinorityReportSmall.pdf (accessed June 2008).

Taggart, P. & Szczerbiak, A. (2002) The party politics of Euroscepticism in EU member and candidate states, *OERN Working Paper* No. 6, April.

Tonge, J. (2005) *The New Northern Irish Politics?* (Basingstoke: Palgrave).

'Battling in Brussels': The DUP and the European Union

GLADYS GANIEL
Trinity College Dublin, Belfast Campus, Northern Ireland

ABSTRACT *Although the Democratic Unionist Party (DUP) does not conform to the model of Europeanization outlined by Ladrech (2002), there is some evidence of change along the lines identified by De Winter and Gómez-Reino (2002) with reference to other European ethnoregionalist parties. For example, the DUP has certainly adapted its behaviour and policies at both local and European levels with a view to exploiting new political opportunities offered by Europeanization. However, De Winter and Gómez-Reino's argument that participation in European institutions has made formerly-Eurosceptic ethnoregionalist parties 'moderate Eurocritics' does not fully apply to the DUP. The DUP continues to demonstrate a number of Eurosceptic characteristics, including ones grounded in extreme religious interpretations of the purpose and process of European integration. Nevertheless, the party's Eurosceptic outlook does not prevent it from being willing to 'battle in Brussels' (as put in its 2009 manifesto for the European elections) in order to serve domestic (party) interests – a tactic not dissimilar to the DUP's approach to Northern Ireland politics in general.*

Introduction

Ladrech (2002) and Mair (2000, 2004) have argued that the direct impact of Europeanization on national political party systems is limited. Regional ethnically-based parties such as the Democratic Unionist Party (DUP) in Northern Ireland fall outside the remit of such analyses. These parties have also been ignored in comparative analyses of Europeanization, with the exception of some treatments of 'ethnoregional' parties (De Winter and Tursan, 1998; De Winter and Gómez-Reino, 2002). But even in these analyses, Northern Ireland parties have often been left out.[1] For analysts of EU politics, Northern Ireland's political parties may (understandably) be considered unique cases or outliers.

When Northern Ireland elected its first representatives to the European Parliament in 1979, the results from the unionist constituency seemed to bear out these assumptions. Rev. Ian Paisley of the DUP, a man at that time considered the extreme voice of unionism, topped the poll. Paisley secured regular European election victories until his retirement in 2004. A common interpretation of this is put forward by Moloney (2008: 222–223):

[H]is successes revealed something very interesting about the Unionist electorate, not least those living in the leafy affluent suburbs of Belfast. In the secrecy of the voting booth they were quite happy to forget all those negative and even frightening aspects of Ian Paisley – his antediluvian religious views, his bullying ways, the embarrassment he brought to the Unionist cause abroad – and use the opportunity of the European election to send a warning message to the British and their Nationalist neighbours by giving Paisley their first preference votes.

The argument that voters treated European elections like referenda on Northern Ireland's constitutional position has also been put forward by Bruce (2007). He contends that European issues as such have hardly mattered, and that the elections served as province wide 'beauty contests' (Bruce, 2007: 109) – with Paisley clearly the Protestant prince.

This seems plausible, given evidence that unionist voters were willing to overlook (if they did not subscribe to) Paisley's religious interpretation of the EU, which many Protestants would consider unusual or extreme (Moloney, 2008: 219–223; Bruce, 2007: 47–49). This interpretation sees the EU as a tool of the Roman Catholic Church, the anti-Christ foretold in the biblical book of Revelations. Paisley has made no attempt to hide these views, with a number of texts explaining the position readily available on his website.

But have such ideological outlooks made the DUP immune from wider processes of Europeanization? Is the party all that different from other ethnoregionalist parties? This article explores how the DUP has acted within the EU (1979–2009) in light of the framework for Europeanization developed by Ladrech (2002). Accordingly, it identifies changes in the party's programmes, organization, patterns of competition, relationships with government, and relationships beyond the national party system. It also determines the extent to which the DUP meets the expectations for ethnoregionalist parties put forward by De Winter and Gómez-Reino (2002). First, they claim that Europeanization has changed the relationship between centres and peripheries. The DUP has adapted its positions and policies at a European level with a view, for example, to securing funding from the 'centre' in the guise of the EU's Special Programme for Peace and Reconciliation (PEACE funding) for local (unionist) communities. Secondly, they argue that Europeanization has made political decisions seem ever more removed from citizens. This process can be observed in the way the DUP has campaigned for European elections, focusing on personalities and on issues internal to Northern Ireland. Finally, they argue that participation in European institutions has made the Eurosceptic ethnoregionalist parties 'moderate Eurocritics' (De Winter and Gómez-Reino, 2002: 500). This has not happened with the DUP, possibly because the party has remained aloof from alliances with other ethnoregionalist parties. The DUP continues to demonstrate a number of Eurosceptic characteristics including objections to the EU, which are grounded in extreme religious interpretations of the Union. Paradoxically, however, the party participates in European institutions and is willing to manipulate opportunities provided by the EU in order to serve Northern Ireland's interests.

The DUP's Paradoxical Approach to the EU

The following sections of this article demonstrate how the DUP has maintained Eurosceptic rhetoric while simultaneously engaging in limited ways with the EU. Paisley's willingness to engage in European institutions whilst holding religious beliefs that regard those institutions as morally reprehensible prefigure, in important ways, his later compromise with 'Sinn Féin/IRA'. Further, the party has demonstrated pragmatic engagement on its priority issues: agriculture, fishing, PEACE funding and opposing the Lisbon Treaty. These issues have been prioritized from Paisley's reign as a Member of European Parliament (MEP) through to that of his successors, Jim Allister (2004) and Diane Dodds (2009).

The Religious Basis of the DUP's Euroscepticism

The DUP's Euroscepticism is closely linked to a religious interpretation of the EU that has been articulated clearly and consistently by Ian Paisley. Unprecedented amongst modern European leaders, the former DUP leader has founded both a political party and a Christian denomination, the Free Presbyterian Church. Paisley locates himself within a wider Protestant fundamentalist/evangelical tradition, claiming the mantle of authentic, Reformed 'Bible Protestantism' (see Bruce, 1986, 2007; Moloney and Pollak, 1987; Smyth, 1987; Moloney, 2008; Cooke, 1996; Brewer & Higgins, 1998; Mitchel, 2003; Ganiel, 2008). Paisley's religious position on the EU links prophecies about the 'end times' with his opposition to the Roman Catholic Church. Yet fundamentalist and evangelical Protestants do not have an agreed position on what exactly will happen in the end times, or the order in which these events will occur; neither does the Free Presbyterian Church have an agreed position on this matter.

Most fundamentalist/evangelical accounts of the end times draw on the books of Revelation and Daniel to piece together a sequence of events, which culminates in the return of Christ. These books are said to foretell the emergence of an 'anti-Christ' who seizes religious and political power on a global scale (see Brewer & Higgins, 1998; Higgins, 2001). What is crucial is the role that the Catholic Church plays in the end times. For some, the Catholic Church is *the* anti-Christ, which will persecute Jews and all true Christians during a period of tribulation. A favourite passage is Revelation 17, where a woman is described as riding upon a beast. This woman is said to symbolize the Catholic Church, the 'whore of Babylon', intent on destroying Christians. Moloney (2008: 221) offers a colourful description of how Paisley conveyed such a message during a sermon in 1984:

> The woman 'riding upon the beast, who has spread herself and her influence and her control and her domination over the beast' was the Catholic Church, he said, the whore of Babylon. And the European Community (EC) was the beast which she rode and controlled. 'She's riding on the beast today,' he shouted at his now spellbound congregation. 'We're in the Common Market and there's

[sic] a hundred million more Roman Catholics in the Common Market than Protestants, so we're in a tiny minority.'

[…]

Behind the Pope was the Devil. 'What holds the Common Market together?' Paisley asked his congregation rhetorically in 1984, 'Satanic power.' That was how so many 'diverse nations with so many problems, so many difficulties, so many political, economic and military strains upon them can suddenly come together'.

Some fundamentalists and evangelicals believe there can be many anti-Christs, including individuals and institutions. This means that the Pope, the EU, and individual politicians or religious leaders could all be considered anti-Christs. During the 1980s, the Free Presbyterian Church's prophecy experts, John Douglas and Bert Cooke, announced, 'after careful study, that the Common Market was a fulfilment of the visions of Daniel and the Book of Revelation' (Moloney, 2008: 221). As Bruce (2007: 49) writes:

> Whichever view is taken, Rome and the papacy are still taken to be the driving force: an identification that is defended by arguing that there is no worldwide organization other than the Roman Catholic Church that has the power, influence, and reach to be the sort of comprehensive anti-Christian force suggested in prophecy.

Identifying the Catholic Church as an anti-Christ is not something new. The 1643 Westminster Confession of Faith, a defining doctrinal document for Presbyterianism worldwide, identified the Pope as an anti-Christ. But such views have passed from mainstream consciousness and are no longer endorsed by most Presbyterian churches. It is not clear how widely known are Paisley's specific religious interpretations of the EU, with its links to the 'Roman Catholic Church/anti-Christ.' But Paisley certainly has not tried to hide them. Sermons and articles about the EU/Pope/anti-Christ are posted on his website. Even if people disagree with the substance of such an elaborate theory of prophecy, Paisley's rhetoric clearly has had anti-Catholic connotations.

This is illustrated by what is perhaps Paisley's best-known action in the European Parliament. In 1988, Pope John Paul II addressed the Parliament in Strasbourg. As he did so, Paisley rose, holding a poster with the words: 'John Paul II Anti-Christ,' and shouting 'I renounce you as the anti-Christ'. He also claimed that the empty seat number 666 in the European parliamentary chamber was reserved for an anti-Christ (Coakley, 2009). Paisley was eventually escorted from the chamber. Moloney (2008: 326) gauged the unionist reaction this way: 'Respectable Unionists shuddered with embarrassment but in the Free Presbyterian heartlands they smiled with pleasure and pride'.

There are two important points to be made here about Paisley, his religion, and the EU. The first is that his religious beliefs about the relationships between Catholicism and the EU arguably contribute to wider currents of anti-Catholicism within unionism (Moloney, 2008). The fact that Paisley continued to be returned to his European post indicates that his beliefs were not unusual or offensive enough to keep people from voting for him. To understand how this works, it is best to conceive of anti-Catholicism, as articulated by Brewer and Higgins (1998: 2), as consisting of negative actions, attitudes, practices and beliefs about:

> individual Catholics, the Catholic Church as an institution or Catholic doctrine, which results in these negative beliefs being invoked as an ethnic boundary marker, which can be used, in some settings, to represent social stratification and conflict. It occurs at three levels – that of ideas, individual behaviour and the social structure. In terms of ideas, anti-Catholicism is expressed in negative stereotypes and pejorative beliefs, notions and language about Catholics and the Catholic Church. At the level of individual action, it shows itself in various forms of direct discrimination, intimidation, harassment and sectarianism against Catholics or the Catholic Church because of their Catholicism. At the level of the social structure, anti-Catholicism expresses itself in patterns of indirect and institutional discrimination and social disadvantage experienced by Catholics because they are Catholics.

For Brewer and Higgins (1998), what Paisley says about the Catholic Church and the EU resides in the level of ideas – rhetoric that can inspire others to direct discriminatory action or violence. Bruce (2001, 2007) has long disputed this. He spends a great deal of time documenting Paisley's denunciation of political discrimination and violence, and argues that his rhetoric did not have a direct influence on Protestant paramilitaries (see Bruce, 2007: 209–245). It is not the task of this article to evaluate whether or to what extent Paisley's anti-Catholic words have spawned violence, but Brewer and Higgins' comprehensive definition of anti-Catholicism makes significant links between words, actions and social structures. At the very least, Paisley's words about the Catholic Church and the EU reflect and reinforce anti-Catholic actions and social structures. In light of this, it could be asked whether Europeanization has increased the DUP's anti-Catholicism. This is unlikely, especially since it is not clear that most members of and voters for the DUP share Paisley's religious interpretation of the EU. Rather, it seems that the EU electoral forum simply provided another platform for Paisley to express anti-Catholic sentiments.

The Justification for Engaging with the European Parliament

The second point to be made concerns Paisley's willingness to compromise his religious beliefs in order to participate in the European Parliament. Moloney (2008: 221–222) records how Paisley decided to stand for the European Parliament despite opposition from senior leaders in the Free Presbyterian Church. He describes a meeting of the church's presbytery in 1977, where Paisley portrayed himself as Daniel in the lion's den:

> He, Ian Paisley from the Ravenhill Road, would be God's voice in the anti-Christian assembly in Strasbourg, a 'firm, strong, unbending Protestant voice to raise the standard'.

The Free Presbyterian elders accepted his argument at that time because they saw him as God's anointed leader. In an interview in the early 1980s, Paisley explained his position: 'I'm going to get all I can for Ulster, every grant we can possibly get our hands on. Then when we have milked the cow dry, we are going to shoot the cow' (interview by Taylor, quoted in Brewer and Higgins, 1998: 108).

These mirror the type of arguments employed by Paisley to justify the DUP's participation in domestic Northern Ireland politics after the 1998 Agreement. The DUP was resolutely anti-Agreement but the party nevertheless came to readily work its institutions, arguing that it would use those institutions to 'smash', or 're-negotiate' the Agreement (Rankin & Ganiel, 2008). Faced with stirrings of discontent within the Free Presbyterian Church after deciding to share power with Sinn Féin in the Northern Ireland Executive, Paisley again justified his decision by drawing on his reputation as Ulster's Protestant prophet. Moloney (2008: 502) cites the May 2007 issue of the Free Presbyterian magazine *The Revivalist*, in which Paisley claimed that his critics were 'doing Satan's work'. The editorial also claimed that Paisley was God's 'specially anointed' leader. Paisley's wife, Eileen, was even more unambiguous in her column (quoted in Moloney, 2008: 502–503):

> Like the Israelites of old treated Moses so they treat today's God-anointed leader. They refuse to believe that God is already working in the most unexpected places and in the hearts of the most unexpected people. Again, like the Israelites, they prefer to remain in the wilderness of the past than move into the promised land of a better and happier future.

Paisley's engagement with the EU – and his religiously-tinged justifications for it – prefigures his later approach to working the institutions of the 1998 Agreement.

The religious dimensions of the DUP's Euroscepticism do not fit easily in either Ladrech's or De Winter and Gómez-Reino's frameworks. Paisley's brand of religiously-based opposition to the EU does not surface in DUP manifestos, so there is no evidence of official party programmatic change. That said, Paisley and by extension the DUP's apparent willingness to compromise religious beliefs and participate in EU institutions may be considered an example of organizational change. But this, rather than demonstrating Europeanization or a moderation of the party's Euroscepticism, is better understood as a selective and calculated form of engagement with the EU.

The DUP's Policies and Priorities in the EU

Setting aside any theological musings, the main reason the DUP opposes further European integration is because it believes this process will dilute the sovereignty of individual nation states (see McCall, 2003). When representing the DUP in Europe, neither Paisley nor Allister aligned with any of the large party groupings. The DUP has opposed EU treaties that it perceived as threats to national sovereignty, it opposes a European constitution, and it opposes the Lisbon Treaty, which it sees as a European constitution in disguise. The party's 2009 European Manifesto (DUP, 2009a: 16) contains the following, under the heading 'Battling in Brussels':

> We oppose the Lisbon Treaty, loss of national vetoes, a President of Europe and the harmonization of immigration and border controls, and defence and foreign policy. The DUP supports a UK-wide referendum on the Lisbon Treaty unconditionally.

Concerns about the dilution of national sovereignty touch on issues of British identity which are, of course, vital to unionist opinion. During the 1980s, some unionists were alarmed by the Europhile discourses of the SDLP's John Hume. Hume saw European integration as a means of diluting national sovereignty and weakening the significance of the link between Northern Ireland and the rest of the UK (Hume, 1996; Todd, 1999; McLoughlin, 2009). The DUP is in favour of keeping the pound and spurning the Euro. The party sets out a number of economic reasons for this (DUP, 2004: 19). The party is also wary of the imposition of European legislation which they view as facilitating the eventual liberalization of current laws on abortion and sexual rights.

Christopher Stalford, a DUP councillor for Laganbank once worked in Allister's European office. He claims (interview with the author, Belfast, 5 April 2008) that DUP policies differ most from those of the Ulster Unionist Party (UUP) in the strength of their Euroscepticism:

> The DUP isn't aligned to any political group in the European Parliament. Ulster Unionists are part of European People's Party–European Democrats (EPP-ED)[2] ... EPP-ED is a federalist party – they believe in the Constitution, they believe in increasing the powers of the Commission, centralizing and taking powers away from sovereign parliaments and into the European structure ... I think the ultimate purpose is to see the creation of a federal Europe ... Ulster Unionists and the Conservative party both are living a lie through their membership of EPP-ED because they're members of a federal party that's committed to a federal Europe whilst at the same time, at home, they make terribly Eurosceptic noises and pander to Euroscepticism. That would be the main area where we would disagree ... I think that the position was that if push came to shove and we were made to choose between joining single currency or leaving the Union – then we would choose to leave. Because I think joining the

Euro is something that would be very bad for our economy and for our country and involve questions about political sovereignty and where does power reside? So I think faced with that position we would choose to leave and I think the Ulster Unionists would choose to stay.

The DUP formulates policies on European issues through its headquarters based central policy unit. Traditionally, the impetus for most policies has come through the sitting MEP. In an interview with the author (East Belfast, 11 January 2008), Allister notes that as a DUP MEP, he freely formulated European policies, none of which were contradicted by party headquarters. Stalford confirms this, saying that 'policies would be fed into headquarters and 99 times out of 100 they would be adopted'. When Allister left the party to form Traditional Unionist Voice in 2007 he remained MEP, his policies on Europe bearing little difference to those of the DUP.

In its manifesto for the 2004 elections for the European Parliament, the DUP highlighted Paisley's achievements in two main areas: securing PEACE funding and agriculture. It is well-established that Paisley, Hume and Nicholson worked together in securing EU peace funding for Northern Ireland (Meehan, 2000; Laffan, 2005). In the party manifesto produced before the 2009 elections, the DUP again prioritized the agri-food sector. The party claimed that EU legislation 'places European farmers at a competitive disadvantage against other parts of the world', pledged reform of the Common Agricultural Policy, and pointed out that the party had secured European support for the Northern Ireland dairy sector (DUP, 2009a: 34).

A priority of the party in later years has been to increase access to EU funds for unionist groups, which have been slower than nationalist groups to access them (McCall, 2003). When Stalford worked in Allister's European office, it was his responsibility to help groups access funds, a task he estimates took 75 percent of his time. Another of Allister's staff members dealt with agriculture.

When he was Finance Minister, Peter Robinson's department was also concerned with securing the continuation of EU peace funding, even as the EU was diverting its funds to Eastern states. Three new European Regional Development Fund Programmes were announced on 14 April 2008, with Robinson attending the launch. The three initiatives are a Sustainable Competitiveness Programme (€614m), PEACE III (€333m) and the INTERREG IVA Northern Ireland/Ireland/Scotland programme (€256m). The addition of Scotland to INTERREG is new and has particularly pleased unionists (Northern Ireland Executive, 2008). In the DUP's consultation response to INTERREG IV, drafted by Allister, the two concerns it highlighted were targeting resources with a stronger economic focus, and strengthening links with Scotland (Allister, 2007).

Interviewed in 2008, Stalford claimed that the 2009 European Parliamentary elections would be about *European* bread and butter issues. And in fact, the DUP's 2009 manifesto did contain more detailed information on European issues when compared with the party's much shorter 2004 manifesto. The issues to which it gave the most prominence were 'Brussels Burden on Business,' 'Internet Safety,' and

'Freedom to Fish.' There was also a list of 16 other specific proposals, including keeping the British pound, a UK-wide referendum on the Lisbon Treaty, a reduction in the allowances of MEPs, EU intervention in Zimbabwe, and greater emphasis on preventing the persecution of Christians throughout the world (DUP, 2009a: 16–17). The party website, redesigned in 2009, contains a section on Europe. Increased mention of the EU in party manifestos may be considered party programmatic change, which Ladrech regards as evidence of Europeanization. But with the DUP, this party programmatic change is recent, reflecting only a very limited degree of Europeanization.

Ladrech (2002) also considers how Europeanization manifests itself in terms of patterns of party competition. In seeking to secure votes, the DUP and UUP are invariably engaged in a battle to present themselves as the primary defenders of the unionist community. When it comes to European elections, neither party can be described as pro-European. Consequently, each party must seek to appeal to voters in ways which are distinctive, but yet resonate with unionist voters who are traditionally hostile to Europe (see Smith, 2000). The DUP has typically presented itself as more Eurosceptic than the UUP. It is difficult, however, to gauge the extent to which UUP voters may have defected to the DUP over the party's position on Europe. Given that unionist party competition is dominated by internal Northern Ireland concerns, even during European election campaigns, it is unlikely that a party's position on Europe is a decisive factor in attracting votes.

The DUP's willingness to identify priority issues and pursue these at the European level demonstrates a willingness to engage with the EU to a limited degree, but without compromising their traditional opposition to European integration. Such behaviour is based on a rationale which has also been utilized effectively at the domestic political level and crucially, one which has been rewarded at the polls. Engagement with Europe in this way is justified because it is based on an approach which serves the practical interests of DUP voters.

The DUP and the 2009 European Parliament Elections

The DUP has rarely framed European parliamentary elections primarily in terms of European issues. As Mair (2000) observes, this is not unusual across European states, as political parties often frame European elections in terms of domestic issues. This feeds into a wider trend of the de-politicization of electorates in Europe. A symptom of de-politicization is a focus on the personalities of candidates, rather than the issues or the candidates' policies. The organization of the DUP's 2004 European election manifesto booklet reflects this particular trend. The first five pages are spent introducing Allister as the new candidate. Then, on pages 6–7, the first 'issue' broached is 'to stop Sinn Féin/ IRA topping the poll.' Pages 8–9 are devoted to a positive review of the DUP's 'Devolution Now' proposals – proposals for government in *Northern Ireland*. Pages 10–11 argue that a vote for Allister will strengthen the DUP's hand in negotiations for devolution. Pages 12–13 declare that there is a revival within unionism, led by the DUP. It is not until page 14 that the booklet actually begins providing information about Europe, opening with a two-page spread celebrating Paisley's record as MEP.

Similarly, a 2009 party press release announcing Dodds' candidacy for the most recent elections contains a statement by the candidate, in which five of its six paragraphs deal with Northern Ireland issues, including stopping Sinn Féin from topping the poll. Just one short paragraph alludes to Europe, and there is no reference to specific EU policies or issues (DUP, 2009b). On the whole, the organization of the 2009 manifesto echoes the 2004 edition. It opens with an introduction to Dodds, then focuses on domestic Northern Ireland issues. The only references to EU politics appear on pages 16 and 17 and are followed by a continued focus on domestic priorities and party politics for the remaining 22 pages.

A major theme of the DUP's 2009 manifesto was the wisdom of the party's decision to enter government with Sinn Féin. The party justified this decision to the unionist electorate as a necessary priority in this election. Accordingly, the manifesto identifies benefits brought about by the DUP's negotiations such as: 'Provisional IRA's terrorist campaign is over', 'there is a Northern Ireland Assembly with a unionist majority', 'Republicans support the police, courts and the rule of law', 'North-South political institutions are now accountable to the Stormont Assembly', 'a peaceful Northern Ireland is attracting foreign investment', and 'No Irish language Act,' amongst other things (see DUP, 2009a: 9, 15). The manifesto also claims that the 'Real Alternative' for unionists 'is not between the current form of devolution and some unionist panacea, but between the present arrangements or Direct Rule with Dublin interference and republican influence' (DUP, 2009a: 21). Finally, as in past years, the manifesto encourages unionists to vote for the DUP candidate in order to prevent Sinn Féin from topping the poll (DUP, 2009a: 4).

It is likely that the DUP's attempts to justify its compromise with Sinn Féin are a response to the campaign of its former party member, Allister. Jim Allister's resignation from the DUP was not due to fundamental disagreements over European issues, but linked to the DUP's decision to enter the Northern Ireland Executive with Sinn Féin in May 2007. Since then, Allister and his Traditional Unionist Voice party has been the most prominent voice of unionist disillusionment with the DUP's compromise. The 2009 European elections produced the worst ever result for the DUP, with Dodds finishing behind Sinn Féin's Bairbre de Brún and the UUP's Jim Nicholson. Allister came fourth, failing to retain his seat. The relatively poor electoral showing for the DUP, however, may not be entirely attributable to Allister's ability to tap into grassroots unionist disillusionment. Other factors likely to have contributed to the drop in support for the DUP include doubts about Dodds' television performances and concerns that DUP representatives may have abused the Westminster expenses system (BBC Online, 2009a). In the aftermath, Robinson seemed to acknowledge unionist disillusionment, telling the BBC (BBC Online, 2009b):

> We have to face up to the fact that while a large portion of the unionist electorate find it very difficult to have Sinn Féin in government, I think that we did

the right thing ... I believe that we have undersold our case. People need to know there was no more acceptable alternative available. I don't believe we have communicated that message sufficiently to our own support base.

The reasons for unionist disillusionment with the DUP are both religious and political, but have little to do with the party's performance in Europe. Religiously-based disillusionment has been articulated by Free Presbyterian Minister, Ivan Foster, and a group calling themselves 'Concerned Free Presbyterians'. Both have railed against the 'immorality' of sharing government with 'terrorists,' and have protested that Paisley, because of his position in the Office of the First Minister and Deputy First Minister, was forced to concede too much in terms of rights for people from the lesbian, gay, bisexual and transgender community (see Moloney, 2008: 489–511). Paisley was eventually forced to relent, stepping down as Moderator of the Free Presbyterian Church when his term expired in January 2008. The reproduction in Moloney's book (2008: 527–531) of notes taken by a 'DUP dissident' at an internal party meeting to discuss the St Andrews' Agreement in October 2006 demonstrate that, for some, plenty of *political* objections remain. On the other hand, Moloney cites evidence that unionists are content with the DUP–Sinn Féin partnership. A survey published in the *Belfast Telegraph* one hundred days after devolution 'showed that 58 percent of DUP voters now backed the deal, compared to 46 percent after the St Andrews' Agreement' (Moloney, 2008: 522). He also notes (2008: 522, 532) that unionist confidence seems to be rebounding, with Protestant 'self-assurance' increasing 42 points between IRA decommissioning in September 2005 and the Assembly's return in 2007.

So, the DUP's disappointing result in the election to the European Parliament in 2009 has primarily been interpreted as a result of its policies in Northern Ireland – not in Europe. The prominence of personalities and extra-European issues in the election campaign seems to fit with a wider trend of the de-politicization of electorates, in which voters perceive that their votes will have little impact on European issues. On the other hand, the party devoted more space than ever before to specific European policies in its 2009 manifesto. This could be interpreted as embryonic programmatic change along the lines of hesitant Europeanization. Even so, the image of the EU presented in DUP manifestos is overwhelmingly suspicious and critical. Engagement is only justified insofar as it is deemed to serve the interests of unionist voters.

Conclusion: Persistent Euroscepticism

There is little evidence that the DUP has been 'Europeanized' in Ladrech's (2002) sense of the term, or even to the extent of other ethnoregionalist parties around Europe. The degree to which any of Ladrech's (2002) five areas of Europeanization can be discerned within the party is limited. In terms of party programmatic change, the DUP's manifestos contain few references to the EU. Even European election manifestos are overwhelmingly dominated by domestic issues. In terms of organization, the EU has not prompted change in the DUP's internal structures. The party's European policies have largely been driven by the sitting MEP, with very little input from the party's central headquarters. The DUP does not have an EU Policy Officer, for example. Neither has involvement in the EU prompted the DUP to forge strong links beyond the national party system, as the party remains unaligned in the European Parliament. Although the DUP has, over time, responded to some specific EU policy issues/areas, the party as a whole is not engaged to any significant extent with the process of European integration. Whether this changes during Diane Dodds' tenure as MEP remains to be seen.

Notably, the one area in which there is some evidence that Ladrech-style Europeanization may have impacted on the DUP is in its competition with the UUP. Neither unionist party can be described as pro-European, but the DUP conscientiously presents itself as more Eurosceptic than the UUP. This may be interpreted as the DUP adopting an anti-EU position to appeal to voters as a means of distinguishing itself from the UUP. But given the extent to which unionist party competition is dominated by internal Northern Ireland concerns, it is unlikely that a party's position on Europe could be a decisive factor in elections – even in elections to the European Parliament, except to the extent that the strength of one's anti-European position reflects the strength of one's Britishness. Indeed, this point may serve to reinforce the argument that 'Europe' is at best an additional medium for local party competition in Northern Ireland rather than a means for transcending it.

Nevertheless, the DUP has been affected in some of the ways anticipated by De Winter and Gómez-Reino (2002). First, the availability of EU funding has meant that the relationship between Northern Ireland as a 'periphery' has changed in relation to a powerful EU centre, with groups in the region competing for PEACE funding. The DUP has adjusted to this context by helping local unionist groups access these funds. Second, and in line with similar processes throughout Europe, it seems that political decisions have become further removed from citizens. Like other ethnoregionalist *and* nationalist parties, the DUP's European election campaigns are contested around personalities and issues that have little direct relevance to what actually goes on in the European Parliament. The DUP does differ from other ethnoregionalist parties, however, in having refused to ally with other ethnoregionalist parties within the EU, as expected by De Winter and Gómez-Reino (2002). Consequently, there is little evidence that participation in EU institutions has invoked any moderation of the traditional and defiant Euroscepticism of the party. Although the DUP has demonstrated a capacity and readiness for selective engagement with EU institutions and policy-making, it remains for the time being definitively outside any model of a 'Europeanized' party. This is, perhaps, to be expected given its proud singularity as a political party in contemporary Europe.

Acknowledgements

The author wishes to acknowledge research assistance by Shae Savoy (transcription) and Sara Templer (data collection). She also wishes to thank Christopher Stalford and Jim Allister for interviews.

Notes

1. For instance, De Winter and Gómez-Reino (2002) include UK regional parties such as Plaid Cymru and the Scottish National Party but make no mention of either unionist or nationalist parties in Northern Ireland.
2. The UUP is now part of the European Conservatives and Reformist Group, which was established after the June 2009 European Parliamentary Elections as an 'anti-federalist' coalition (see Murphy, 2009).

References

Allister, J. (2007) *European Union Programme for Cross Border Territorial Co-Operation (Interreg IV): Consultation Response*, available at: www.jimallister.org (accessed July 2009).
BBC Online (2009a) DUP must learn from Euro poll, 9 June 2009, available at: http://news.bbc.co.uk/1/hi/northern_ireland/8090607.stm (accessed July 2009).
BBC Online (2009b) DUP's worst ever Euro poll result, *BBC Online*, 8 June, available at: http://news.bbc.co.uk/1/hi/northern_ireland/8090294.stm (accessed July 2009).
Brewer, J. & Higgins, G. (1998) *Anti Catholicism in Northern Ireland 1600–1998: The Mote and the Beam* (Basingstoke: Macmillan).
Bruce, S. (1986) *God Save Ulster! The Religion and Politics of Paisleyism* (Oxford: Oxford University Press).
Bruce, S. (2001) Fundamentalism and political violence: the case of Paisley and Ulster Evangelicals, *Religion*, 31, pp. 387–405.
Bruce, S. (2007) *Paisley: Religion and Politics in Northern Ireland* (Oxford: Oxford University Press).
Coakley, J. (2009) A political profile of Protestant minorities in Europe, *National Identities*, 11(1), pp. 9–30.
Cooke, D. (1996) *Persecuting Zeal: A Portrait of Ian Paisley* (Dingle: Brandon).
DUP (2004) *The DUP's Vision for Europe: Europe 04* (Belfast: DUP).
DUP (2009a) *Strong Leadership in Challenging Times: Manifesto 2009* (Belfast: DUP).
DUP (2009b) *Latest News: DUP Leader Congratulates Diane Dodds*, available at: www.dup.org.uk/articles.asp?ArticleNewsID=611 (accessed July 2009).
De Winter, L. & Gomez-Reino Cachafeiro, M. (2002) European integration and ethnoregionalist parties, *Party Politics*, 8(4), pp. 483–503.
De Winter, L. & Tursan, H. (Eds) (1998) *Regionalist Parties in Western Europe* (London: Routledge).
Ganiel, G. (2008) *Evangelicalism and Conflict in Northern Ireland* (New York: Palgrave).
Higgins, G. (2001) Great expectations: the myth of the anti-Christ in Northern Ireland, Unpublished PhD dissertation (Belfast: Queens University).
Hume, J. (1996) *John Hume: Personal Views* (Dublin: TownHouse).
Ladrech, R. (2002) Europeanization and political parties: towards a framework for analysis, *Party Politics*, 8(4), pp. 389–403.
Laffan, B. (2005) The European context: a new political dimension in Ireland, North and South, in: J. Coakley, B. Laffan & J. Todd (Eds) *Renovation or Revolution? New Territorial Politics in Ireland and the United Kingdom*, pp. 166–184 (Dublin: UCD Press).
Mair, P. (2000) The limited impact of Europe on national party systems, *West European Politics*, 23(4), pp. 27–51.
Mair, P. (2004) The Europeanization dimension, *Journal of European Public Policy*, 11(2), pp. 337–348.
McCall, C. (2003) Shifting thresholds, contested meanings: governance, cross-border co-operation and the Ulster Unionist identity, *European Studies: A Journal of European Culture, History and Politics*, 19, pp. 81–103.
McLoughlin, P.J. (2009) The SDLP and the Europeanization of the Northern Ireland problem, *Irish Political Studies*, 24(4), pp. 603–619.

Meehan, E. (2000) Europe and the Europeanization of the Irish question, in: M. Cox, A. Guelke & F. Stephen (Eds) *A Farewell to Arms? From 'Long War' to 'Long Peace' in Northern Ireland*, pp. 199–213 (Manchester: Manchester University Press).
Mitchel, P. (2003) *Evangelicalism and National Identity in Ulster, 1921–1998* (Oxford: Oxford University Press).
Moloney, E. (2008) *Paisley: From Demagogue to Democrat?* (Dublin: Poolbeg).
Moloney, E. & Pollak, A. (1987) *Paisley* (Swords: Poolbeg).
Murphy, M.C. (2009) Pragmatic politics: the Ulster Unionist Party and the European Union, *Irish Political Studies*, 24(4), pp. 589–602.
Northern Ireland Executive (2008) 614 million EU programme tops trio launched by Robinson, 14 April, available at: www.northernireland.gov.uk/news-dfp-140408-614million-eu-programme (accessed July 2009).
Rankin, A. & Ganiel, G. (2008) DUP discourses about violence and their impact on the Northern Ireland peace process, *Peace and Conflict Studies*, 15(1), pp. 115–135.
Smith, M.L. (2000) The European connection and public opinion, in: D. Kennedy (Ed.) *Living with the European Union: The Northern Ireland Experience*, pp. 169–196 (Basingstoke: Macmillan).
Smyth, C. (1987) *Ian Paisley: Voice of Protestant Ulster* (Edinburgh: Scottish Academic Press).
Todd, J. (1999) Nationalism, Republicanism and the Good Friday Agreement, in: J. Ruane & J. Todd (Eds) *After the Good Friday Agreement: Analysing Political Change in Northern Ireland*, pp. 49–70 (Dublin: UCD Press).

Pragmatic Politics: The Ulster Unionist Party and the European Union

MARY C. MURPHY
University College Cork, Ireland

ABSTRACT   *In the context of its waning political fortunes, the European Union (EU) represents the only electoral realm where the Ulster Unionist Party (UUP) has maintained a stable presence. The party's traditionally negative approach to the EU has changed over time, shifting from opposition to pragmatism or realism, and has involved programmatic and organizational change. Such developments, however, are not symptomatic of a process of Europeanization as defined by Ladrech (2002). Instead they are indicative of the ways in which the UUP has sought to use the European arena as a means to secure domestic political and electoral advantage. Changing approaches to the EU have occurred in tandem with the emergence of a rational civic form of unionism during the 1990s. Occasioned by wider political developments, this 'new unionism' marked a radical shift in UUP strategy. It was an approach grounded in pragmatism and built upon a modernization agenda involving organizational change. The UUP–EU dynamic is built on similar foundations. The impact of 'new unionism' on the UUP party is thus broadly spread, embracing new and pragmatic approaches to both constitutional politics and policy positions, including the EU. Crucially, it should not be confused with a process of Europeanization.*

Introduction

The Ulster Unionist Party (UUP) has a long political history. One of the oldest political parties on the island of Ireland, its electoral fortunes have recently shifted from a position of hegemony in the period 1921–1972, to a position of increasing marginalization. The emergence of rival unionist parties from the late 1960s onwards undermined the overwhelming dominance of the party as a voice for unionism within Northern Ireland. Despite the challenges, the party remained the largest party representing unionists in Northern Ireland and played an instrumental role in drafting the 1998 Belfast Agreement. The party participated in the newly created Northern Ireland Executive as the largest political party in Northern Ireland and party leader, David Trimble, became the first First Minister in Northern Ireland. The electoral fortunes of the party, however, began to change thereafter. In 2005, the Westminster General Election produced the worst ever election result for the UUP. The party was reduced to a single Member of Parliament (MP) and had effectively been overtaken by the Democratic Unionist Party (DUP) as the largest unionist party in Northern Ireland.

The party's changing fortunes can be traced to developments during the 1990s. In response to domestic political realities linked to the evolution of the peace process, the party reluctantly embraced what has been labelled 'new unionism' (English, 2002). 'New unionism' has involved the cultivation of a more pragmatically-focused party, the development of new relationships and policy positions and ultimately, the weakening of the traditional character of the party. The changes were profound and challenging and paradoxically, they impacted negatively on the electoral performance of the party.

In tandem with these changes, the party's traditionally negative approach to the EU has waned over time, shifting from opposition to pragmatism. This may suggest some element of Europeanization as defined by Ladrech (2002). Deeper examination however, suggests that new approaches to Europe are informed by internal party dynamics and other political pressures, and not by external Europeanizing forces. The focus of 'new unionism' on pragmatism extends to other policy domains and is reflected in the party's approach to Europe. Domestic politics and the demands of devolution are the primary focus for the UUP party. In a review of the literature on Europeanization, Mair (2004) notes that the preferences of political leaders (in this case key party figures) is a factor in mediating the impact of the forces of Europeanization. Also important is the political and cultural context, which can further mediate Europeanizing influences. All of these considerations are relevant to the UUP experience.

This article applies the Ladrech Europeanization framework to a study of the UUP and the European Union (EU). Programmatic/policy and organizational adjustments within the UUP are evident in terms of deeper consideration of the EU and an increased engagement with Europe by the party. The relationship between this and the forces of Europeanization however are dubious. Domestic developments have been as, if not more significant in promoting new pragmatic party practices and perspectives on Europe. In terms of patterns of party competition; party–government relations; and relations beyond the national party system, evidence of Europeanization is negligible. The party's adaptation to the EU has been grounded in pragmatism and this has been a key feature of recent developments within the UUP. The impact of 'new unionism' should not be confused with a process of Europeanization.

The Ulster Unionist Party

Until 2005, the UUP was the largest political party in Northern Ireland. In constitutional terms, the party supports the maintenance of Northern Ireland's position as an integral part of the UK. The defence of the constitutional status of Northern Ireland has traditionally represented the basis for the party's very existence.

The party is distinctly British and is currently rekindling and formalizing its one-time close links with the Conservative Party in Britain. In early 2009, the UUP and

Conservative Party agreed a pact to fight elections jointly in Northern Ireland. In June 2009, the party's Member of the European Parliament (MEP) Jim Nicholson ran in the European elections under the banner of *Ulster Conservatives and Unionists – New Force* (UCUNF). Although the parties continue to exist separately, they agree joint election manifestos and candidates. For the UUP, the move is an attempt to reinvigorate the party and ultimately claim back lost electoral ground (see Empey, 2008). For the Conservative Party, in particular its leader David Cameron, the venture is a means of portraying the party as a British party which encompasses all of the UK and Northern Ireland (see Cameron, 2008).

The decision to join forces with the Conservative Party does not enjoy universal support within the party ranks. This reflects the history and tradition of a party which has been described as a movement rather than a party (see Hume, 1996), thus lacking a strong ideological basis. According to Tonge and Evans (2001: 112): 'Since its formation, the UUP has attempted to act as catch-all communal political party, representing the interests of all unionists irrespective of social backgrounds'. A number of UUP members are offended by the way in which an alliance with the Conservative Party undermines the traditional catch-all character of the party (see McGimpsey, 2008). The party's only MP, Lady Sylvia Hermon, has indicated publically that she is unlikely to contest the next general election under a Conservative Party banner. Of course, the UUP has previously been linked to the Conservative Party. Those links became strained after 1972 and were eventually severed. UUP Leader, Sir Reg Empey, claims that the new alliance differs from earlier experience. He notes a changing shift in Conservative thinking under David Cameron which serves to legitimize the UUP decision to reassess and rebuild old relationships (Empey, 2008).

The UUP alliance with the Conservative Party however, is only one of a number of changes experienced by the party in recent years. During the 1990s, political circumstance forced difficult change upon Ulster Unionists. The UUP was effectively compelled to do a deal with nationalism or risk being excluded (on weakened terms) from a final peace settlement. This new variety of unionism, or 'new unionism' as it has been labelled, is ostensibly associated with former UUP leader, David Trimble. New unionism can be characterized by a readiness 'to make a new deal with nationalism' (English, 2002: 97). The consequence has been the emergence of a form of unionism which displays a more sophisticated understanding of contemporary political forces, in both the domestic and international context. Developments such as the fall of the British Empire, membership of the EU and UK constitutional change (particularly the embrace of devolution) forced leading Unionists to reappraise unionism and to encourage the party rank and file to support a form of domestic and international political engagement based on pragmatism. The reluctant engagement with Irish nationalism which this entailed led to much soul-searching within the party and at its worst, resulted in serious divisions. Internal party difficulties and splits worsened after 1998 with the party divided between pro- and anti-Agreement sentiments and culminated in the disastrous Westminster election results of 2005.

Unionism and unionist culture on the whole has been subject to immense pressures since the proroguing of Stormont in 1972 (see Farrington 2008). These pressures became even more profound during the 1990s when serious differences emerged within the party in relation to engagement with the peace process. UUP participation in the peace process was a highly sensitive matter. The party was 'divided over whether to embrace a rational civic or traditional cultural form [of Unionism]' (Tonge, 2005: 78). Supporters of rational civic unionism supported the 1998 Agreement and saw it as a means to secure the Union. Traditional cultural unionists, on the other hand, opposed the settlement viewing it as a means of undermining the Union and appeasing Republicans. Ultimately, the party has shifted towards a form of rational civic unionism as evidenced by recent structural and organizational reforms which have severed formal relations with the Orange Order and nurtured an alliance with the UK Conservative Party. The consideration of such profound changes is not grounded in any strong ideological outlook but rather in a perception that unionist interests are best protected by supporting the pluralist dimensions of the 1998 Agreement, accepting the legitimacy of constitutional nationalism and tolerating power-sharing with cross-border bodies (Tonge, 2005). Pragmatism has therefore defined the approach of the UUP to the peace process (for further discussion, see Farrington, 2001). This approach and outlook is not solely confined to the constitutional question – it has also been embraced in the context of the party's engagement with the European Union.

The Europeanization of the UUP

In examining the Europeanization of the UUP, there are two dimensions to be considered. Firstly, to what extent is there evidence of Europeanization of the UUP, and secondly, how do we explain it, i.e. what factors influenced the party's decision to adapt its structures, organization and/or behaviour? In framing responses to these questions, Ladrech's (2002) framework for analysing the Europeanization of political parties is utilized.

Policy/Programmatic Change

Research suggests that regionalist parties across Europe are typically Europhile. Indeed one author has characterized such parties as being 'consistently pro-EU' (Jolly, 2007: 124). Unlike its counterparts in other parts of Europe, however, the UUP does not have a Europhile character. Goodman (1996: 219) has described the UUP approach to the European Union as 'hesitant pro-Europeanism'. Opposed to deeper integration, the party favours the notion of a Europe of sovereign nation-states. However, the party is prepared to 'accept the reality of the EU and work constructively within it' (Hainsworth, 1996: 31). Moxon-Browne (1983: 163) presents a similar perspective: 'membership was a fact of life and the best had to be made of it'. In this respect the UUP acknowledges the opportunities provided by the single market, recognizes the benefits of the Common Agricultural Policy (CAP) for

Northern Ireland and welcomes the financial support to the region from the EU. Its stance may be summarized as pragmatic but lacking a wholehearted embrace of fundamental EU principles.

Evidence of Europeanization of the UUP can be identified with reference to an outlook and approach to European matters which have evolved over time. The pragmatic approach to the EU which is apparent today has not always been in evidence. Initial reactions to the prospects of UK membership of the EU were less than positive. Although the UK did not hold a referendum on accession to the then European Economic Community (EEC), a majority of UUP MPs opposed membership in a free vote in Westminster. The 1975 referendum on the UK's membership of the EEC returned a slim majority in favour of continued membership in Northern Ireland. Party perspectives on the central issue were characterized by 'obfuscation' (Moxon-Browne, 1983: 157). Issues were simplified and distorted rendering the quality of the debate poor – unsurprising considering the timing of the referendum, which coincided with a period of intense communal conflict in the region. A Northern Ireland Attitude Survey (NIAS) survey three years later produced similar results to the referendum outcome. Interestingly, however, it provided a party breakdown of views. UUP voters were marginally against continued membership (52.7 percent) (Moxon-Browne, 1983).

In the intervening years, the party's opposition to EU membership has remained largely steadfast notwithstanding a willingness to work the system to Northern Ireland's advantage. The traditional hostility to the EU is grounded in a fear of the erosion of the sovereignty of the Westminster parliament and a belief that any form of internationalization will aid nationalists in Northern Ireland. McGarry and O'Leary (1995: 304) go so far as to suggest that: 'Rather than promoting accommodation, European integration has increased unionist insecurities and reinforced their intransigence'. They go on to claim that unionists 'see themselves as captive participants in an integrative project over which they have no control'. Yet this has not prevented the party from developing a less hostile approach to the EU. For the most part, this has been pioneered by the party's MEP, Jim Nicholson. He defines himself as a 'Eurorealist' who 'approaches the EU from the position of a mainstream Unionist, *supporting co-operation between free nations for mutual advantage*' (emphasis in the original) (UUP, 2004). He also recognizes the benefits of the EU for Northern Ireland, particularly in the context of regional funding (see Hainsworth & McCann, 2004: 99–100).

Aside from principled objections to the European integration project and its implications for the integrity and future of the UK state, the UUP has also voiced opposition to specific EU actions. Attempts to link the resolution of the Northern Ireland conflict to the EU have been rejected by the UUP. Unionists have never viewed the EU as a forum within which unionists and nationalists might be reconciled. Indeed talk of such a possibility tended to further harden UUP attitudes to Europe, particularly when coupled with strong Social Democratic and Labour Party (SDLP) support for the EU.

Party policy on the European Union has traditionally been under-developed. Election manifestos provide some indication of this. There is little reference to the

EU in early election manifestos. Indeed the 1973 UUP Assembly Manifesto makes only scant reference to Europe. In a short section entitled 'Ulster in Europe', only three vague and somewhat ambiguous points are made:

- Ulster's farming and industrial interests will need to be protected in the EEC.
- We shall organize a central marketing strategy.
- We shall improve transport facilities between Ulster, Europe and Great Britain.

In contrast, later election manifestos display a more sophisticated understanding of the EU and an intention to exploit the Union for Northern Ireland's advantage. Recent UUP European election manifestos are explicitly focused on EU issues. The 1999 European election took place against a challenging backdrop in that it was bound up in debates about the 1998 Agreement. Discussion of the Agreement was inevitable during the campaign. Nevertheless, Nicholson's manifesto had a strong European flavour albeit one which demonstrated a Eurosceptic outlook. However, it did include specific proposals in relation to better defending Northern Ireland interests in Europe via the creation of a regional office in Brussels (Hainsworth & McCann, 2000: 136–137). During the 2004 European election campaign, Jim Nicholson again 'tried to keep the focus on Europe' and made much of his European experience and credentials (Hainsworth, 2004: 101).

Interestingly, other UUP election manifestos are gradually affording greater acknowledgment of the European dimension to national and regional governance. The EU is invariably referenced in relation to the party's position on agriculture and fisheries (see UUP Westminster Election Manifestos, 2005, 2001 and 1997). A Eurosceptic position is also evident in relation to opposition to a European superstate (UUP, 1997) and the EU Constitution (UUP, 2005).

The introduction of devolution has involved substantial change for all political parties in Northern Ireland and represents a challenge for parties and politicians who are now required to engage with everyday public policy issues. Although EU matters are reserved, there is nevertheless an onus on the devolved administration to manage policies which have a strong EU dimension. UUP manifestos for elections to the Northern Ireland Assembly devote some consideration to the EU and make specific recommendations in relation to best representing Northern Ireland's interests. The 2007 manifesto advocated the 'creation of an Assembly Committee on European Affairs – providing focus to Northern Ireland's relationship with the European Union' (UUP, 2007: 34). The 2003 manifesto made reference to the creation of the Office of the Northern Ireland Executive in Brussels (ONIEB), portraying its opening as an example of how the UUP's involvement in the Assembly can work effectively (UUP, 2003: 4).

One of the more high profile examples of UUP perspectives on Europe was the decision of the party to back the Maastricht Treaty in Westminster in 1993. A pragmatic approach to the EU was evident in this uncharacteristic decision. Support for the treaty was not based on conviction but instead on the fear that the alternatives may have been worse, i.e. a collapse of the government and the election of a Labour

Party government which would seek the reunification of Ireland by consensus. The UUP also believed that its support for the Conservative government would grant it privileges for the lifetime of the parliament. The decision to support Maastricht therefore had everything to do with domestic political priorities and little to do with Europe. Political pragmatism linked to the domestic agenda, as opposed to a moderation of party position on Europe explains the vote.

In terms of programmatic change, the UUP has on the face of it experienced some degree of Europeanization since the UK's accession to the EU in 1973. Ladrech (2002: 396) suggests that such developments are likely a consequence of 'enhanced European policy expertise among party specialists ... [and] agreement with the leadership to integrate the European dimension into references to domestic policy'. However, although there is increased quantitative consideration of the EU in party manifestos, qualitative analysis of such content suggests that it is not based on a shift in party policy towards enhanced support for European integration. Clearly, the party has gradually allowed itself to engage with the EU, but crucially this is in a manner which is decidedly practical and pragmatic. The UUP has supported EU initiatives and policies which benefit Northern Ireland but which do not undermine the sovereignty and integrity of the UK state such as, for example, the drive to secure EU structural funding and support for Northern Ireland farmers. Principled objections to the European integration project within the UUP remain apparent. The party's position on the Lisbon Treaty is ambiguous and reflects differing opinions within the party organization and among UUP voters. The party's MEP voted against the Lisbon Treaty in a European Parliament (EP) vote, going against European People's Party and European Democrats (EPP-ED) policy (of which he was then a member). This position does not reflect party policy. The UUP has not articulated explicit opposition to the Lisbon Treaty, but instead has focused on calls for the UK government to hold a referendum on the treaty. Pragmatic and selective engagement with the EU and vague party perspectives on the EU's future constitutional shape cannot be considered symptomatic of a process of Europeanization.

Organizational Change

The UUP's MEP has traditionally been the focus for the party's outlook and approach to the EU.[1] However, both of the party's two MEPs to date have faced considerable challenges in nurturing interest in EU matters within the broader party. The overwhelming focus of the UUP (and all political parties in Northern Ireland) has traditionally been on the constitutional question. In this context, it was invariably left to the party's MEP alone to define and pursue the UUP's EU programme. Party leaders may have sporadically intervened, but for the most part neither James Molyneaux nor David Trimble demonstrated a strong interest in EU politics (certainly when compared with former SDLP leader John Hume). The UUP's presence in Europe is a consequence of electoral pressures, and not principled interest or support. This is not to undermine the sustained European electoral success since 1989 of current UUP MEP Jim Nicholson. His elevation to the post of Quaestor within the EP;[2] his work on behalf of Northern Ireland's agricultural sector; and his recent appointment as spokesman on Regional Affairs for the Conservative Party in the EP have garnered him increased stature and respect within his own party. He is also a member of the UUP Party Executive Committee. This committee governs many areas of party administration, including membership and candidate selection, and is an important component of the party machine. The significance of MEP membership of this committee however has not promoted a wider engagement by the party organization with matters European. According to a leading party figure, the UUP's policy approach to the EU is led by the party's MEP and only in instances where a specific issue may be controversial is wider party input or consultation deemed necessary. Otherwise the judgement of the MEP is accepted and trusted. Some cynics may also claim that the MEP's membership of the Party Executive is more a consequence of the current incumbent's support for the 1998 Agreement and/ or his closeness to recent party leaders than it is of his European credentials.

Although the presence of the party's EP representative at the heart of the party's decision-making organ may on the face of it appear significant, it does not signal a 'greater profile of European policy and the leadership's need to manage it more closely' (Ladrech, 2002: 397). Ladrech's suggestion that the inclusion of key EU personnel at the heart of the party machine implies a measurable increase in the profile of the EU within the party is not borne out in the case of the UUP. Clear evidence of the Europeanization of the party organization is lacking.

Notwithstanding the apparent limits of Europeanization across the party organization, individual UUP figures have begun to engage more actively and visibly with the EU than hithertofore. A number of UUP members of the Northern Ireland Assembly (MLAs) are playing increasingly energetic roles in areas with an EU context. The introduction of devolution in 1999 has changed the dynamics of governance within Northern Ireland and has forced all Northern Ireland parties to adapt to new political realities and responsibilities. In his capacity as First Minister, David Trimble engaged directly with the EU. He visited Brussels and met with senior political and administrative figures. He was active in lobbying for an extension of the PEACE programme and supported the opening of the ONIEB. The current Northern Ireland administration is very different in composition to that of the original. The UUP now has just two Ministerial positions within the Northern Ireland Executive. Party leader, Sir Reg Empey, holds the office of Minister for Employment and Learning. Although the European 'flavour' to this Department is less than that for other policy areas (such as agricultural or environmental policy), the Minister has responsibility for the management and implementation of the European Social Fund (ESF) in Northern Ireland. The Minister has also visited Brussels and in 2007 he engaged directly with key officials including the European Commissioner for Employment, Social Affairs and Equal Opportunities. In his capacity as party leader, Sir Empey has also met with European Commission President Jose Manuel Barroso on the subject of the EU's Taskforce on Northern Ireland and he continues to maintain visible and regular relations with the EU.

Other UUP MLAs are also involved in EU affairs. Danny Kennedy is Chair of the Committee for the Office of the First Minister and Deputy First Minister. European issues are among the matters for which the Committee has responsibility for overseeing. Under the Chairmanship of the UUP MLA, the Committee published terms of reference for the consideration of EU issues in October 2008. The process involves reviewing the Northern Ireland Assembly's role in relation to European issues and includes consultation with key representatives and stakeholders.

Closer engagement with the EU is often focused on funding and a necessity to manage the EU dimension to specific ministerial portfolios. Indeed, the behaviour and activities of politicians may be construed as a necessary function of their participation in devolved structures. The trigger for engaging with Europe therefore is often dictated by domestic political circumstance rather than by changed party policy or altered party organization. Specific activities and approaches on the part of individual politicians are not explicitly linked to EU-related organizational change within the party. Instead they replicate the culture of pragmatism which has marked the approach to other policy issues by the UUP in recent years. Furthermore, changed conduct *vis-à-vis* Europe on the part of individual members of the UUP is not reflected across the wider party organization but instead is concentrated amongst a small number of elite party members. The EU has not permeated the wider party organization. The notion therefore that the UUP party organization has been Europeanized is, at the very least, premature.

Patterns of Party Competition

Ladrech (2002: 397) suggests that the European arena may be a fruitful location for parties to opportunistically target voters, by pushing a strong pro- or anti-EU position. In their study of ethnoregionalist parties, De Winter and Gómez-Reino (2002: 493) claim that 'parties obtain better results at the European elections than at the parliamentary elections in their country'. In this context, the EU arena is seen as one where 'political visibility and legitimacy at the European level' can be gained (De Winter & Gómez-Reino, 2002: 494). This has not been the experience of the UUP. Indeed, the European contest has typically been a persistently challenging electoral arena for the party. Nevertheless, the party has continuously returned a candidate to one of the three EP seats allocated to Northern Ireland, since the introduction of direct elections in 1979. However, they have traditionally polled third in these elections. This feature of EP election outcomes can be explained by the fact that such elections are treated as 'a contest for political leadership in Northern Ireland and as a vote for or against British sovereignty' (Goodman, 1996: 213). EP elections in Northern Ireland have typically been conducted against a domestic backdrop which has reinforced the unique nature of Northern Ireland's party system with its emphasis on the constitutional question. In 1994 for example: 'The DUP's stated intention was to make the Euro-election akin to a referendum on the Downing Street Declaration' (Hainsworth, 1995: 201). A similar context was apparent in 1999. On this occasion, the European election campaign was bound up with debates on the Agreement. Because of the focus on domestic politics, EP elections are occasions for 'intra-unionist and intra-nationalist struggles' (Hainsworth & McCann, 2000: 135). The battle between the DUP and UUP has always been particularly antagonistic. The force of personality has undoubtedly played a role. The 1999 EP election was billed as a personal contest between John Hume and Ian Paisley for the first seat. Against such internationally known figures, the relatively low profile UUP candidate is unable to compete on the same terms. He was effectively 'overshadowed by the two longstanding antagonists' (Elliott, 1990: 99) and invariably owed his seat to what one commentator has labelled 'the magnanimity of the DUP leader's supporters' (Cochrane, 2001: 324).

The 2004 election was a slightly different affair. The personalities had changed (with the retirement of DUP leader, Ian Paisley and SDLP leader, John Hume) and the tone of the electoral contest was less focused on domestic affairs. This however, was not to the benefit of the UUP. The party did not succeed in capitalizing on Jim Nicholson's European experience and credentials against new lesser known candidates. The MEP was re-elected, coming in third place on the third count. The inability of Nicholson to appeal to the broader unionist community (particularly after the departure of Paisley) was a reflection of 'doubts ... about the workings of [the] Agreement and about the benefits accrued to that community thereby' (Hainsworth & McCann, 2004: 110). The unrelenting implicit and explicit focus on domestic politics has left little room for the UUP to exploit the European election arena by concentrating on the party's European credentials and outlook. Unlike other regions of Europe, EP electoral contests do not provide a basis for a party such as the UUP to experience any substantial degree of Europeanization.

The 2009 elections to the EP marked a departure for the UUP. The party's alliance with the Conservative Party saw the UUP incumbent seek re-election under the banner *Ulster Conservatives and Unionists – New Force*. This alliance allowed the UUP to fight the campaign on different terms to previously. In particular, it allowed the party to make a clearer distinction between itself and the DUP. In European terms, the outlook of the UCUNF is less Eurosceptic than the DUP. The election manifesto praises the EU's contribution to healing division and spreading democracy across Europe and also expresses support for the single market and deregulation. The manifesto is less positive with respect to the Lisbon Treaty and points to concerns in relation to notions of creeping federalism within the Union.

The UUP alliance with the Conservative Party however is not expressly about the development of a clearer EU outlook and profile and cannot be construed as evidence of the Europeanization of the party. It does however fit with the pragmatic ethos of 'new unionism' in constituting an attempt to revive and re-invigorate the party. During the negotiation process which preceded the electoral alliance between the UUP and Conservative Party, Sir Reg Empey (2008) stated:

> If nothing else, our ongoing talks with the Conservative Party have opened up a possible route to something much more productive than the present

stalemate. Politics is about the willingness to explore all options. That is why the Ulster Unionist Party engaged in the Talks process that produced the Belfast Agreement. It is why we are talking to the Conservative Party now.

Links with the Conservative Party allows the UUP to claim that it is the best protector of Unionist interests by virtue of their close and formal links with a major UK political party. This strategy potentially allows the party to appeal to larger numbers of unionist voters. Since the 1998 Agreement, Northern Ireland politicians are required to deal with everyday policy issues. It is this new political environment which makes the current UUP association with the Conservative Party different from the earlier relationship. The latter was intently focused on the constitutional question, the former has a substantially stronger ideological basis (which explains the unease felt by some UUP members). Former Conservative Party leader, William Hague, has welcomed the restructuring of relations between the two parties claiming 'it [is] "good for Northern Ireland" as it [offers] local voters a place in the UK political mainstream' (*Irish Times*, 26 May 2009). The new relationship between the parties also offers the possibility of greater national influence. Speaking at the UUP's Annual Conference in Belfast in December 2008, Conservative Party Leader David Cameron spoke of Northern Ireland needing MPs 'who have a real prospect of holding office as ministers in a Westminster government'. The UUP can use such possibilities to appeal to voters in ways which give them an advantage relative to their DUP foes.

The first electoral outing for the UCUNF proved successful for the UUP. For the first time, UUP candidate Jim Nicholson was the first unionist candidate returned, coming in ahead of the DUP's Diane Dodds who polled disappointingly. The result reflected a marginal increase in voter support for the UUP. The party gained 17.1 percent of the vote, up from 16.6 percent in 2004. However, their victory over the DUP was clearly facilitated by the presence of three unionist parties on the ballot sheet and the resultant split in voting which this entailed. Regardless of interpretations of the result however, the notion that the new alliance between the Conservatives and the Ulster Unionists is, in any way, an example of Europeanization, is imprudent. The 2009 elections to the EP have served as a useful (and encouraging) electoral testing ground for a political experiment which, from the UUP's perspective, is unquestionably about the renewal of Ulster Unionism and not the politicization of the party's EU strategy.

Party–Government Relations and Relations beyond the National Party System

No Northern Ireland political party has ever participated in national government. This effectively means that Northern Ireland political parties have not had privileged contact with the EU through the executive, as has been the case for other political parties at other regional levels across Europe. Political parties which have traditionally had little likelihood of ever participating in executive level politics are somewhat sidelined and excluded from the cut and thrust of EU politics as a consequence of the increasing domination of EU issues and politics by national executives. With reference to the UUP and party–government relations, the Ladrech framework is currently redundant.

In terms of relations beyond the national party system, evidence of the Europeanization of the UUP is highly limited. The party's MEPs have been members of a number of EP political groupings. John Taylor was aligned to the European Democratic Group and later joined the Group of the European Right which was commonly regarded as a far right political grouping (see Hix, Noury & Roland, 2005). Jim Nicholson has been a member of the EPP–ED Group and was previously allied to the late James Goldsmith's Europe of Nations Group. More recently, Nicholson's political allegiances in the EP have shifted again. After the June 2009 EP elections, the Conservative Party created the new anti-federalist European Conservatives and Reformists Group of which Nicholson is a member.[3] UUP member Chris McGimpsey (2009) highlights the implications of this arrangement for the MEP posing the question: 'Will the "Euro-realist" edge closer to being a "Euro-sceptic"?'. The lack of stability and consistency in terms of alliances between the UUP and European political groupings is unusual. Research by De Winter and Gómez-Reino (2002: 494) has concluded that, with reference to ethno-regionalist political parties: 'An emerging European polity has ... facilitated the development of contacts and has transformed party cooperation into standard practice'. This has clearly not been the experience of Ulster Unionists. There is no foundation for Europeanization of UUP relations beyond the national party system.

Conclusion

The UUP has experienced profound change in recent years. The shift to 'new unionism' has been a difficult one and has involved participating in a new era of devolved politics in Northern Ireland. Changes to the party organization have also been antagonistic and exposed internal divisions. Poor electoral performances have drastically reduced party representation and strength at all levels of political representation, bar the European. The decision to engage proactively with the Northern Ireland peace process during the 1990s marked a turning point for the UUP and was accompanied by a shift towards a rational civic form of unionism grounded in pragmatism. The opposition which this engendered over time, both within the party and among traditional UUP voters, stimulated further change. A new leader, continued changes to the party organization and an electoral alliance with the Conservative Party continue to reflect the pragmatic character of the UUP.

In tandem, the evolving character of the UUP–EU dynamic has been similarly pragmatic. Changes to the programmatic/policy orientation and the organization of the party vis-à-vis the EU has been apparent. Greater mention of the EU in party manifestos, the central position of the party's MEP within the party structure and an engagement by key UUP politicians with the EU, via their involvement in devolved politics, potentially suggests a deeper consideration of Europe by the party. In effect however, the developments have a superficial quality. They do not represent a deeper interest in Europe for Europe's sake. They are instead based on political and strategic domestic calculations, i.e. the EU is treated as a tool for improving party fortunes. Furthermore, the changes do not embrace all party levels. The process is effectively elite-driven. Root and branch evidence of Europeanization is wanting. The same can be said for other dimensions of the Ladrech framework where the absence of evidence of Europeanization is even more marked. In relation to party competition, party-government relations and relations beyond the national party system, the impact of the EU hardly registers. The UUP's resistance to the forces of Europeanization is arguably linked to what Mair (2004: 344) has termed 'deep-rooted political and organizational cultures … long-lasting collective identities, and … differential strategic empowerment'. Penetration of the party by the EU is minimal because it is being 'managed' by key party figures, who do not wish to compromise the UUP's domestic agenda and evolving character.

De Winter and Gómez-Reino (2002: 500) refer to 'new political opportunities for ethnoregionalist parties at the European level' providing a spur for processes of Europeanization. The experience of the UUP does not fit with this trend. The stimulus for what little Europeanization has taken place is to be found within Northern Ireland and is based primarily on exploiting the EU arena for domestic advantage. This finding fits with broader patterns of UUP party development and evolution since the 1990s. The impact of new unionism on the UUP party appears to be broadly spread, embracing new and pragmatic approaches to both constitutional politics *and* policy positions, including the EU. It is crucial to our understanding of both the Ulster Unionist Party and the process of European integration more widely that this pragmatism is not mistaken for evidence of deep Europeanization.

Notes

1. John Taylor, the party's first MEP, served for ten years from 1979 to 1989. He was succeeded by the current incumbent, Jim Nicholson.
2. This is the highest parliamentary office ever held by a Northern Ireland MEP and means that Jim Nicholson sat on the Bureau of the European Parliament. This is the key decision-making body which manages the running of the parliament.
3. The group has had an inauspicious start. There is some disquiet in relation to its membership. The Polish Law and Justice Party whose members have joined the group has been criticized for its position on gay rights. There is also some opposition within Conservative Party ranks as to the wisdom of leaving the larger EPP–ED grouping. The early expulsion of a Conservative Party MEP from the grouping has been controversial. Edward McMillan-Scott attempted to win a Vice-Presidential post without being put forward by the group.

References

Cameron, D. (2008) A new political force in Northern Ireland, Speech to the Annual Conference of the Ulster Unionist Party, Belfast, 6 December.
Cochrane, F. (2001) *Unionist Politics and the Politics of Unionism since the Anglo-Irish Agreement*, 2nd ed. (Cork: Cork University Press).
De Winter, L. & Gómez-Reino Cachefeiro, M. (2002) European integration and ethnoregionalist parties, *Party Politics*, 8(4), pp. 483–503.

Elliott, S. (1990) The 1989 election to the European Parliament in Northern Ireland, *Irish Political Studies*, 5(1), pp. 93–100.
Empey, R. (2008) Sir Reg Empey: our talks with the Tories may open brand new avenues, *Belfast Telegraph*, 20 August.
English, R. (2002) The growth of new unionism, in: J. Coakley (Ed.) *Changing Shades of Orange and Green: Redefining the Union and Nation in Contemporary Ireland*, pp. 95–105 (Dublin: UCD Press).
Farrington, C. (2001) Ulster Unionist political divisions in the twentieth century, *Irish Political Studies*, 16(1), pp. 49–71.
Farrington, C. (2008) Mobilisation, state crisis and counter mobilisation: Ulster Unionist politics and the outbreak of the troubles, *Irish Political Studies*, 23(4), pp. 513–532.
Goodman, J. (1996) The Northern Ireland question and European politics, in: P. Catterall & S. McDougall (Eds) *The Northern Ireland Question in British Politics*, pp. 212–228 (London: Macmillan).
Hainsworth, P. (1995) The 1994 European Parliament election in Northern Ireland, *Irish Political Studies*, 10, pp. 200–208.
Hainsworth, P. (1996) Northern Ireland and the European Union, in A. Aughey & D. Morrow (Eds) *Northern Ireland Politics*, pp. 129–138 (London and New York: Longman).
Hainsworth, P. & McCann, G. (2000) Continuity amidst change: the 1999 European election in Northern Ireland, *Irish Political Studies*, 15(1), pp. 135–142.
Hainsworth, P. & McCann, G. (2004) Change at last: the 2004 European election in Northern Ireland, *Irish Political Studies*, 19(2), pp. 96–111.
Hix, S., Noury, A. & Roland, G. (2005) Power to the parties: cohesion and competition in the European Parliament 1979–2001, *British Journal of Political Science*, 35(2), pp. 209–234.
Hume, D. (1996) *The Ulster Unionist Party 1972–1992 (A Political Movement in an Era of Conflict and Change)* (Belfast: Ulster Society Publications).
Jolly, S.K. (2007) The Europhile fringe? Regionalist party support for European integration, *European Union Politics*, 8(1), pp. 109–130.
Ladrech, R. (2002) Europeanization and political parties: towards a framework for analysis, *Party Politics*, 8(4), pp. 389–403.
Mair, P. (2004) The Europeanization dimension, *Journal of European Public Policy*, 11(2), pp. 337–348.
McGarry, J. & O'Leary, B. (1995) *Explaining Northern Ireland* (Oxford: Blackwell).
McGimpsey, C. (2008) A union that adds up for Cameron, but not for the people, *The Observer*, 7 September.
McGimpsey, C. (2009) Marriage of convenience or despair? *Fortnight*, 463.
Moxon-Browne, E. (1983) *Nation, Class and Creed in Northern Ireland* (Aldershot: Gower).
Tonge, J. (2005) *The New Northern Irish Politics?* (Basingstoke: Palgrave).
Tonge, J. & Evans, J.A.J. (2001) Faultlines in Unionism: division and dissent within the Ulster Unionist Council, *Irish Political Studies*, 16(1), pp. 111–131.
Ulster Unionist Party (1973) *Peace, Order and Good Government*, Unionist Assembly Manifesto (Belfast: Ulster Unionist Party).
Ulster Unionist Party (1997) *Secure the Union, Build your Future*, Westminster General Election Manifesto (Belfast: Ulster Unionist Party).
Ulster Unionist Party (2001) *Westminster and Local Government Elections Manifesto* (Belfast: Ulster Unionist Party).
Ulster Unionist Party (2003) *Ulster Unionists Manifesto*, Northern Ireland Assembly Elections (Belfast: Ulster Unionist Party).
Ulster Unionist Party (2004) *European Election Manifesto* (Belfast: Ulster Unionist Party).
Ulster Unionist Party (2005) *Westminster and Local Government Elections Manifesto* (Belfast: Ulster Unionist Party).
Ulster Unionist Party (2007) *For All of Us*, Northern Ireland Assembly Manifesto (Belfast: Ulster Unionist Party).

The SDLP and the Europeanization of the Northern Ireland Problem

P. J. MCLOUGHLIN
Queen's University Belfast, Northern Ireland, UK

ABSTRACT *This article explores the various ways in which the Social Democratic and Labour Party (SDLP) has used Europe – as a source of financial aid, political support, ideas and inspiration – in its attempts to resolve the Northern Ireland conflict. In this, the piece considers the SDLP, not as a subject, but rather as an advocate of the Europeanization of the Northern Ireland problem. In particular, it looks at the role of John Hume, a founding member and later leader of the SDLP, who inculcated a strongly pro-European outlook within the party. In doing so, the article considers the success of Hume and the SDLP in their efforts to bring a European influence to bear on Northern Ireland, especially in relation to the peace process and the 1998 Agreement. However, it also looks at both the limitations of this influence, and the problems involved with the SDLP's pro-European approach, particularly since Hume's departure as party leader in 2001. In conclusion, the article suggests that the party may have been 'over-Europeanized', with its long-term focus on European issues and ideas now becoming electorally disadvantageous. In this way, the Europeanization of the Northern Ireland problem, and by extension the SDLP, has proven costly to the party.*

Introduction

The Social Democratic and Labour Party (SDLP) is generally viewed as the most pro-European party in Ireland. This tendency is particularly associated with the founding member and arguably the principal ideologue of the SDLP, John Hume. It is for this reason that the article focuses primarily on Hume's thinking in relation to Europe, and his leadership of the SDLP between 1979 and 2001.

Although Hume was the chief architect of the SDLP's pro-European approach, he was not without support amongst the party rank and file. Indeed, research amongst the SDLP's grassroots has recorded a strong preference for the term 'European' in describing the party, this ahead of other labels such as 'nationalist' or 'social democratic' (Tonge, 2005: 104). For this reason, the present article takes a different approach to other party analyses in this volume. It does not so much consider the Europeanization of the SDLP, but rather looks at how the party sought to Europeanize the Northern Ireland problem. For the SDLP, particularly under Hume, was more an *advocate* than a subject of the processes identified by authors such as Ladrech (2002).

The SDLP also differs from the 'ethnoregionalist' parties with which it has been associated in the wider literature on European integration and minority nationalisms (Müller-Rommel, 1998; De Winter & Gómez-Reino Cachafeiro, 2000; Mitchell & Cavanagh, 2001). Certainly, the SDLP has sought to exploit the 'structure of political opportunities' (De Winter & Gómez-Reino Cachafeiro, 2000: 483) offered by Europe, just as regional parties such as the Scottish National Party or Esquerra Republicana de Catalunya have done. Indeed, consideration of Hume's activities as an MEP in the 1980s and 1990s will clearly demonstrate this point. But firstly the article looks at Hume's ideological influence and his role in policy-making in the SDLP from the early 1970s. This shows that Hume was developing a pro-European outlook within the party long before he became SDLP leader, and indeed before he came to represent the party in the Strasbourg parliament from 1979. In this respect, it can be argued the SDLP's pro-Europeanism was not 'learned' in the way that it was by other regional parties. The SDLP did not simply 'discover' the benefits of the European Community (EC) during the 1980s, since Hume had encouraged an affiliation with the ideals of European integration from the time of the party's formation in 1970. As such, whilst the SDLP did – like other regionalist parties – use the EC and later European Union (EU) in the pursuit of its own ethno-national agenda, it also had a deeper ideological connection with the European project.

The aim of this article, then, is to explain how the SDLP – primarily through Hume – tried to engage Europe in its efforts to resolve the Northern Ireland problem. It will show how the party sought economic aid and political support from Brussels, but also how it used integrationist ideas and indeed the very example of post-war European reconciliation as a model for political progress in the region. In doing so, the article will consider the success of the SDLP in its efforts to bring a European influence to bear on Northern Ireland, especially in relation to the peace process and the 1998 Agreement. However, it will also look at both the limitations of this influence, and the problems involved with the SDLP's pro-European approach, particularly since Hume's departure as party leader.

Europe and Hume

As early as February 1971 – when the SDLP was still in its infancy, and British and Irish entry into the EC was still in process – Hume (1971: 5) wrote an article for the *Fortnight* magazine in which he made the case for Europe as a context in which the Northern Ireland problem should be easier to resolve:

> while countries like France and Germany, who only 25 years ago were engaged in mutual carnage are today building bonds of friendship, in Ireland there is little or no sign of the communities coming together. It seems somewhat contradictory that each part of Ireland seems willing to participate separately

in the planned integration of Europe, but not in the planned integration of this little island.

However, even these early comments – and in particular the last line of this quotation – suggested that Hume's thinking went beyond the idea of Europe providing a model of political reconciliation. It also appeared that he saw the project of European integration as means towards Irish reunification.[1]

Such thinking was carried through to the SDLP's first published political proposals, the *Towards a New Ireland* document of 1972. Although this article drew on contributions from a number of policy-makers in the early SDLP, it was Hume who wrote the final version (Devlin, 1993: 185; Murray, 1998: 13–18), and his hand is evident throughout. Most notably, like Hume's *Fortnight* article, *Towards a New Ireland* celebrated European integration as a paragon of political reconciliation (SDLP, 1972: 2):

> Old and bitter enemies are settling their differences and are working together in a new and wider context of a United Europe. We in this Island cannot remain in the seventeenth century. We cannot participate in this vision while at the same time continuing our outdated quarrel.

However, *Towards a New Ireland* was more explicit than Hume's *Fortnight* piece in its proposed solution to this quarrel: 'it would be in the best interests of all sections of the Communities ... if Ireland were to become united on terms which would be acceptable to all the people of Ireland' (SDLP, 1972: 2). To this end – and again evoking the European model – *Towards a New Ireland* suggested political institutions which would facilitate co-operation between the North and South of Ireland, harmonizing structures and services in the two jurisdictions, and paving the way towards their eventual unification (SDLP, 1972: 6).

Like many of the ideas in *Towards a New Ireland*, this neo-functionalism (see Haas, 1968) – common to theories of European integration in this period – would remain central to the SDLP's political thinking. In articulating a peaceful, gradualist approach to Irish reunification, the party frequently cited post-war Europe as an example of how former antagonists could overcome their differences through a process of co-operation in areas of common social and economic interest. Similarly, the European model was used to support the idea of a pluralist all-Ireland constitution, one capable of accommodating all traditions and identities on the island (Hume, 1979: 310):

> [T]he peoples of Europe have been locked in the savagery of two world wars ... that goes far beyond anything that we have experienced on this island. Yet ... as a result of an agreed process, they have been able to create one parliament to represent them, one community – and the Germans are still German, the French are still French. They ... have a unity in diversity. ... Can we too build a unity in diversity?

As well as these ideological affiliations, the SDLP also sought to create practical links with Europe. It was much aided in this by Hume's appointment in 1977 as a political adviser to Dick Burke, Ireland's EC Commissioner for Transport, Trade and Administration. 'That…was very valuable to me', Hume recalled: 'I built a lot of major contacts in Europe and I got to know the European scene inside out' (quoted in Drower, 1995: 84). For this reason, Hume was well-positioned to begin working the EC machinery towards his own ends when he was elected to the Strasbourg Parliament in 1979.

Europe, the SDLP, and Organizational Change

Ladrech cites organizational change as one of the key identifiers in the Europeanization of political parties. However, in this, Ladrech is not overly concerned with the effect that Europe might have on an individual party's constitution: 'Explicit statutory change in parties may not be readily evident, although changes in practices and power relations may occur' (2002: 397). In relation to the latter, Europe certainly impacted on the SDLP, playing some role in the resignation of two of its most senior founding members, departures which opened the way towards Hume's leadership of the party. Firstly, Paddy Devlin claimed that his resignation resulted from ideological differences with Hume, and what he saw as the increasingly nationalist direction of the SDLP in the late 1970s (Devlin, 1993: 278–83). However, other senior SDLP members have suggested that Devlin was also aggrieved by Hume's selection, ahead of him, as the party's European candidate (Murray, 1998: 63; Murphy, 2007: 258). This interpretation is given credence by the fact that, after leaving the SDLP, Devlin stood for the United Labour Party in the Strasbourg poll, but on a broadly anti-European platform. As such, Séamus Mallon, later deputy leader of the SDLP, suggested that: 'Devlin's resignation happened to coincide with the fact that he did not get the [SDLP] nomination for Europe. The reality was that if he had, he would not have felt it necessary to resign and he would have fought the election on an SDLP ticket' (quoted in Murphy, 2007: 258).

Gerry Fitt also claimed that his resignation as SDLP leader in 1979 was a response to the more nationalist tone which he felt the party was then assuming. However, biographies of both men have suggested that Hume's election to Strasbourg – with a record vote for the SDLP – undermined Fitt's position as party leader, and thus contributed to his subsequent departure (White, 1984: 204; Murphy, 2007: 272–273). As White argued: 'the European election confirmed that Hume was popularly regarded as the real leader of nationalist opinion in the North' (White, 1984: 204).

Both Fitt and Devlin represented the more traditionally socialist wing of the SDLP. As such, Devlin in particular held a more traditionally leftist suspicion of the EC (Devlin, 1993: 278). Accordingly, with their departure, and Hume's subsequent election as party leader, he was free to steer the SDLP down an ever more European path. This seems to confirm Ladech's thesis, suggesting an effect – albeit indirect – which Europe had in changing the leadership and the overall direction of the SDLP.

Europe and the SDLP under Hume

Under Hume, the SDLP used the 'structure of political opportunities' offered by the EC – the chance to procure external funding, build international alliances, and so on – in much the same way as other small, regional parties in Europe (De Winter & Gómez-Reino Cachafeiro, 2000; Mitchell & Cavanagh, 2001). However, the SDLP approached the EC in a different manner to the 'ethnoregionalist' parties identified by De Winter and Gómez-Reino Cachafeiro. Most notably, whereas these parties began to coalesce as a distinct 'family' in the EC parliament in the early 1980s, from the moment of its election in 1979, the SDLP joined the Socialist political bloc at Strasbourg. Through the course of the 1970s, the SDLP had built links with parties from the European Left, and so was immediately accepted into this grouping. As such, the SDLP began from a very different position to that of other regional parties. Due to the pro-European outlook which Hume had been articulating throughout the 1970s, and in the contacts he had made in this period, the SDLP had already established a favourable reputation amongst influential actors in the EC Parliament. This gives credence to the idea that the SDLP was not simply a subject, but rather an active player in the Europeanization of the Northern Ireland problem.

Similar evidence is provided by the manifesto on which the SDLP was elected to the European Parliament. Moreover, examination of this document allows for engagement with the principal mode of party Europeanization in Ladrech's theoretical schema: programmatic change. Indeed, Ladrech suggests that changes to individual party programmes provide one of the most explicit examples of Europeanization (2002: 396). However, the SDLP manifesto for the 1979 election shows that, even before its participation in the EC Parliament, the party was already very much engaged with the issues with which it would be dealing at Strasbourg. In this regard, it compared favourably with the other major parties contesting the election in Northern Ireland, whose manifestos tended to focus largely on the implications of European membership for British sovereignty over the region. Though the SDLP also made oblique references to this subject, the greater part of its lengthy manifesto discussed issues relating to employment, agricultural development, the fishing industry, energy, and education. Moreover, the document showed great awareness of the instruments, policies and procedures through which the EC could best serve Northern Ireland's interests in these areas (SDLP, 1979). Indeed, the detail included in the SDLP's manifesto suggested that, if the party had been Europeanized, it was primarily though Hume's own experience of working within the Brussels bureaucracy over the previous two years. This led to an outlook where, although it remained conscious of the unique political problem in Northern Ireland, the SDLP showed an early eagerness to work positively within the EC to help address the social and economic conditions which exacerbated this problem. Thus, rather than the party's subsequent experience of working in the European Parliament, it was Hume's own, pre-existing affiliation with the European project which provided the original dynamic for the Europeanization of the SDLP's political programme.

The SDLP's 1979 manifesto also made much of its membership of the European Confederation of Socialist Parties. Working within this alliance, it suggested, would help the party to initiate action in the Strasbourg Parliament aimed at resolving Northern Ireland's social and economic problems (SDLP, 1979: 2–3). In this regard, the SDLP remained true to its word – and with no little help from its leftist allies. Indeed, during his time working in Brussels in the late 1970s, Hume had established good relations with leading figures in the Socialist Confederation. As such, on election to Strasbourg, he was immediately offered a place on the Socialists' front bench, acting as the group's treasurer. This put Hume in an ideal position from which to lobby his new political colleagues. Thus, within six months of becoming an MEP, he had gained enough support to table a resolution calling for an investigation into the ways that the EC could help the Northern Ireland economy. The subsequent Martin Report (1981) was adopted by the Regional Policy Committee – of which Hume was a member – and so Northern Ireland's ailing and conflict-damaged economy first began to receive special aid from Brussels (White, 1984: 229–230; Mitchell & Cavanagh, 2001: 258).

This breakthrough was even more notable in that Hume was able to secure support for the Martin Report from the two Ulster unionist members of the European Parliament, Ian Paisley and John Taylor. Throughout the 1980s, Hume continued to collaborate with Paisley and Taylor to secure many millions more in European aid for Northern Ireland. Then, in the 1990s, again he combined with the unionist MEPs in lobbying efforts that led to the establishment of the EU's Special Programme for Peace and Reconciliation (PEACE funding), designed to support the burgeoning peace process by providing monies for inter-communal and cross-border reconciliation projects (Laffan, 2005: 175). In this respect, it could be argued that Hume was little different from his unionist counterparts, simply seeking to 'squeeze' the EU for all that it would give to Northern Ireland. But unlike the unionist MEPs, Hume actually believed in European integration. Thus, in seeking funds from Brussels, he would cite the founding ideals of the project, and articulate the aim of increased economic equality between the various regions of Europe as a basis for greater political integration (SDLP, 1979: 3–4; Murray, 1998: 211–212). Hume clearly wanted financial assistance to help Northern Ireland's immediate economic problems, but also to help fulfil the integrationist ideal of political harmony in Europe.

As well as economic assistance, Hume also sought political support from Brussels. In particular, he hoped to make the EU a source of diplomatic pressure on London, and a means to steer the British government towards a more progressive policy on Northern Ireland. Most significant in this regard was his part in prompting the EC to commission a formal inquiry into the conflict in the early 1980s. Notably, the outcome of this, the Haagerup Report (1984), appeared to endorse many of the SDLP's ideas for a resolution of the Northern Ireland problem, in particular advocating a joint London–Dublin approach as the best way towards political progress. This, and Hume's lobbying of Brussels in general, clearly played a part in nudging London towards the Anglo-Irish Agreement (AIA) which was signed a year later (Kennedy, 1994: 179).

After the announcement of the AIA, Hume was keen to stress the European dimension of the accord. The EC, he suggested, had helped alter the terms of the debate between Britain and Ireland, and thus prepared the way for the 1985 Agreement (Hume, n.d.):

> Sovereignty and independence, the issues at the heart of wars in Europe and the issues at the heart of the British–Irish quarrel, have changed their meaning. The basic needs of all countries have led to shared sovereignty and interdependence ... All of this is reflected in the new approach to British–Irish relations ... [and] the Anglo-Irish Agreement ... None of that could have happened had the new European order not changed the roots and nature of the British-Irish quarrel.

In this, Hume showed that he did not champion the EC simply for the economic aid it provided to Northern Ireland, or the political support which it offered to his party. He still drew upon the integrationist project as an ideological resource, hoping to evoke new ways of thinking about the Northern Ireland problem. However, this use of Europeanist ideas – of shared sovereignty, interdependence, and the possibility of wholly new forms of political association – become even more pronounced in Hume's and his party's arguments in the years that followed. Indeed, as pro-integrationist as the SDLP had been hitherto, from the late 1980s, the party became even more enthusiastic about the part which Europe might play in resolving the Northern Ireland problem. The SDLP's optimism in this regard was clearly encouraged by developments taking place in the EC at this time, but also by the tentative shifts in Northern Ireland politics that were occurring in the late 1980s, shifts that would subsequently spawn the peace process.

Europe, the SDLP and the Peace Process

Hume and his party were not alone in their growing enthusiasm for Europe in the late 1980s and early 1990s. Indeed, at this time, such a trend was evident amongst the liberal intelligentsia in various member states. This was clearly related to the increased momentum of the integrationist project from the late 1980s: the development of the Single European Market from 1986, the Maastricht Treaty of 1992, and with this the transformation from the economic co-operation of the EC to the political association of the EU, led the most fervent Europeanists to believe that they were moving towards the realization of 'post-national' superstate. In this context, various commentators on Northern Ireland began to speak – in a way not dissimilar to the SDLP – of how the process of European integration could lead to the transcendence of the conflict (Boyle, 1991; Kearney & Wilson, 1993; Pollack, 1993: 205–215; Delanty, 1996).

Amidst this new-found fervour for European integration, Hume's discussion of the subject became charged with even greater optimism. In his mind, the radical changes taking place in Europe created an environment in which the various parties to the Northern Ireland problem might finally escape absolutist notions of national sovereignty (Hume, 1993: 229–230):

> Common membership in a new Europe moving towards unity has provided a new and positive context for the discussion and exercise of sovereignty in these islands ... The new European scene offers a psychological framework in which such issues can no longer be pushed in absolutist terms.

In this, Hume even appeared to embrace something of the 'post-nationalist' discourse that was emerging in the early 1990s (Hume, 1993: 227, 229):

> [T]he democratic nation-state is no longer a sufficient political entity to allow people to have adequate control over the economic and technological forces that affect people's opportunities and circumstances. The task is ... to optimise the real sovereignty of the peoples of Europe rather than ossify our democratic development around limited notions of national sovereignty ... [T]he nation-state is not the last word in polity creation.[2]

Looking at the political proposals that the SDLP were submitting to the inter-party talks that were also taking place in Northern Ireland in the early 1990s, it seems that the party was trying to achieve what Hume was suggesting here – that is to resolve the problem by moving it beyond the bounds of traditional nation-state sovereignty. Most notable was the SDLP's *Agreeing New Political Structures* document, submitted to the Mayhew talks in 1992. This paper went as far as to recommend that the EU play a direct role in the governance of Northern Ireland, with a delegate from the European Commission sitting on a regional executive alongside representatives of the British and Irish governments, and three locally elected politicians. In addition, the SDLP proposed a 'North–South Council/Council of Ministers' to develop co-operation between the two parts of the island and, as one of its special functions, to deal with European issues which had an all-Ireland dimension (Kennedy, 2000: 156, 158).

These proposals were immediately rejected by the unionist representatives at the Mayhew talks. Unsurprisingly, they opposed any idea of a role for Dublin in the governance of Northern Ireland, but felt that the involvement of the European Commission would signal a further dilution of British sovereignty over the region. However, aside from unionist objections, the London government was not hugely impressed by the SDLP's plan for a European role in Northern Ireland. Even more significantly, when he was asked to comment on the party's proposals at a Belfast press conference, the President of the European Commission, Jacques Delors, explicitly rejected the idea that Brussels could be directly involved in the governance of the region (*Irish Times*, 4 November 1992).

Despite this, some concession to the SDLP's European ideas was apparent in the Joint Declaration for Peace – or the Downing Street Declaration (DSD) as it is more commonly known – made by the British and Irish governments the following year. Here the two governments recognized the need for 'new approaches to serve interests common to both parts of the island of Ireland, and to Ireland and the United Kingdom as partners in the European Union' (HMSO, 1993: para. 3). This limited recognition of a European dimension to the Northern Ireland problem – and a consideration of the way that cross-border co-operation of the kind championed by the SDLP could contribute to its resolution – was fleshed out in the Frameworks Documents of 1995. Indeed, the part of the Frameworks Documents which provoked most controversy was that detailing the institutions which London and Dublin were contemplating as a way to promote social and economic interchange between the two parts of Ireland. The two governments recommended that such institutions should have executive powers and the capacity to develop in such a way as to 'keep pace with the growth of harmonization and with greater integration between the two economies' (HMSO, 1995: para. 38). In addition, the Framework Documents showed that the British and Irish governments had given considerable thought to the SDLP's suggestion that many EU-related issues could be addressed more effectively on an all-Ireland basis (HMSO, 1995, para. 26).

Although the Frameworks Documents horrified unionists, unsurprisingly, they received a warm welcome from the SDLP. Hume and his party saw in the proposals exactly the type of structures which they had often suggested as a means to facilitate co-operation between the two parts of Ireland. Institutions such as these, Hume suggested, would allow the people of Ireland to follow the European example, where collaboration in areas of common social and economic concern would lead to the gradual dissolution of political difference (Hume, 1996: 132). Also, the prospect of harmonization between the two Irish economies matched with arguments which the SDLP had first made in its 1972 proposals, *Towards a New Ireland*. As such, Hume and his party saw the Framework Documents as opening the way towards the incremental reunification of Ireland which they had long advocated.

Europe, the SDLP and the 1998 Agreement

The Framework Documents sent a shockwave through the Protestant community. One of the principle casualties was the Unionist Party leader, James Molyneaux. His 'wait-and-see' style of leadership was seen as lacking in the face of a political process which the SDLP, in collaboration with Dublin, appeared to be driving. Molyneaux's replacement as Ulster Unionist Party (UUP) leader, David Trimble, promised a bolder approach, one which would engage with the process to ensure that unionist interests were upheld. Foremost amongst Trimble's objectives was the neutralization of the dynamic North–South structures which the two governments had proposed in the Framework Documents. In this regard, Trimble was successful. Indeed, the 1998 Agreement which his party helped to negotiate saw a significant dilution in the strength of the all-Ireland institutions that were mooted in 1995.

Despite this, the structures of the Agreement still bear an essential resemblance to the European-style cross-border arrangements long championed by Hume and the SDLP (Meehan, 2006). Most obviously, like the institutions of the EU, they provide formal mechanisms of inter-jurisdictional co-operation. Moreover, though their competencies are circumscribed, the scope and powers of the Agreement's North-South structures can be extended by agreement between the Northern Ireland Assembly and Dáil Éireann. Accordingly, the SDLP hoped that these structures would instigate a process similar to that seen in post-war Europe, where increased contact and co-operation between elites from the two parts of Ireland would build both personal trust and political momentum. In this, it was clear that neo-functionalism continued to influence the thinking of Hume and his colleagues.

The main all-Ireland institution to be created by the Agreement was the North-South Ministerial Council (NSMC). Though less powerful than the North–South body which the SDLP had suggested at the Mayhew talks, the NSMC clearly drew upon the party's 1992 proposals. Most notably, as with the SDLP's version, the NSMC showed a particularly European influence. Indeed, even in its basic mode of operation – meeting in both plenary and in different sectoral formations – this institution closely resembles the practice of the EU's Council of Ministers (Laffan, 2005: 173). Also, again like the SDLP's 1992 model, the NSMC was given specific authority to deal with EU matters which had an all-Ireland dimension. In addition to the NSMC, the Agreement also created a number of cross-border 'implementation bodies'. These were intended to promote co-operation in particular areas of common interest between the two parts of Ireland, for example agriculture or tourism. However, one of the new bodies was given an exclusively European remit. The Special EU Programmes Body (SEUPB) assumed responsibility for the administration of all existing and future cross-border programmes developed by Brussels. In this, by establishing an all-Ireland basis to the management of certain EU matters, both the NSMC and the SEUPB are close to the thinking of Hume and the SDLP, and reflect specific proposals which they had submitted to the settlement process (Murray, 1998: 205–206, 217, 218; Kennedy, 2000: 156, 158; Laffan, 2005: 182).

However, European influences were also evident in the internal structures of government which the 1998 Agreement created for Northern Ireland. Indeed, partly because the UUP was allowed to dilute the potential of the Agreement's North-South institutions, in return, the SDLP had much of its way in the negotiations on internal mechanisms of government (Mallie & McKittrick, 2001: 266–270; Bew, Gibbon & Patterson, 2002: 236–237). Most importantly, the UUP accepted the SDLP's proposals for executive level and fully inclusive power-sharing arrangements. Again, this created a system with European parallels, consociationalism having a distinctly continental pedigree (see Lijphart, 1977). Indeed, this is something which the SDLP had long stressed in its advocacy of power-sharing as an alternative to adversarial, British-style majoritarian democracy. Also, the d'Hondt mechanism which decides the composition of the Northern Ireland executive is the same as that used to allocate political offices according to the share of seats in the European Parliament. This is no coincidence: the SDLP insisted that the d'Hondt mechanism was included in the Agreement, arguing that this was the surest method towards proportional representation in the executive (Hennessy, 2000: 125).

In summary, at the close of the negotiations on the 1998 Agreement, the SDLP – and particularly the party leader – could feel satisfied that at least some of the Europeanist thinking which they had tried to inject into the peace process was made manifest in the final outcome.

Europe and the SDLP after Hume

Hume's final electoral contest as SDLP leader came in the Westminster poll of June 2001. It is notable that, during this campaign, the Sinn Féin leader, Gerry Adams, poured scorn upon the 'post-nationalism' with which the SDLP had been associated in the 1990s, instead asserting a more traditional position (Tonge, 2008: 145). Of course, this was not the sole reason why Sinn Féin finally overtook the SDLP as the largest nationalist party at this election. However, the outcome did suggest that any talk of a fading of nationalist identification in Northern Ireland was premature, as the more staunchly nationalist Sinn Féin edged ahead of its moderate rival.

Sinn Féin extended its lead over the SDLP in the Northern Ireland Assembly elections of 2003, but it was the European poll of the following year that truly confirmed the new-found dominance of the republican party. Indeed, in this contest – the first European election in which Hume was not standing as the SDLP candidate – the party's support collapsed, with its number of first preference votes dropping by over 50 percent from the poll in 1999 (Hainsworth & McCann, 2004: 107).[3] Accordingly, this result showed not only how the tide had turned against the SDLP, but also raised questions about Catholic attitudes towards Europe – long considered to be more favourable than those of the Protestant community. After all, by supporting Sinn Féin in much greater numbers, Catholics were sending to Strasbourg a party far more critical of the EU, and a party which would not be building upon the vast network of contacts which Hume had created during his quarter century as an MEP – a network which had delivered a great deal, particularly in financial terms, to Northern Ireland. As such, this rapid transfer of allegiances naturally created doubts about how wedded the nationalist community was to Hume's European vision.

The 2004 election also allows for engagement with another aspect of Ladrech's Europeanization thesis, namely the idea that Europe affects patterns of party competition. Ladrech (2002: 397–398) notes how parties in different states have used Europe in an opportunistic fashion, seeking to mobilize voters on a pro- or anti-EU platform. This, clearly, has always had some relevance to the electoral contest between the SDLP and Sinn Féin. Indeed, whilst there were more important issues dividing the two parties in the 1980s – and although this article has argued that the SDLP's pro-Europeanism was ideological rather than opportunistic – during this period, Hume did stress his party's support for the EC as another point of difference with Sinn Féin (*Irish News*, 17 May 1984; SDLP, 1984: 2). As such, he and his colleagues may have felt vindication as much as relief in the European election of 1984. For this came at a time when a continuing surge in support for

Sinn Féin had led many commentators to predict that the party was about to usurp the SDLP as leaders of the nationalist community. However, after fighting the 1984 poll on an anti-European platform, Sinn Féin saw the first drop in its vote since the party began to contest Northern Ireland elections in 1982 (Mitchell, 1999: 98). Thus, the SDLP's support for Europe, and Hume's successful acquirement of substantial European funds for Northern Ireland in the early 1980s, may have played some part in securing his Strasbourg seat, and thus arresting the momentum of Sinn Féin in this period.

However, looking back from the vantage point of the 2000s – when Sinn Féin did finally overtake the SDLP – it is obvious that there were far more important factors that prevented the party from doing so at an earlier point. Foremost amongst these was Sinn Féin's support for the Irish Republican Army's (IRA) campaign of violence. Once the party began to move towards a peaceful political strategy in the 1990s, its vote started to rise significantly (Mitchell, 1999: 98). Moreover, the outcome of the 2004 election only confirmed what psephologists had always suggested, namely that the SDLP's previous support in European polls had been based on a large personal vote for Hume. Indeed, it was his charisma and calibre as a political leader as much as his views on Europe which won Hume such a huge number of votes in these contests.[4] Also, the particularly large mandates which he received in the European elections of 1994 and 1999 – the biggest ever in terms of the SDLP's share of the vote – can be seen as an endorsement of his peace-making efforts in the 1990s.

This would help to explain the subsequent collapse of SDLP's support in the European election of 2004. In keeping with Ladrech's thesis, the party's candidate for this contest, Martin Morgan, had contrasted the SDLP's pro-Europeanism with the opposition and ambivalence of other parties seeking election. Indeed, it was argued that the SDLP's pro-European reputation, along with its membership of the Party of European Socialists, would guarantee that Northern Ireland retained an effective voice at Strasbourg: 'Only an SDLP MEP will have the contacts and influence to keep delivering for farming, fishing and rural communities.' In this respect, Morgan also emphasized his predecessor's highly successful record in Europe: 'I will continue to build on what John Hume has delivered for our community – for workers, for women, for farmers … And I will deliver' (SDLP, 2004). However, the outcome of the election showed that the SDLP's reputation and established influence in Europe was not enough to retain its Strasbourg seat. The reason for this was that most nationalist voters did not make their choice on the basis of which party was the most pro-European, but which they perceived as being most likely to protect their communal interests. By the early 2000s, in the context of the contested implementation of the 1998 Agreement, and in the face of an ever-strengthening DUP, it is clear that most nationalists felt that Sinn Féin best fulfilled this role.

Much the same can be said in reference to the most recent European election, in June 2009. Here again, the SDLP candidate, Alban Maginness, sounded familiar notes in emphasizing his party's pro-Europeanism, the value of its political affiliation at Strasbourg, and the SDLP's former record of representation:

Northern Ireland needs a strong, credible, pro-European voice at the very heart of Europe. ... The SDLP is the only major party offering that ... Our membership of the Party of European Socialists ... gives us real influence where it matters. You know that we used that influence to deliver for you in the past when John Hume was our MEP. We want to deliver that again for you. (SDLP, 2009: 4)

Clearly alluding to Sinn Féin's bid to top the poll ahead of its unionist opponents, the SDLP leader, Mark Durkan, also asked voters to focus on European issues rather than inter-ethnic rivalry: 'This election must not become a sectarian vanity contest. Other parties will want it to be all about who will emerge as top-dog. That's because they have no record in Europe to run on or no positive agenda for the future' (SDLP, 2009: 3). However, despite Durkan's plea, the election did become an inter-communal competition rather than a contest to see which party best represented Northern Ireland's interests in Europe. In that context, again Sinn Féin won out over the SDLP.

In this regard, it could be argued that the SDLP has become 'over-Europeanized'. For whilst Ladrech suggests that parties will use Europe – either support of or opposition to – in an attempt to mobilize voters, it seems that the SDLP has gone past the point where its pro-Europeanism was an electoral advantage. Indeed, by overly focusing on European issues, the party has lost sight of the fact that most voters in Northern Ireland are more concerned with how their communal interests are represented, and which party will best protect those interests from the challenge of 'the other side'. Of course, it would be difficult for the SDLP to act otherwise. Not only would it be hard to out-flank Sinn Féin in terms of ethnic posturing, but this would contradict the SDLP's formative philosophy as a party which aspires to win Protestant support or at least build bridges with the unionist community (see McLoughlin, 2008). Notwithstanding the failure of the SDLP to meaningfully realize such lofty ambitions, it would be difficult to abandon them altogether without undermining the party's founding principles. As such, the SDLP may be seen as a victim of a situation in Northern Ireland in which inter-communal conflict has ended, but inter-communal competition remains strong. In this context, the party's efforts to focus on what *should* be the issues at European elections – social and economic matters, and how Northern Ireland's interests in these are best represented at Strasbourg – are largely overlooked.

Accordingly, the 2004 and 2009 elections also suggest the limited impact of the SDLP's attempt to Europeanize attitudes in Northern Ireland. As noted at the outset of this article, rank and file members of the SDLP have certainly embraced a pro-European outlook, suggesting that Hume has left some legacy in this regard. However, beyond the party faithful, there is little evidence to suggest that voters in Northern Ireland have been profoundly influenced by Europeanist thinking (McGarry, 2001: 301–304). In this respect, the SDLP seems little different to other regionalist parties, where De Winter and Gómez-Reino Cachafeiro (2002: 492, 500) suggest that the Europeanization of attitudes among party elites is not, necessarily, replicated among party electorates.

Conclusion

The SDLP has certainly been Europeanized. However, by and large, this has been achieved through the party's own initiative, and particularly the efforts of John Hume. Indeed, in many respects, Hume pre-empted the Europeanization of the SDLP. He did so by fostering a pro-European outlook within the party long before it had the opportunity to actually engage with European institutions and processes. This reflected a personal passion on Hume's part, and a firm belief that Europe could aid the path towards peace in Northern Ireland. As such, Hume was attempting to Europeanize the Northern Ireland problem as much as he was trying to Europeanize his own party.

Regarding the former aim, Hume had some success. Numerous authors have noted the positive effect which European integration has had on Northern Ireland (McCall, 1999; Laffan, 2005; Meehan, 2006; Hayward, 2009), and Hume and the SDLP can rightly claim to have played a significant part in this. Indeed, as demonstrated above, at every available opportunity, Hume and his colleagues sought to use Europe – as a source of financial aid, political support, ideas and inspiration – to help resolve the Northern Ireland conflict. Moreover, the 1998 Agreement – a settlement which the SDLP played no small part in making (Murray, 2002) – certainly shows a European influence (Laffan, 2005; Meehan, 2006).

However, it is also clear that Europe has not had the radical impact on Northern Ireland which the SDLP – and indeed many others – had imagined amidst the 'Europhila' of the late 1980s and early 1990s. For example, Brussels played no direct role in the resolution of the conflict, and certainly nothing like the part envisaged by the SDLP in its ambitious proposals to the Mayhew talks in 1992. Similarly, Europe does not appear to have had any great influence on political attitudes in Northern Ireland. The experience of the SDLP in the Strasbourg polls of 2004 and 2009, but also the evidence of other electoral and survey data, casts doubts on the idea that European integration has caused any significant erosion of oppositional political identities in the region (McGarry, 2001: 301–304). Northern Ireland may be post-conflict, but it is certainly not post-nationalist.

Hume's efforts to inscribe pro-European thinking into the ideology of the SDLP have also left an ambivalent legacy for the party itself. As recent European elections have shown, the SDLP is still very engaged with the issues relevant to these polls, and is eager to emphasize its record of effective representation of Northern Ireland's interests *vis-à-vis* these issues at Strasbourg. However, the party's abject failure at these elections suggests that the SDLP has become over-Europeanized. It is overly-focused on European issues, even when it is clear that these are not the deciding factor for voters at these elections. But this has echoes of a problem with significance for the European project as a whole: the increasing disconnection between political elites and voters. Like other pro-European parties, and indeed the governments in each member state, the SDLP needs to renew its efforts to convince voters that further integration is the best way forward for Europe. With the generous funds that Northern Ireland once received from Brussels now largely diverted to the new and needier EU members of the East, and with fading memories of the political support that Strasbourg provided to the region in darker times, this will be no easy task.

Acknowledgements

The author would like to thank the two anonymous referees of this article for their constructive comments, and Katy Hayward and Mary C. Murphy for their advice and patience as editors of this special edition of *Irish Political Studies*. The article was written with the support of the Irish Research Council for the Humanities and Social Sciences and subsequently the International Research Initiative, Queen's University Belfast.

Notes

1. Hume was not the first Irish nationalist to use the idea of European integration in this way. Seán Lemass justified Ireland's original application to join the EC in 1961 on the basis that it would advance the cause of Irish reunification, an argument taken up by many subsequent southern Irish leaders, most notably Garret FitzGerald.
2. For a broader discussion of Hume's perceived 'post-nationalism', see McLoughlin (forthcoming, 2010).
3. Although there was a lower turnout in 2004, Sinn Féin saw significant increases in its number of first preference votes and its overall percentage of the poll. This suggested that defection as much as abstention accounted for the dramatic decline in the SDLP's vote between 1999 and 2004.
4. This effect was amplified by the fact that Northern Ireland is treated as a single constituency in European elections. This allowed those who would not normally have the opportunity to vote for Hume to do so on these occasions.

References

Bew, P., Gibbon, P. & Patterson, H. (2002) *Northern Ireland, 1921–2001: Political Forces and Social Classes* (London: Serif).
Boyle, K. (1991) Northern Ireland: allegiances and identities, in: B. Crick (Ed.) *National Identities: The Constitution of the United Kingdom*, pp. 68–78 (Oxford: Blackwell).
Delanty, G. (1996) Northern Ireland in a Europe of regions, *The Political Quarterly*, 67(2), pp. 127–134.
Devlin, P. (1993) *Straight Left: An Autobiography* (Belfast: Blackstaff).
De Winter, L. & Gómez-Reino Cachafeiro, M. (2000) European integration and ethnoregionalist parties, *Party Politics*, 8(4), pp. 483–503.
Drower, G. (1995) *John Hume: Peacemaker* (London: Victor Gollancz).
Haas, E.B. (1968) *The Uniting of Europe: Political Social and Economic Forces 1950–1957* (Stanford: Stanford University Press).
Hainsworth, P. & McCann, G. (2004) Change at last: the 2004 European election in Northern Ireland, *Irish Political Studies*, 19(2), pp. 96–111.
Hayward, K. (2009) *Irish Nationalism and European Integration: The Official Redefinition of the Island of Ireland* (Manchester: Manchester University Press).
Hennessy, T. (2000) *The Northern Ireland Peace Process: Ending the Troubles?* (Dublin: Gill and Macmillan).
HMSO (1993) *Text of the Joint Declaration by the Prime Minister, Rt. Hon. John Major, MP and the Taoiseach, Mr. Albert Reynolds, TD on 15 December, 1993* (Belfast: HMSO).

HMSO (1995) *Framework Documents: Including Part 1 – A Framework for Accountable Government in Northern Ireland Produced by Government of Great Britain and Northern Ireland and Part 2 – A New Framework for Agreement Produced by Government of Great Britain and Northern Ireland and Government of Republic of Ireland* (Belfast: HMSO).
Hume, J. (1971) John Hume's Ireland, *Fortnight*, 1(6), pp. 5–6.
Hume, J. (1979) The Irish question: a British problem, *Foreign Affairs: An American Quarterly Review*, 58(2), pp. 300–313.
Hume, J. (1993) A new Ireland in a new Europe, in: D. Keogh & M.H. Haltzel (Eds) *Northern Ireland and the Politics of Reconciliation*, pp. 226–233 (Cambridge: Cambridge University Press).
Hume, J. (1996) *A New Ireland: Peace, Politics and Reconciliation* (Boulder, CO: Roberts Rinehart).
Hume, J. (n.d.) A new Ireland in a new Europe (Linen Hall Library, Northern Ireland Political Collection, SDLP Box 3).
Kearney, R. & Wilson, R. (1993) Northern Ireland's future as a European region, in: R. Kearney (Ed.) (1997) *Post-Nationalist Ireland: Politics, Culture, Philosophy*, pp. 60–73 (London: Routledge).
Kennedy, D. (1994) The European Union and the Northern Ireland question, in: B. Barton, & P.J. Roche (Eds) *The Northern Ireland Question: Perspectives and Policies*, pp. 166–188 (Aldershot: Avebury).
Kennedy, D. (2000) Europe and the Northern Ireland problem, in: D. Kennedy (Ed.) *Living with the European Union: The Northern Ireland Experience*, pp. 146–168 (Basingstoke: Macmillan).
Ladrech, R. (2002) Europeanization and political parties: towards a framework for analysis, *Party Politics*, 8(4), pp. 389–403.
Laffan, B. (2005) The European context: a new political dimension in Ireland, North and South, in: J. Coakley, B. Laffan & J. Todd (Eds) *Renovation or Revolution? New Territorial Politics in Ireland and the United Kingdom*, pp. 166–184 (Dublin: UCD Press).
Lijphart, A. (1977) *Democracy in Plural Societies: A Comparative Exploration* (New Haven: Yale University Press).
Mallie, E. & McKittrick, D. (2001) *Endgame in Ireland* (London: Hodder and Stoughton).
McCall, C. (1999) *Identity in Northern Ireland: Communities, Politics and Change* (Basingstoke: Palgrave).
McGarry, J. (2001) Globalization, European integration, and the Northern Ireland conflict, in: M. Keating & J. McGarry (Eds) *Minority Nationalism and the Changing International Order*, pp. 295–324 (Oxford: Oxford University Press).
McLoughlin, P. J. (2008) Horowitz's theory of ethnic party competition and the case of the SDLP, 1970–79, *Nationalism and Ethnic Politics*, 14(4), pp. 549–578.
McLoughlin, P.J. (forthcoming, 2010) *John Hume and the Revision of Irish Nationalism* (Manchester: Manchester University Press).
Meehan, E. (2006) Europe and the Europeanisation of the Irish question, in: M. Cox, A. Guelke & F. Stephen (Eds) *A Farewell to Arms? Beyond the Good Friday Agreement*, 2nd ed., pp. 338–356 (Manchester: Manchester University Press).
Mitchell, P. (1999) The party system and party competition, in: P. Mitchell & R. Wilford (Eds) *Politics in Northern Ireland*, pp. 91–116 (Oxford: Westview Press).
Mitchell, J. & Cavanagh, M. (2001) Context and contingency: constitutional nationalists in Europe, in: M. Keating & J. McGarry (Eds) *Minority Nationalism and the Changing International Order*, pp. 246–263 (Oxford: Oxford University Press).
Müller-Rommel, F. (1998) Ethnoregionalist parties in Western Europe: theoretical considerations and framework for analysis, in: L. De Winter & H. Türsan (Eds) *Regionalist Parties in Western Europe*, pp. 17–27 (London: Routledge).
Murphy, M. (2007) *Gerry Fitt: A Political Chameleon* (Cork: Mercier).
Murray, G. (1998) *John Hume and the SDLP: Impact and Survival in Northern Ireland* (Dublin: Irish Academic Press).
Murray, G. (2002) The Good Friday Agreement: an SDLP analysis of the Northern Ireland conflict, in: J. Neuheiser & S. Wolff (Eds) *Peace at Last? The Impact of the Good Friday Agreement on Northern Ireland*, pp. 45–59 (London: Berghahn Books).

Pollack, A. (Ed.) (1993) *A Citizens' Inquiry: The Opsahl Report on Northern Ireland* (Dublin: Lilliput Press).
SDLP (1972) *Towards a New Ireland* (Belfast: SDLP).
SDLP (1979) *A New Horizon* (n.p.).
SDLP (1984) *Strength in Europe* (Nu Print).
SDLP (2004) *SDLP for Europe: Best Record, Best Agenda: SDLP European Manifesto 2004* (Belfast: SDLP).
SDLP (2009) *A Vision for Europe, Ambition for You: SDLP European Manifesto 2009* (Belfast: SDLP).
Tonge, J. (2005) *The New Northern Ireland Politics?* (Basingstoke: Palgrave).
Tonge, J. (2008) 'Commentary' on Michael Cunningham's 'The Political Language of John Hume', in: C. McGrath & E. O'Malley (Eds) *Irish Political Studies Reader: Key Contributions*, pp. 142–146 (London: Routledge).
White, B. (1984) *John Hume: Statesman of the Troubles* (Belfast: Blackstaff).

Index

Page numbers in *Italics* represent tables.
Page numbers in **Bold** represent figures.

abortion 20, 25, 165
abstentionism: Sinn Féin 147, 148
accountability 151
Adams, G. 64, 151, 197
Afghanistan 67
agriculture 166
Ahern, B. 22
Ahern, N. 132
Alliance of Liberals and Democrats for Europe (ALDE) 88
Alliance Party of Northern Ireland (APNI) 2
Allister, J. 161, 166, 167, 168
Amsterdam Treaty 5, 13, 34, 63, 65; Green Party 135; referendum 18, 20
Anglo-Irish Agreement (AIA) 192, 193
anti-imperialism 60
Argentina 60
armed struggle 148
Attac 26

Banotti, M. 102
Barrett, J. 25
Barroso, J.M. 180
Barry, P. 100
Battlegroups 66
Belfast Agreement (1998) 173, 187, 200; Social Democratic and Labour Party (SDLP) 195, 196, 197
Belfast Telegraph 169
Benoit, K.: and McElroy, G. 88
A Better Deal (Sinn Féin) 152
Beyond Neutrality (Mitchell) 66, 99
Brewer, J.: and Higgins, G. 163
British Ecology Party 129
Bruce, S. 160, 162

Bruton, J. 96, 97, 100, 102

Cameron, D. 175, 183
Campaign Against the EU Constitution (CAEUC) 25
campaign dynamics 16
Canovan, M. 24
Carney, J. 19
Catholicism 25, 163
centralization 131, 132, 137
Charter of Fundamental Rights 25, 121
citizen participation 16, 127, 133, 136
civic education 15, 16
civil society groups 19, 20, 21, 28
Clinton, M. 102, 103
Cochrane, F. 182
Cóir (Justice) 25
Cold War 62, 63
Cole, A. 119
Cole, R. 20
Comhaontas Glas/Green Alliance 129
Common Agricultural Policy (CAP) 91, 98, 107, 114, 166, 176
common defence policy 57, 62, 70; Fianna Fáil 66
common foreign policy 57, 63
Common Foreign and Security Policy (CFSP) 51, 63; European Security and Defence Policy (ESDP) 52
Common Market 17, 113, 118, 147, 161, 162
Common Market Study Group 17
Common Security and Defence Policy (CSDP) 54, 55
Communist Revolutionary League 26

Comparative Manifesto Project (CMP) 32, 33, 41
Concerned Free Presbyterians 169
Confederation of Socialist Parties 119
conflict resolution 2
Connolly, C. 121
Conservative Party 175, 176, 182, 183
Constitution 17, 18
Constitutional Treaty 26, 121, 135, 136; Dutch referendum 26; French referendum 26
Cooke, B. 162
Cooney, P. 103
Corish, B. 113
Cosgrave, L. 99, 100
Coughlan, A. 18, 19
Coughlan judgement 18, 24
Cowen, B. 22, 77, 84, 88, 89, 90
critical engagement 144, 150, 156, 157
Crotty judgement 28, 103
Crotty, R. 18
Crowley, B. 80, 88
Cushnahan, J. 103

Darcy, R.: and Laver, M. 16
de Brún, B. 27, 149, 154, 155
De Rossa, P. 118, 121
de Valera, S. 77
De Winter, L.: and Gómez-Reino, M. 159, 160, 181, 184
decentralization 46, 132
decentralization policy 32, 41, 42
defence 56; European 56, 57
Delors, J. 194
Democratic Left 65
Democratic Unionist Party (DUP) 5, 6, 159-70
Denmark 116
deregulation 45
Devlin, P. 190
devolution 167, 168, 174, 178, 180
d'Hondt mechanism 196
Direct Rule 168
Dodds, D. 161, 170
Doherty, P. 153, 154
domestic identity: Fine Gael 102
domestic issues: Democratic Unionist Party (DUP) 167; Green Party 133

Dooge, J. 61, 62, 100
Dooge Report 61
Douglas, J. 162
Downing Street Declaration (DSD) 194
Doyle, A. 102, 103
dual ethnic party system 1
Duffy, M.: and Evans, G. 2
Dukes, A. 97
Durkan, M. 199

Ecology Party of Ireland 129
Economic and Monetary Union (EMU) 34, 76, 87, 114, 118
elections (2007): policy dimensions 40, 41
electoral politics 148
elite commitment 95
elite withdrawal 8, 14, 16, 19, 21, 22
Elliott, S. 182
Empey, R. 175, 180, 182
English, R. 175
entrepreneurship 25
environment 45
environmental issues 131, 133
ethnoregionalist parties 159, 160, 170, 181, 184, 185, 188, 190
Euro 34, 165
Euro-enthusiasm 4
Euro-positivism: Fianna Fáil 89, 90, 91
Eurobarometer 15, 27
Europe of Nations Group 184
European army 20, 146
European capitalism 147
European Central Bank 77
European Co-ordination Committee of Green Parties 129
European common security 71
European Community (EC) 161; Social Democratic and Labour Party (SDLP) 188
European Confederation of Socialist Parties 192
European Constitution 68; Democratic Unionist Party (DUP) 165
European Constitutional Treaty: Dutch referendum 14; French referendum 14
European Council 52
European defence 60, 65
European defence policy 55, 58, 63; Fianna Fáil 66

European Democratic Group 184
European Economic Community (EEC)
   15, 17, 18, 51; defence 57; Fine Gael
   95, 106; Ireland's accession 55, 75;
   membership 58; referendum (1972) 17;
   Sinn Féin 143, 144, 145; Ulster Unionist
   Party (UUP) 177
European enlargement 151
European Federation of Green Parties 130
European Green Party (EGP) 70
European identity 27
European integration 3, 4, 6, 9; debate 34;
   Democratic Unionist Party (DUP) 165,
   170; evolving attitudes 13; Fianna Fáil
   84; Fine Gael membership 106; Green
   Party 35, 127, 133, 134, 136, 138; impact
   3, 31; issue 35; literature 32; Northern
   Ireland 200; opposition 39; party
   manifestos **33**; party positions 32, **36, 37,
   40**; policy 42; policy positions 35; public
   consensus 4; Sinn Féin 35, 144, 149,
   155; Social Democratic and Labour Party
   (SDLP) 189, 192, 193; support 27, 39;
   Ulster Unionist Party (UUP) 177
European interference: Fianna Fail 76,
   77, 78
European Liberal, Democratic and Reform
   Party (ELDR) 88, 89
European Monetary System (EMS) 114
European Parliament 6; Democratic Unionist
   Party (DUP) 163, 164
European Parliament elections 3, 7, 16,
   105; Democratic Unionist Party (DUP)
   160, 167, 168, 169; Fianna Fáil 81, 82,
   83; Fine Gael 103, 104, 105, 106; Green
   Party 130, 137; Labour Party 115, *115*;
   Sinn Féin 147, *149*; Sinn Féin manifesto
   150; Social Democratic and Labour
   Party (SDLP) 198; Ulster Unionist Party
   (UUP) 178, 182
European People's Party-European
   Democrats (EPP-ED) 95, 97, 100, 184;
   Fine Gael's membership of 101, 102,
   103, 108
European policy: Fine Gael 98, 99, 100;
   Sinn Féin 150, 151, 153
European Political Co-operation 59
European Rapid Reaction Force 66

European referendum 14, 83, 84; results
   (1972-2008) *15*
European Regional Development Fund
   Programmes 166
European Security and Defence Policy
   (ESDP) 5, 6, 51, 55, 58; agenda 52; and
   neutrality (1970s) **55**; and neutrality
   (1980s) **59**; and neutrality (2000s) **67**;
   party positions 52, 53; provisions 69, 70
European Social Fund (ESF) 180
European Union (EU) 2, 4, 5, 6, 9, 63, 134,
   151; accountability 39, 42; accountability
   vs. authority **38**; authority 39, 42;
   changing nature 52; democratization
   139; enthusiasm 8; Fine Gael 104;
   foreign policy 146; funds 31, 166; Green
   Party 133; impact 3; knowledge of
   23, 24; Labour Party 122, 123; lack of
   knowledge 13; military alliance 57; open
   labour market 31; policy dimension **34**;
   Sinn Féin 143; Social Democratic and
   Labour Party (SDLP) 188; support 10;
   treaties 4, 8, 14; treaties voting
   intentions *119*; Ulster Unionist Party
   (UUP) 174, 176
European Union (EU) membership 3, 9;
   benefits 19, 85; Fianna Fáil 85; Ireland
   129; Labour Party 112
European Union (EU) referendums 14, 16,
   65; in Ireland **14**; turnout 19; voting
   behaviour 16
Europeanism 75; Fianna Fail 91
Europeanization 3, 4, 51, 52, 62, 100;
   acceptance 10; conditionality 4, 5, 6;
   definition 112; Democratic Unionist
   Party (DUP) 160, 163, 167, 169; effects
   9; elite-led 4, 8, 9; Eurosceptic parties
   127, 128; Fine Gael 95, 108; impact 159;
   Labour Party 111, 113-20, 120, 121;
   limits 8; party systems 112; patterns 10;
   political parties 138; pragmatism 4, 6, 7;
   resistance 4; restricted 76; Sinn Féin 143,
   157; Social Democratic and Labour Party
   (SDLP) 191; sub-national priorities 4, 7,
   8; Ulster Unionist Party (UUP) 174, 176,
   177, 179, 184, 185
Eurosceptic parties 127, 128
Euroscepticism 5, 26, 27, 38, 77, 134;

Democratic Unionist Party (DUP) 160, 161, 162, 163, 164; Green Party 35, 136; Sinn Féin 35
Evans, G.: and Duffy, M. 2
Evans, J.A.J.: and Tonge, J. 175
Expert Survey (2007) 45, 46; party importance scores *49, 50*; party positions *47, 48*

Falklands War 59, 60
family values 25
farmers 107, 179
federalism 182
Fianna Fáil 1, 7, 9, 35, 42, 57, 59, 75-91; high profile negotiators 87; organization **79**; programmatic pragmatism 76-8
Fine Gael 1, 7, 8, 35, 42, 57, 95-108; membership 106; within Europe 100-3
Fingal Green Group 130
Finland 131
Finlay, F. 111
Fitt, G. 190
FitzGerald, E. 114
FitzGerald, G. 56, 57, 61, 97, 100, 102, 107, 117
foreign policy 53, 56, 58, 62, 150; goals 54; Irish 62; Sinn Féin 145
Frampton, M. 146
France 54, 188
Free Presbyterian Church 161, 162, 164, 169
fringe activists 16, 24
The Future of the EU and Ireland's Role in Shaping that Future (Sinn Fein) 153

Gallagher, M. 111
Gallagher, P. 88
Ganley, D. 5, 25, 26
Garland, R. 130
general elections: campaigning 23
Germany 54, 131, 188
Gilmore, E. 122
Gómez-Reino, M.: and De Winter, L. 159, 160, 181, 184
Goodman, J. 181
Gormley, J. 130, 133, 134, 135, 136
governance issues 15
Green Action Now Group (GANG) 129
Green Party 1, 2, 5, 7, 19, 27, 127-

39; Germany 129; organizational development 128, 129, 130, 131, 132
Griffiths, A. 144
Group of the European Right 184

Haagerup Report 192
Hague Conventions 69
Hague, W. 183
Hainsworth, P. 176, 181
Hakovirta, H. 58
Halligan, B. 114
Harkin, M. 23
Haughey, C. 60, 61
Hermon, S. 175
Higgins, G.: and Brewer, J. 163
Higgins, J. 156
high politics 51
Hillery, P. 56, 61
Hix, S. 104, 120
Hooghe, L. 70, 71
Hume, J. 165, 179, 182, 187, 189, 190, 192, 193, 194

identity 7, 53, 56
immigration 31, 41, 46; Fianna Fáil 42
imperialism 146
independence 20, 53
industry 21
intra-ethnic competition 2
Iraq 67
Irish Alliance for Europe 21
Irish Campaign for Nuclear Disarmament 20
Irish Congress of Trade Unions (ICTU) 17, 20
Irish economy 76, 77, 78
Irish Farmers' Association (IFA) 22, 107
Irish Green Party 127-39
Irish identity 27
Irish Labour Party 4, 111-24
Irish nationalism 146, 175
Irish neutrality 54, 55, 56, 57, 58, 61, 66, 71; Fine Gael 68, 99; threat 67, 151
Irish party manifestos 32
Irish referendum game: rules 18, 19
Irish Republican Army (IRA) 198; decommissioning 169
Irish reunification 7, 154, 189

Irish Social and Political Attitudes Survey (ISPAS) 54

Karsh, E. 58
Keatinge, P. 54, 58
Kennedy, D. 181
Kenny, E. 101, 102
Keogh, D. 112

Labour Party 1, 8, 20, 35, 111-24; Europeanization 113-20; transnational party networks 118, 119, 120
Labour Youth 121
Ladrech framework 96, 98, 99, 112, 160, 174, 176
Ladrech, R. 3, 9, 53, 75, 143, 155, 159, 179, 190
Laver, M.: and Darcy, R. 16
LeDuc, L. 16, 24
Left-Right dimension 46
Lemass, S. 61
Libertas 5, 25, 26, 104
Lisbon dilemma 28
Lisbon Treaty 8, 13, 22, 25, 26, 34, 52; Democratic Unionist Party (DUP) 165, 167; Green Party 136, 137; knowledge levels 23; Labour Party 112, 121, 122; rejection 132; Sinn Fein 153; support 31; Ulster Unionist Party (UUP) 179, 182
Lisbon Treaty referendum 22, 23, 67, 75, 143, 146; abstention 24; Fine Gael 96, 106; referendum I 14, 21; referendum I campaign 24; referendum I voting motivations 86, 87; referendum II 28; referendum II Fianna Fail 90; Sinn Fein 151, 152; voting patterns *123*
local democracy 132, 133, 134, 135, 136, 139
local and European elections (2009) **83**
localism 75, 76, 82

Maastricht Treaty 13, 34, 63, 193; campaign 18; Green Party 135; referendum 20, 65; Ulster Unionist Party (UUP) 178, 179
McCreevy, C. 22, 77
McDonald, M.L. 145, 146, 149, 150, 152, 153, 156, 157
McElroy, G.: and Benoit, K. 88

McGarry, J.: and O'Leary, B. 177
McGimpsey, C. 184
McKenna judgement 18, 24, 63
McKenna, P. 18, 132
Maginness, A. 198, 199
Mair, P. 3, 104, 159, 185; and Weeks, L. 111
Mallon, S. 190
Maloney, E. 164
Martin, M. 22, 77
Martin Report 192
Maskey, A. 146
media 24
Members of the European Parliament (MEPs) 7; Democratic Unionist Party (DUP) 161, 166; Fianna Fáil 78, 80, **81**, 89; Fine Gael 97, 102, 103; Green Party 130, 132; Labour Party 115; Sinn Féin 150; Ulster Unionist Party (UUP) 175, 182
Members of Parliament (MPs): Ulster Unionist Party (UUP) 173
military force 53
military neutrality 51, 54, 55, 62, 64, 66, 68, 71
Mitchell, G. 103
Mitchell, P. 2
Moloney, E. 159, 160, 161
Molyneaux, J. 179, 195
Morgan, M. 198
Morrison, D. 148
Mouvement pour la France 26
Moxon-Browne, E. 176
mutual defence clause 55

National Forum on Europe 21; road shows 23
National Platform for Employment, Democracy and Neutrality 20
nationalism 60
neo-functionalism 189, 196
Netherlands 25
neutrality 5, 20, 51, 52, 53, 56, 58; active 51, 62, 64, 65, 68, 71; and ESDP **55**, **59**, **67**; Fianna Fáil 56, 60, 61, 68; Fine Gael 56, 61, 62; Green Party 64, 70, 134; Labour Party 62, 63; party positions 52, 53; public thinking 53; Sinn Féin 64, 144, 145, 146, 152; support 54

new unionism 173, 174, 175, 182, 184, 185
Nice Treaty 5, 8, 13, 19, 21, 25, 34, 66
Nice Treaty referendum 67, 68, 143; Green Party 134; referendum I 14, 15, 16, 19, 21; referendum I abstention 14; referendum I no vote 14; referendum II 21; Sinn Fèin 151, 152
Nicholson, J. 177, 179
North Atlantic Treaty Organization (NATO) 20, 52, 57, 70, 145
North-South Ministerial Council (NSMC) 196
Northern Ireland: party system 1, 2
Northern Ireland issue 41, 46; Social Democratic and Labour Party (SDLP) 188

Ó Broin, E. 156, 157
Ó Neachtain, S. 80
O'Dea, W. 77
O'Leary, B.: and McGarry, J. 177
Olsen, J.P. 138
opinion polls 13
Orange Order 176
organizational change 3, 9, 100; Democratic Ulster Party (DUP) 169; Fine Gael 103; Labour Party 114, 115, 116; Sinn Fèin 155, 156; Ulster Unionist Party (UUP) 179-81
O'Toole, F. 151

Paisley, E. 164
Paisley, I. 159, 160, 161, 162, 163, 164, 169, 182
Paris Treaty 58
Partnership for Peace 64, 65, 76
party competition 3, 9, 59, 71, 104, 167; Democratic Unionist Party (DUP) 170; Labour Party 116, 117; Sinn Féin 156, 157; Social Democratic and Labour Party (SDLP) 197; Ulster Unionist Party (UUP) 181, 182, 183, 185
Party of European Socialists (PES) 115, 119, 120, 198, 199
party evolution 10
party principles 6
party system 3; Northern Ireland 1, 2; Republic of Ireland 1

party-government relations 4; Labour Party 117, 118
PEACE funding 160, 166, 170, 192
Peace and Neutrality Alliance (PANA) 20, 21, 113
peace process 150, 154, 174, 176, 184, 187, 188, 192, 193; Sinn Féin 149
Pearse, P. 145
People Before Profit Alliance 123
People's Movement 132
permissive consensus 52
Petersberg tasks 63, 69
political attachment 7
political elite 8
political systems 1; European Union (EU) impact 3
popular disillusionment 95
populism 24, 25; Fianna Fáil 25; and the no campaigns 24, 25, 26; rise 25; Sinn Féin 25
populist capture 8, 14, 21, 23, 24, 25, 26
positive neutrality 61, 151
Positive Neutrality in Action (Sinn Féin) 69
post-nationalism 197
power sharing 196
pragmatism 76, 150, 173, 174, 175, 176, 181
professionalization 131, 132, 137
programmatic change 3, 9; Democratic Unionist Party (DUP) 164, 169; Green Party 132, 133, 134, 135, 136, 137; Labour Party 113, 114; Sinn Féin 154, 155; Social Democratic and Labour Party (SDLP) 191; Ulster Unionist Party (UUP) 176, 177, 178, 179
programmatic pragmatism: Fianna Fáil 76-8
Progressive Democrats (PDs) 1, 35, 42
proportional representation 196
Protestant paramilitaries 163
Puirséil, N. 111
Putnam, R. 54

Quinn, R. 114, 118, 121

Raidió Teilifís Éireann (RTÉ) 18, 19
Rainbow Coalition 64
Rathmines Radicals 129

Referendum Act (1998) 63
referendum campaigns 19
Referendum Commission 18, 20, 21, 64; role 28
referendums 6, 15, 16; campaigning 23; in Europe 15, 16; Ireland **17**; research 16; turnout 20; voter turnout 16; voting 15; voting behaviour 54
religious right 25
representative democracy 15
Republic of Ireland: party system 1; Sinn Féin 151
republicanism 146, 156, 157
resistance 5
Reynolds, A. 20, 87
Robinson, M. 55, 56
Roche, D. 21, 28, 69, 76, 77
Roman Catholic Church 160, 161, 162
Rome Treaty 32, 58
Rural Environmental Protection Scheme 91
Ryan, R. 62, 103

St. Andrews' Agreement 169
Sands, B. 147, 157
Sargent, T. 130, 131
Sarkozy, N. 122
Scottish National Party 188
security environment 52
security policy 51
September 11th terrorist attacks 67
Seville Declaration 68, 146
Single European Act (SEA) 13, 17, 18, 54, 61, 65; Labour Party 63, 113; referendum 34; referendum campaign 19
Single European Market 193
Sinn Féin 5, 6, 19, 27, 143-57, 161
Sinnott, R. 23
Smith, M. 68
Smyth, R. 156
Social Charter 118
social democracy 111; European 112
Social Democratic and Labour Party (SDLP) 7, 8, 177, 187-200
social Europe 151, 152
social policy 41
social values 45
social-moral issues 15
Socialist International 119

Socialist Party 123, 156
Socialist Workers' Party 19
sovereignty 20, 58, 88, 150, 151, 193, 194; Democratic Unionist Party (DUP) 165; Sinn Féin 144, 145, 146; Ulster Unionist Party (UUP) 177, 179
Special EU Programmes Body (SEUPB) 196
Spring, D. 117, 118
Stalford, C. 165, 166
Structural and Cohesion Funds scheme 31
sustainable development 150
Sutherland, P. 96, 100
sympathy 46

tax policy 131
taxes *vs.* spending 45
Taylor, J. 184
terrorism 69
Tonge, J. 176; and Evans, J.A.J. 175
trade unions 25
Traditional Unionist Voice 166, 168
transnational party networks 118, 119, 120
transparency 151, 152
Treaty: Amsterdam 5, 13, 34, 63, 65; Lisbon 8, 13, 22, 23, 25, 26, 31, 34, 52; Maastricht 13, 34, 63, 193; Nice 5, 8, 13, 19, 21, 25, 34, 66; Paris 58; Rome 32, 58
Trimble, D. 173, 175, 179, 180, 195

Ulster Conservatives and Unionists-New Force (UCUNF) 175, 182
Ulster Unionist Party (UUP) 6, 165, 167, 173-85
Union for Europe of the Nations (UEN) 88, 101
unionism 159, 163, 167, 173, 175, 176
United Labour Party 190
United Nations (UN) 60; peacekeeping 60, 62, 65; primacy 69
United States of America (USA) 52
universal suffrage 147

voter ignorance 16
voting: elections 10; referendums 10
voting public 8

Warsaw Pact 145
Weeks, L.: and Mair, P. 111
Western European Union (WEU) 57, 64
Westminster Confession of Faith 162
White, B. 190
Workers' Party 116, 123
World Trade Organization (WTO) 22

Young Fine Gael (YFG) 97, 107; Campaign for Europe posters **98**
Youth Defence 25
Youth of the European People's Party (YEPP) 97

Zimbabwe 167

The Europeanization of Party Politics in Ireland, North and South

National experience of European Union membership tends to centre upon the behaviour, actions and discourses of political parties. This book is the first of its kind to examine and compare the 'Europeanization' of all main political parties in the Republic of Ireland and Northern Ireland.

The book presents an in-depth study of the tenuous place of 'Europe' amid the changing dynamics of party politics on the island of Ireland. Although elements of Europeanization are evident in all the parties considered here (including those most critical of European integration), they have been significantly curtailed by enduring resistance to – and conditions placed upon – EU influence within the parties themselves. Even parties' 'European' policies are often characterized by pragmatism and the prioritizing of national or local party concerns.

Beyond Ireland, the systematic testing of the Europeanization thesis presented here identifies ways in which the essential interests of national and regional political parties can moderate the impact of the EU on wider public debate. Furthermore, it reveals the often-decisive importance of the (sub-) national domestic political context in determining the nature and depth of Europeanization processes. This has implications not only for the future of Ireland's relationship with the EU but also for the nature of European integration itself.

This book was published as a special issue of *Irish Political Studies*.

Katy Hayward is Lecturer in Sociology at the School of Sociology, Social Policy and Social Work, Queen's University Belfast.

Mary C. Murphy is College Lecturer in Politics at the Department of Government, University College Cork.

Dr Hayward and Dr Murphy are co-conveners of the European Studies Specialist Group of the Political Studies Association of Ireland.